Education and Society in Modern India

ABOUT THE AUTHOR

Dr. R. Annadurai is working as Director-in-Charge in Centre for Educational Research at Madurai Kamaraj University in Madurai, Tamil Nadu. He was served Fourteen years in College of Education and University, Experience in field of Education. He is Editor in Chief for International Journal of Educational Research, Development and Extension (IJERDE) at Centre for Educational Research-MKU- He has served as member in the visiting team conducted by NCTE, Bangalore. He was presented the research papers in many National and International conferences and organizing many Conference, Seminar and Workshop related to academic Activities.

ABOUT THE BOOK

The twenty first century that poses many challenges and enormous pressure on our daily life, work and society. Information and communication technologies (ICT) transform all aspect of education and distance education (DE), The expression open and distance learning reflect both the information that all or most of the teaching is conducted by somebody who is gone from the learner, and that the project aims to include better proportions of sincerity and flexibility, whether in terms of right of entry, curriculum or other elements of organization. Now-a-days the role of Information and Communication Technology, in the education sector plays an important role, especially in the process of empowering the technology into the educational activities. Education sector can be the most effective sector to anticipate and eliminate the negative impact of ICT. A country can grow only if it makes the maximum use of its resources. India is blessed with huge population of 1200 million, and children below 7 form the bulk of the population.

❐

Education and Society in Modern India

Dr. R. Annadurai
Director-in-Charge in Centre for Educational Research
Madurai Kamaraj University
Madurai, Tamil Nadu

AMIGA PRESS INC.

AMIGA PRESS INC.
H.O:- 28-A, Indra Park, St.No-9
Near-Chander Nagar, Krishna Nagar
Delhi: - 110051 (India)
Tel: - 011-22504028, +91-98736-57000
Email: - amigapress@gmail.com
info@amigapress.co.in
amigaeditorial@gmail.com
amigapub@gmail.com

Website: - www.amigapress.co.in

This edition is published by Amiga Press Inc.

ISBN: 978-93-84533-59-5

First Published 2020

Printed and bound in India by Replika Press Pvt. Ltd.

Contents

❐

1

Environmental Health Education for Public

Public health is defined by the World Health Organization as not merely the absence of disease, but the state of physical, mental and social well-being. To achieve that state, community efforts have to be made towards prevention of disease and prolonging life. This is done by maintaining and providing a sanitary environment, controlling communicable and non-communicable diseases, educating the community on health and health-related topics, organizing nursing and mcdical scrviccs for thc carly diagnosis and prevention of disease and developing a social machinery to ensure an adequate standard of living, by maintaining health and longevity, which are human birthrights to each and every individual.

Environmental health is a broad branch of public health that addresses and emphasizes on all human-health related aspects of the environment that are detrimental in the improvement of health outcomes. It is defined as the theory and practice of assessing, correcting, controlling and prevention of factors that affect the quality of lives of people in the community. As such, environmental health is integrated within the concept of public health to create and maintain environments that prevent disease and promote good public health of the communities.

Health education can help people understand and value different screening procedures, such as those involved in MCH services. It teaches about the early symptoms and signs of important diseases (e.g. leprosy and tuberculosis) so that people can recognize them and go for check up at an early stage. It can help them co-operate in reporting diseases in surveillance programmes for such diseases as measles, rabies and malaria. It can help people to understand diseases better and to cooperate with the medical services in carrying out treatment properly- for example, continuing with treatment for tuberculosis until cured. While people are attending for treatment, health educators can give them new and up-to-date information about how to prevent diseases such as malaria and gastroenteritis.

Health education posters in clinic waiting areas can also be used to spread information. Environmental health is affected by a lot of factors that are naturally present in every environment and are external to a person of physical, chemical, biological and psychosocial nature. It stresses on following a preventative approach rather than an end-of-pipe approach which addresses a health problem after its occurrence, to provide not only for the present communities, but to future generations as well.

DEFINITION

Environment

"Environment is the complex of physical, chemical, and biotic factors (such as climate, soil, and living things) that act upon an organism or an ecological community and ultimately determine its form and survival".

Environmental Health

"Environmental health refers to aspects of human health (including quality of life) that are determined by physical, chemical, biological, social and psychosocial factors in the environment".

Health Education

"Health education is a profession of educating people about health. [1] Areas within this profession encompass environmental health, physical health, social health, emotional health, intellectual health, and spiritual health, as well as sexual and reproductive health education".

NEED FOR ENVIRONMENTAL HEALTH

We need safe, healthy and supportive environments for good health. The environment in which we live is a major determinant of our health and wellbeing. We depend on the environment for energy and the materials needed to sustain life, such as:

1. Air quality, including both ambient outdoor air and indoor air quality, which also comprises concerns about environmental tobacco smoke.
2. Hazardous materials management, cluding hazardousste management, contaminated site remediation, the prevention of leaks underground

storage tanks and the prevention of hazardous materials releases to the environment and responses to emergency situations resulting from such releases.

3. Housing, including substandard housing abatement and the inspection of jails and prisons.
4. Childhood lead poisoning prevention.
5. Land use planning, including smart growth.
6. Liquid waste disposal, including city waste water treatment plants and on-site waste water disposal systems, such as septic tank systems and chemical toilets.
7. Medical waste management and disposal.
8. Recreational water illness prevention, including from swimming pools, spas and ocean and freshwater bathing places.

Health Effects Related to the Environment

Outdoor Air Pollution	Respiratory Conditions, Cardiovascular Disease, hung Cancer
Unsafe drinking water	Diarrhoeal (gastrointestinal) illnesses
Contaminated Recreational water	Diarrhoeal(gastrointestinal) illnesses; eye, ear, nose and throat infections
Mosquitoes, ticks and other vectors	Malaria, dengue fever, Rickettsial disease
UV (ultraviolet light) exposure	Too much: melanoma, non melanoma skin cancer, eye cataracts Too little: vitamin D deficiency, leading to rickets, osteoporosis and osteomalacia
Second hand smoke exposure	In infants: low birth weight, sudden unexpected death in infancy (SUDI)
	In children: asthma, lower respiratory infections, middle ear infections In adults: ischaemic heart disease, stroke, lung cancer
Household crowding Cold and damp housing	Infectious diseases, including lower respiratory infections Excess mortality
Climate change	Infectious diseases, including giardiasis, cryptosporidiosis and salmonellosis; heat stroke
Hazardous substances	Poisoning, burns, dermatitis

PEOPLE CAN LEARN FROM

- verbal (spoken) explanations
- demonstrations (being shown)
- observing (looking at) what others do

- getting information from books, posters, videos, pamphlets and other printed materials
- things are explained clearly in words they understand
- they feel happy when they are being taught
- pictures and diagrams are used to explain difficult ideas
- Solid waste management, including landfills, recycling facilities, composting and solid waste transfer stations.

ENVIRONMENTAL PROTECTION

Prevention and control systems should be designed to protect both workers' health and the general environment. Environmental consequences include the effect of fine particles on atmospheric visibility, damage to buildings, effects on vegetation and animals, and health effects on people outside the plant. As in the workplace, the first priority is to prevent the generation of airborne dust, and, if generation cannot be prevented, then secondly, its removal. Measures that minimize waste generation should be given priority, and any inevitable waste disposal should be so planned as to avoid environmental damage.

CONCLUSION

Environment and development-related health effects are becoming of increasing concern world-wide, in both developing and developed countries. As problems become more complex and widespread, resources with which to tackle them are dwindling. New approaches needed to address the challenges must be based on integrated, holistic policy and planning mechanisms at all tiers of government, involving all relevant partners and sectors. In this connection, there is a clear need to improve information for policy- and decision-making, in order that it support the new ways of thinking and approaches to addressing cross-cutting problems.

❐

2

Innovative Teaching Techniques for Distance Education

The twenty first century that poses many challenges and enormous pressure on our daily life, work and society. Information and communication technologies (ICT) transform all aspect of education and distance education (DE), The expression open and distance learning reflect both the information that all or most of the teaching is conducted by somebody who is gone from the learner, and that the project aims to include better proportions of sincerity and flexibility, whether in terms of right of entry, curriculum or other elements of organization. The great growth in ICT has unbreakable this trend. The ODL has the probable to create new patterns of teaching and learning. the Internet as a means of information access and allotment and the explosive growth of the World Wide Web (Web) have changed distance teaching from a transmit mode to an interactive one. staff is all at the turning point and being pressured to increase their efficiency and to change instructional strategy to provide accommodation changes and educational reform. There is a need for the new icon and the new roles of faculty within the changing DE environment. This article deals with the distance education and the innovative teaching techniques .

INNOVATIVE TEACHING TECHNIQUES (ITT)

Internet

The Internet as a medium of learning is explored to the maximum for the creative use and positive impact of such knowledge on the learning process. Topics from recent advances in the subject are allocated to them. Through Internet search, the students acquire the latest know how on the assigned topics and compile the projects in the form of a brochure.

Web-based Instruction (WBI) is defined broadly as any form of innovative approach for delivering instruction to a remote audience in which the Web is included as a tool (Relan & Gillani, 1997). Presently, several Web sites have been developed to provide learners with access to instructional resources from a distance. However, Hill (1996) noted that, most course-based or learning sites simply post course materials. In such instances, use of the Web falls far short of the potential this medium affords. According to Casey (1998), currently used Web models of learning can be identified as one of the followings:

1. **The Web as Electronic Book:** Many institutions have moved to use the Web to present information in a more structured way for teaching process. Students use the screen to read materials, activate multimedia demonstrations, and take self-correcting quizzes or other activities. The course material is mostly factual information, which is to be learned from the Web page and any accompanying media. There is no interaction between teacher and the students through the Web.
2. **The Web as Teacher:** Some Web-based courses include some form of personal communication between students and other students via the use of email and perhaps chat rooms.
3. **The Web as a Communication Medium between Teacher and Students:** In this model, students learn from the teacher but "through" the Web and not "from" the Web. Thus, the Web acts as the communication medium for the necessary interaction. A model such as these aims to mirror a face-to-face learning environment, within which the students will be able to establish some form of human relationship with the teacher. (Ruksasuk, 1999).

Computer Assisted learning (learning through CD-ROM)

The opportunities associated with the development of computer-based technology in contributing to effective science education have grown exponentially within the past decade. The multimedia software available on CD-ROM plays a powerful role with applications in labs and lectures, tutorials and project work.

Seminars

To have interaction, weekly seminars are held and all the students are required to participate actively. The best speaker of the seminar from the entire batch is given an award. The awards are given to inculcate a competitive spirit among the students and bring the best out of the students.

Virtual laboratories

Virtual laboratories detail the preparation, essential equipment, and method relevant to the practical and students then actively perform experiments themselves with simulated responses. Virtual laboratory presents a range of equipment on-screen and may offer a very high degree of interactivity. Training through audiovisual aids can play an important role in medical education.

Students as Project Coordinators

The department inculcates leadership qualities in students. The students actively participate as coordinators of the on-going departmental research projects, by which they are encouraged.

Teleconferencing

It is a new mixed model approach for DE combining satellite teleconferencing with hands-on activity session. It was developed to adjust for many of the disadvantages associated with DE and traditional in person training. The mixed model used live teleconference speakers, video clips, interactive call-in sessions and local sessions.

CONCLUSION

The field of education all over the world is swept by a paradigm shift that is the result of a new awakening in the teaching-learning process. The onus is now on the learner and the teacher is now looked upon as a facilitator. Understanding that the traditional chalk and talk method can no longer enthuse the students, the college continuously strives to innovate methods that will sustain their interest and make the learning process more productive and interesting. Innovative teaching can take many forms. Educators must learn to change with the times and the methods offered for instructing students. These changes will ultimately benefit the students and the education system. The ability to adapt to these changes may be one of the most important attributes for today's educators. The teaching /learning process to create information literate distance students.

❐

3

Miming and Remind: A Web Tool for Teaching and Learning

Teaching is taking place in rapidly changing conditions. It is optimal didactic and educational solution encompassing goals and contents as well as forms and teaching methods allowing for preparing students to face the challenges of the contemporary world.

Web based learning is often called online learning or e- learning because it includes online course content. Discussion forums via email, videoconferencing, and live lectures (video streaming) are all possible through the web. Web based courses may also provide static pages such as printed course materials. Web based learning is the study and ethical practice of facilitating learning and improving performance by creating, using and managing appropriate web processes and resources.

Web-based learning tools have made it easier for teachers to instruct students, and for students to collaborate with those teachers and with other students and parents. These tools aren't magical, but they may seem to challenge definition at times since they save time, help the educators to stay organized, and often take up little space on a computer. Some of these tools or applications are Web-based, which means that they can be accessed from any computer.

Undeniably, the utilization of teaching with web tools and increases their understanding of the knowledge of subjects. In accordance with the teaching by web tools is supposed to help students understand and may solve their problems.

Fig. 3.1: Actions of 60 Seconds in internet in 2019

MIMIND

Mimind is a mind mapping tool designed to create and share ideas and activities, such as project planning, brainstorming ideas, designing, thought structuring, summarizing ideas, discussions, poster presentation, project demonstrations and many other creative applications. It can download miMind for iOS and MacOS directly on your iPhones, iPads and MacBooks from the respective App Stores. Similarly, miMind for android will be put in from the Google Play Store on all android devices. A beta version for Windows PCs is currently on the market with the link at the highest of this page.

FEATURES OF MIMIND

- It is very easy and user-friendly, intuitive, navigate, and unique interfaces.
- This tool is simple, flexible and smart.
- It can be export too many formats: images (jpeg/jpg, png, tga, bmp / bitmap), pdf, text, xml files.
- There is no advertisements, no need to sign-up, completely free.
- Multi-level, logical, hierarchical frameworks, many layout schemes.
- Lines and curves, shapes (square, rectangle, oval, circle, hexagon, cloud, octagon, etc.).
- Online backup storage is availed and restore.
- Undo redo, collapse expand, zoom scroll, crop rotates, drag.
- Copy paste, duplicate, detach reattach nodes also availed.

USES OF MIMIND

- Note taking, scrapbooks, slides, presentation, flash cards.
- Project planning and management at work, home and businesses.
- Helps with staying focused, goal settings, colour-coding, assignments, qualitative analysis, budgeting.
- Creative writing: a novel, fictions, speech, summary.
- Add images, audios and memories.
- Maps: topological networks, not-to-scale road maps, vector drawing.
- Trees: multi-layered, binary, radix, decision.
- Diagrams: graph, flow charts, abstract design, class (UML), state, data flow, complex, venn and
- Much more: Imagination is Limitless.

REMIND

Remind is a communication platform that helps schools and districts to reach and engage with their communities and build the relationships that lead to better learning. Anyone can send quick, simple messages to any device for Free. It should be improve the student success through effective two-way communication. Update the communication and improve the engagement across the learner's community.

- **Advantages:** With over seventy languages and choices to share files and links, it›s easy to keep students and parents informed and involved. Multimedia content like text, photos, videos, pdf and voice clips are possible to share in this tool.
- **Limitations:** while not aware use, it could be more enabling than empowering; families in varying parts of the digital divide may have unequal access.
- Bottom Line: Well-designed, extremely effective electronic communication tool has the potential to stay students and families connected with their colleges.

CONCLUSION

Web based educational tools is an important and fast growing segment of educational technology. It largely overlaps with the field of e-Learning, but it must be noted that learning represents only one aspect of education. It is covers many other educational services, such as teaching, authoring, assessment and collaboration. Above the web tool Mimind and Remind is the very imperative tool in the field of teaching and learning. It is not only the classroom tool, the teacher can connect the students with effective interaction in anytime, anywhere and any place. In this web based tool creates the interest, curiosity to learn the much content among the learners. This condition leads to enhance the academic performance of the students. Undeniably, the utilization of teaching with web tools and increases their understanding of the knowledge of subjects. In accordance with the teaching by web tools is supposed to help students understand and may solve their problems. It may be in creative interactive class and all the students will perform well in academics. There is no doubt this kind of web based learning tools enhance the quality of higher education.

❐

4

New Technologies Transforming the Classroom

There are many new technologies being used in classrooms today: social networking, online teaching, class blogs and wikis, podcasting, interactive whiteboards, and mobile devices. There are many ways in which we can benefit from the new technologies being developed today. For one, new technologies make distance learning easier. It also allows for faster feedback and improved collaborative efforts between large groups of people. Technologies like podcasting and websites allow students to learn and participate in discussions even when they miss classes due to sickness. Class blogs and wikis widen the avenue for discussion and give students a chance to participate outside of the classroom. Interactive whiteboards makes teaching easier, giving students better visual aids and teachers an easier time in presenting lessons; while mobile devices allow teachers to deliver information to students in a lightning-fast manner. Online teaching and distance learning is a fast growing industry. People today are not confined anymore by geographical or cultural boundaries. People want to learn and people want to give out information. In today's world that is growing ever smaller thanks to technology, classrooms aren't just confined anymore to the four walls of traditional schools. Education through technology is the way of the future.

New Technologies Transforming the Classroom

1. **Class Websites:** A modern classroom will have a personalized website which helps students, teachers and parents to be in touch always. This web application provides a single place for everyone in the class to communicate any related things round the clock. The website will have access to announcements, events and calendars and students can have a look at the upcoming assignments and syllabus. The website can even include additional sections such as blogs where students can share their views on any subjects or polls and contests as part of some celebration or decision making.
2. **Interactive Whiteboards:** The period of one-way lectures with a black board and chalk are now getting outdated. The interactive whiteboards that can be connected to computer are really changing the way different subjects are covered in class. These large computer monitors are also visually appealing for students and teachers can easily handle multimedia presentations. Teachers and students even have the option to draw or write on them with ease using its touch screen capabilities. Similarly, note taking is taking a new form with lightweight and flexible digital displays replacing paper note books.
3. **3D Printing:** With this technology, students will have access to 3D models of different elements covered in their subjects. A 3D view helps them to have a deeper level understanding of certain lessons which they otherwise have only limited access when referring just text book pictures. Some working mini-models of certain applications can be set up in class to better learn about some principles. This technology erases the limitations of experimenting options for students. Without giving much emphasis to time and costs, they can freely experiment their preferred designs. The complex concept models can be reconstructed to easily convey tough subjects.
4. **Online Social Networking:** An online platform within a classroom will be an added advantage for students to socialize with their classmates and teachers. Teachers can act as moderators and students can utilize this platform to share their ideas freely with friends. Such opportunities for students can help them to identify their role in taking up learning as a personal responsibility. This can also act as a source for interactive learning where they can discuss their home works and projects and make learning more productive. The social networking tools can play crucial roles in improving engagement, interaction and team building activities in the classroom.

5. **Big Data:** Data generation within classrooms is on the rise every year which includes assignments, attendance, projects and weekly tests. Monitoring all these data in a regular manner is necessary to get an assessment of student's performance which is a tough job. Big data is an efficient tool that helps to manage this monitoring pretty easily by analyzing significant patterns and trends. With this technology, data can be utilized in an efficient manner by saving a lot of time.
6. **Student Response System:** Teachers can receive instant feedback about their classes with such response systems. The modern tools such as Google Forms and Socrative are making the job really easy after every class which helps teachers to develop better strategies in the next class if needed. They can make necessary changes based on the understanding level of the students. This is also a good way to make in-class quizzes or polls at the time of decision making with regard to any event.
7. **Flipped Learning** Flipped Learning is a form of blended learning where students learn their lessons at home by watching video lectures and studying content online, and then doing their homework in class. Basically instead of learning directly from the teacher students learn from each other through a process of small groups using critical problem solving. By using Wi-Fi enabled classroom technology and various mobile-app solutions you can create the interactive environment that students benefit the most from. The value for educators comes from generating powerful analytics to measure student responses while also having the ability to stay engaged with your students in and out of the classroom.
8. **Cloud Computing:** This kind of advanced technology avoids the burden of students to carry their home works, heavy text books and assignments. They can just log in to their device to access their work saved at home system from their class. They can access the reading materials from digital library whenever they have an internet connection. Students can work on the projects anytime with the convenience of their device. The cloud technology also opens a world of virtual classroom learning experience when they can log in from their systems even at the comfort of their home.
9. **Document Cameras:** The advanced document cameras are now replacing the old era projectors for displaying learning content in the classroom for a wider audience. With precise display of text in big screen, students can get a visual treat of interesting lessons. The advanced models can easily capture movies with audio in addition to images. This technology provides ease of convenience in teaching with possibilities of even displaying content from SD cards.

10. **Augmented Reality (AR):** Engaging students in a classroom is the key to gain their interest for learning and this is possible up to a great extent with augmented reality (AR). The technology provides students an indirect vision of a real-world setting. They get an experience of getting physical with elements which are bettered with sensory inputs and graphics. With improved engagement and interaction, learning can be all fun for students. The endless possibilities of this technology help students to think out of the box and excel in the learning.
11. **Communication Apps:** These are becoming a must-have tool in today's classroom. Whether it is Teacher Kit or Remind 101, communication between teachers, students and parents are a lot easy than before. The child's activities in school can be monitored by parents with a virtual presence. They can also be intimated about any upcoming events or happenings in school. Students will get reminders from teachers regarding project deadlines and homework assignments which make the job a lot easy for teachers.
12. **Virtual Field Trips:** With limited time to go out of classrooms and explore different places and subjects, the virtual field trips are proving really beneficial for modern classrooms. With the endless possibilities of World Wide Web, the students can experience a guided exploration. This online learning experience can be customized depending on the subjects to be covered. Teachers also add tools for visualization, modelling and simulation along with this digital trip to enable them to think critically. They can engage in data collection and analysis, scaffolding and discussion to get the better out of this experience. Virtual studios are also slowly becoming an important tool in today's classroom.
13. **Artificial Intelligence:** As each student prefer a varied learning style, the regular teaching methods may not be feasible for everyone. Their different progress rates and pace in learning can be better handled with artificial intelligence. With this technology, they would be able to pick up lessons in their preferred pace. The machine learning and artificial intelligence can play a key role in improving the weak areas of different students with customised learning.
14. **Biometrics:** Even when this technology is dominant in security industry, its possibilities are opening a new phase in the education sector. The eye tracking are finding its use for teachers to learn how the students understand and absorb the lessons. In libraries, the iris patterns can be used to know the identity of the students who are borrowing books which avoids the manual labour and saves time. The facial recognition and fingerprints are also helpful in easing off the class attendance.

CONCLUSION

Easy information access is the key to a successful learning phase and these future technologies are designed to bridge the online and offline gaps. With the use of modern technology in classrooms, students are getting all freedom to express their voice and creativity while learning new concepts in a different way. A sense of pleasure and the opportunities to explore new technology helps students to approach the world of learning in a positive mode. The modern classroom experience has really changed the way students perceive education and they love this phase of life than ever before. With more and more technologies to be introduced in the near future, tomorrow's classrooms would be a better place for students.

❐

5

ICT Enabled Learning Environments

Now-a-days the role of Information and Communication Technology, in the education sector plays an important role, especially in the process of empowering the technology into the educational activities. Education sector can be the most effective sector to anticipate and eliminate the negative impact of ICT. Technology in another side can be the most effective way to increase the student's knowledge. The use of ICT in education adds great value to teaching and learning by enhancing the effectiveness of learning. It adds an extra dimension to the process and the environments of teaching-learning that were not previously available. After the inception of ICT in colleges and schools, the students find learning in a technology enhanced environment more stimulating, entertaining and engaging than in a traditional classroom environment. In that way the students can access information in the areas for their requirement. WWW and Internet are the most two important tool which is supporting for communication and Information transfer. The Internet and www have occupied great place supporting the students and the research scholars in all the areas.

ICT RESOURCES IN LEARNING ENVIRONMENT

The resources are divided into two types depends on its features. They are;

- Online resources, which may include the online resources, are providing information to its users via internet and WWW. Online resources are considered virtual one. Users are able to use the information in intangible manner. Some examples of on-line resources are (i) E-journal (Full Text & Bibliographic Databases), (ii) E- books, (iii) On-line Databases, (iv) Web sites
- Other type resources may include the off line resources that are keep inside the library in the form of electronic materials. Users can be able to touch physically and use it. Some examples of resources are (i) CD ROM, (ii) Diskettes, (iii) Other portable computer databases

ROLE OF ICT IN TRANSFORMING LEARNER ENVIRONMENTS

Research has shown that the appropriate use of ICTs can catalyze the paradigmatic shift in both content and pedagogy that is at the heart of education reform in the 21st century. If designed and implemented properly, ICT supported education can promote the acquisition of the knowledge and skills that will empower students for lifelong learning. When used appropriately, ICTs especially computers and Internet technologies enable new ways of teaching and learning rather than simply allow teachers and students to do what they have done before in a better way. These new ways of teaching and learning are underpinned by constructivist theories of learning and constitute a shift from a teacher-centered pedagogy in its worst form characterized by memorization and rote learning to one that is learner-centered.

Active Learning

ICT-enhanced learning mobilizes tools for examination, calculation and analysis of information, thus providing a platform for student inquiry, analysis and construction of new information. Learners therefore learn as they do and, whenever appropriate, work on real-life problems in-depth, making learning less abstract and more relevant to the learner's life situation. In this way, and in contrast to memorization-based or rote learning, ICT-enhanced learning promotes increased learner engagement. ICT-enhanced learning is also 'just-in-time' learning in which learners can choose what to learn when they need to learn it.

Collaborative Learning

ICT-supported learning encourages interaction and cooperation among students, teachers, and experts regardless of where they are. Apart from modeling real-world interactions, ICT-supported learning provides learners the opportunity to work with people from different cultures, thereby helping to enhance learners' teaming and communicative skills as well as their global awareness. It models learning done throughout the learner's lifetime by expanding the learning space to include not just peers but also mentors and experts from different fields.

ICT TOOLS IN LEARNING ENVIRONMENT

As we know the importance of ICT in education, we also should be aware of the increasing needs of ICT tools that are being applied to assist teaching and learning in the classroom. Among thousands of tools available in the educational fields nowadays, there are five which have caught my attention in terms of their practicality and interactivity.

Social Networks

A recent survey from the Pew Internet & American Life Project found that 73 percent of online teens use social-networking sites. Updating their Facebook or MySpace page has become a regular activity for teens as is using these services to catch up on what their peers are doing. But, for the most part, teens are using social networking while they are away from school. Many schools actually ban access to services like Face book and Twitter and often configure filtering programs to block students from accessing them.

- Advantages of Social Networking in the Classroom
- Make literature real. Have students create a Face book page for a character from literature you are studying like.
- Follow famous people. Many famous people are on Twitter. Have students follow someone related to what you are studying, such as following President Obama when looking at government.
- Twitter treasure hunt. Use GPS treasure hunting to send students in search of educational clues.
- Study geography. Use a combination of Twitter and Google Earth to help teach geography-based lessons.
- Connect with other classrooms. Collaborate with another classroom, no matter where they are in the world, to expand learning opportunities.
- Recent public updates. The recent public updates on Twitter shows the most recent posts from all users and is a great tool to use when studying current events.

- Field trips. Use Skype to bring the field trip into the classroom when it is difficult or impossible for students to go to the source.
- Conference with parents. Stay connected with parents through social media to communicate their child's progress.

Edu blogs

- Edu blogs can do a lot, and it would be impossible to list everything in one place. Edu blogs are great for group projects, e-Portfolio, school newspapers, reflection journals, class web sites and much more.Edu blogs are:
- Safe and Reliable: Blogs can be completely private or open to the public. Since we only host education related content, Edu blogs are allowed by most school filters where other blogging platforms are not.
- Student Friendly: It is as simple to add to and update a blog as it is to send an email. Teachers can easily create and manage as many student blogs as needed.
- Rich with Features: A few of the most popular features include discussion tools, video embedding, Face book and Twitter integration, and calendars.
- Customizable: With over 100 different themes which allow for control of colors, images, and layout.
- Research-Based: Engage students in their learning and enhance instruction through collaboration, student portfolios, and endless classroom uses.

Wikipedia

Wikipedia represents a radical step in information access and availability. As writer and educator Will Richardson has noted, Wikipedia's goal is nothing less than "collecting the sum of human knowledge" in a vast, constantly growing digital repository. Such an enormous mission is made at least partly possible by allowing anyone in the world to edit the site's entries and thus make their own contribution to the overall pool of knowledge (the site derives its name partly from "wiki," a term for any website that allows multiple users to easily add or change content). Wikipedia currently features active encyclopedias in more than 90 languages with plans for the development of many more. As in conventional encyclopedias, Wikipedia's English language encyclopedia contains articles about topics traditionally considered important, but it also includes entries on all manner of contemporary popular culture and current events.

Smart Board

Presentation tools are increasing in popularity for educators who want to share ideas and information with large or small groups of students. Interactive applications are in demand for educators who want to involve their students in learning with technology. The electronic interactive whiteboard is a device that combines both of these attributes; offering shared learning experiences for large or small groups as well as for distance learning. The interactive electronic whiteboard is great for demonstrations. In the survey, many technology teachers and specialists reported enthusiasm for the board in staff development or computer class to show students how to use a particular application. Because the presenter can run the application from the board, using his finger like a mouse, it is easy to show the important features of particular software. The board can accommodate different learning styles. Tactile learners can benefit from touching and marking at the board, audio learners can have the class discussion; visual learners can see what is taking place as it develops at the board. All ages of students respond favourably to board use. Interactive whiteboards were originally used in the business world for group meetings. As they have gained popularity in schools, teachers have reported success with the youngest learners through students in academic settings.

E-Readers

E-readers are electronic devices that can hold hundreds of books in digital form, and they are increasingly utilized in the delivery of reading material. Students both skilled readers and reluctant readers have had positive responses to the use of E-readers for independent reading. Features of E-readers that can contribute to positive usc include their portability and long battery life, response to text, and the ability to define unknown words. Additionally, many classic book titles are available for free in E-book form.

Flipped Classrooms

The flipped classroom model, involving lecture and practice at home via computer-guided instruction and interactive learning activities in class, can allow for an expanded curriculum. There is little investigation on the student learning outcomes of flipped classrooms. Student perceptions about flipped classrooms are mixed, but generally positive, as they prefer the cooperative learning activities in class over lecture.

CONCLUSION

Now-a-days the role of Information and Communication Technology, especially internet in the education sector plays an important role, especially in the process of empowering the technology into the educational activities. Education sector can be the most effective sector to anticipate and eliminate the negative impact of ICT. Technology in another side can be the most effective way to increase the student's knowledge. Being aware of the significant role of ICT in our life, especially in the educational activities, education authorities should be wise enough in implementing the strategies to empower ICT in supporting the teaching and learning process in the classroom. ICT is not just the bloom of the educational activities, but also it will be the secondary option to improve the effective and meaningful educational process. ❒

6

A Study on Emotional Intelligence, Adjustment and Academic Achievement in Relation to their Social Maturity

Today `humanity' is perhaps sitting on the top of volcano and is facing many challenges in bringing about a healthy society. Every one today appears to be tenser than the past either due to lack of understanding and confidence among themselves or because of psychopathic morbidities like parent child relationship, loveless domestic life, broken families, global terrorism and narrow considerations. Values have sunken to gain their selfish motives to sustainable development. People can be both humanly pro-social and destructively anti-social as they are not necessarily aware of their values, some may even conflict with conscious values. The necessity of making a choice commonly leads to a specific `cognitive strain' and it appears to be difficult to make up one's mind especially, when each alternative offers values that the other does not and the choice is an important one. It is at times minimal or immense, at times ridden or open and at times constructive or destructive, any time in making a choice at the cost of another, conflict is a perceived incompatibility of actions and goals that prevents, obstructs interfere, injuries or in some way makes another activity less likely or less effective.

Concept of Conflicts

The term `conflict' is used in so many ways in our day to day set up. There may be conflicts between the ideologies of two sects, cultures, religions and organisations. Conflict may be aroused between husband and wife, father and his son, the teacher and the taught. They may also show their presence among brothers and sisters, members of an organisation or community, states of a country and countries of the world at large. Apart from these external or outer conflicts, there are inner or internal conflicts which are called psychological conflicts.

Statement of the Problem

A study on value conflicts and mental health of students at the Higher Secondary level in relation to their social maturity.

Objectives

To find out the dimension of value conflict of higher-secondary students.

1. To find out the level of mental health of higher secondary students
2. To find out the level of social maturity of higher secondary students
3. To find out whether the different dimensions of value conflict viz. Fortitude, Self - Reliance, Probity, Affection, Assertion and Idealism exhibit different levels of (i.e.) low, average and high social maturity among students studying in higher secondary level.
4. To find out whether categories of mental health exhibit different levels (i.e.) low, average and high social maturity.
5. To find out whether there is significant association between value conflict and mental health of students studying at higher secondary level.
6. To find out whether there is significant difference between scores of value conflict of students studying at higher secondary level.

Limitations

- The study is done only in Chennai City.
- The XI Standard Students are taken as the sample.
- The study is done with 302 samples.

Tools

- Value Conflict Scale prepared by R.L. Bharadwaj (2006).
- Social Maturity Scale prepared by Dr.Nalini Rao (2009).
- Mental Health Inventory prepared by Droved and Augustine (2010).

Sample

The present study is mainly concerned with XI standard students studying in schools following the syllabus of Tamil Nadu State Board of Secondary Education. For the study, a sample of 302 students of standard XI studying in Chennai City during the academic year 2006-2007 were taken.

TABLE. 6.1: Showing the Details of the Composition of Students in the Sample

Type of Management	Name of the School	Number of Students	
		Boys	Girls
Government	Government Higher Secondary School for Boys, Saidapet, Chennai - 15.	53	-
	Lady Willingdon Higher Secondary School for Girls, Triplicane, Chennai - 5.	-	67
Government Aided	St. Joseph Higher Secondary School, Bharathi Nagar, Chennai - 39.	52	-
	K.K.Nirmala Girls' Higher Secondary School, Ashok Nagar, Chennai - 83.	-	48
Private	Madras Christian College Matric. Higher Secondary School, Chetpet, Chennai - 31.	41	-
	Fathima Matriculation Higher Secondary School, Kodambakkam, Chennai - 24	-	41

Pilot Study

Before finalizing the final from the tools and collecting data for main study, a pilot study was attempted. It was conducted in the month of September, 2017 on 30 XI Standard students drawn from each school selected randomly from the whole sample to establish reliability and validity of the various tools used in the study.

Analysis of the Data

Categories of Value Conflicts

Value conflicts have been categorized into six dimensions, viz., fortitude, self - reliance, probity, affection, assertion and idealism. The percentages of these categories are shown below.

TABLE. 6.2: Showing the Criteria of Classifying the Sample based on Categories of Value Conflicts

Dimensions of value conflicts	Percentage
Fortitude	51.7
Self - reliance	62.9
Probity	49.3
Affection	48.7
Assertion	59.3
Idealism	64.6

From the above table, it is clear that the dimension of value conflicts of the higher secondary student is idealism. Hence, Hypothesis I which states that, The dimension of value conflict is idealism in nature» is accepted.

Categories of Mental Health

The quartile points for the distribution of the mental health score have been computed and those falls above 'Q3' are taken as the high group, those below 'Q1' are termed as low mental health group. The moderate group lies in between these two group scores. The details are computed below.

TAB:E. 6.3: Showing the criteria of classifying the sample into three groups of mental health

Groups	Mental Health Score range	Number of students	Percentage
Low	0 - 28	44	14.6
Moderate	29 - 39	205	67.9
High	40 - 49	53	17.5
Total		**302**	**100**

It is observed that the mental health of XI standard students is average in nature. Hence, Hypothesis II which states that, «The level of mental health of higher secondary students is average in nature» is accepted

Categories of Social Maturity

The quartile points for the distribution of social maturity score have been computed and those full above 'Q3' are taken in the high group, those below 'Q1' are in the low group. The moderate group lies in between these two group scores. These details of the categories are stated as follows.

TABLE. 6.4: Showing the Criteria of Classifying the Sample into three Groups of Social Maturity

Groups	Social Maturity Score range	Number of students	Percentage
Low	0 - 28	69	22.8
Moderate	219 - 257	226	74.8
High	258 - 297	7	2.3
Total		**302**	**100**

It is observed that the social maturity of XI Standard students is average in nature. Hence, Hypothesis III which states that "The level of social maturity of higher secondary students is average in nature" is accepted.

Association between Value Conflicts and Social Maturity

The association between the variables, value conflicts and social maturity has been assessed through chi - square test, the details of which are found in the following table.

TABLE. 6.5: Showing the Chi - Square Distribution to Find out the Association between Value Conflicts and Social Maturity

Value conflicts	Social Maturity			Total
	Low	Moderate	High	
Low	28 (10.5)	17 (34.4)	1 (1.1)	46
Moderate	38 (4.57)	159 (149.7)	3 (4.6)	200
High	3 (12.8)	50 (41.9)	3 (1.3)	56
Total	**69**	**226**	**7**	**302**

$$\chi 2 = \frac{\sum (f_2 - f_e)^2}{f_e}$$

$$= 51.67680$$

At df = 4; table value = 13.28 at .01 level

It is observed that the calculated value (51.68) is greater than the standard table value (13.28). So, it is clear that there is significant association between the value conflicts and social maturity of students. Hence, Hypothesis IV which states that, *"The different dimensions of value conflict viz. fortitude, self-reliance, probity, affection, assertion and idealism will exhibit different levels of social maturity (i.e.) low, average and high social maturity among students studying at the higher secondary level"* is accepted.

Association between Mental Health and Social Maturity

The association between the variables, mental health and social maturity has been assessed through chi-square test; the details are computed as follows.

TABLE. 6.36: Showing the Chi - Square Distribution to Find out the Association between Mental Health and Social Maturity

Mental Health	Social Maturity			Total
	Low	Moderate	High	
Low	24 (10.05)	19 (32.93)	1 (1.02)	44
Moderate	39 (46.84)	162 (153.41)	4 (4.75)	205
High	6 (12.11)	45 (37.43)	2 (1.23)	53
Total	**69**	**226**	**7**	**302**

$$\chi 2 = \frac{\sum(f_o - f_e)^2}{f_e}$$

$$= 31.43703$$

At df = 4; table value = 13.28 at .01 level

It is observed that the calculated value (31.44) is greater than the table value (13.28). So it is clear that there is significant association between the mental health and social maturity of students. Hence, Hypothesis V which states that, *"The different categories of mental health (i.e.) low, average and high will exhibit different levels of social maturity"* is accepted.

Association between Value Conflicts and Mental Health

The significant association between the variables value conflicts and mental health has been assessed through chi - square test, the details of which are found in the following table.

TABLE. 6.7: Showing the Chi - Square Distribution to Find out the Association between Value Conflicts and Mental Health

Value Conflicts	Mental Health			Total
	Low	Moderate	High	
Low	19 (7.46)	24 (30.46)	3 (8.07)	46
Moderate	21 (32.45)	150 (132.45)	29 (35.09)	200
High	4 (9.08)	31 (37.09)	21 (9.83)	56
Total	**49**	**200**	**53**	**302**

$$\chi 2 = \frac{\sum(f_o - f_e)^2}{f_e}$$

= 48.36707

At df = 4; table value = 13.28 at .01 level

It is observed that the calculated value (48.37) is greater than the table value (13.28). So it is clear that there is significant association between value conflicts and mental health of students. Hence, Hypothesis VI which states that, *"There is significant association between value conflicts and mental health of students studying at the higher secondary level"* is accepted.

Influence of Sex on Value Conflicts

The mean scores of value conflicts of boys and girls have been computed and the difference is tested for significance as shown below.

TABLE. 6.8: Showing the Significant Difference between the Mean Scores of Value Conflicts of Male and Female XI Standard Students

Group	Number of Students	Mean	Standard Deviation	Standard Error	Critical ratio	Level of Significance
Male	145	75.0000	9.387	0.780	1.28	N.S.
Female	157	73.5606	10.167	0.811		

The calculated table value (1.28) is less than the standard table value (1.96) at .05 level. So, it is clear that there is no significant difference between the mean scores of value conflicts of male and female students. Hence, Hypothesis VII which states that, *"There is no significant difference between the mean scores of "value conflicts" of students studying at the higher secondary level with respect to sex"* is accepted.

TABLE. 6.9: Showing Multiple Comparisons of the Significant Difference of the Mean Scores of Value Conflicts of Students Studying in Different Type of Management of Schools

Groups compared	Number of Students	Mean	Standard Deviation	Standard Error	Critical Ratio	Level of Significance
Government Vs Government Aided	119	71.5630	8.649	0.793	1.29	N.S.
	101	73.2178	10.095	1.005		
Government Vs Private	119	71.5630	8.649	0.793	6.12	0.01
	82	79.4268	9.153	1.011		
Government Aided Vs Private	101	73.2178	10.095	1.005	4.36	0.01
	82	79.4268	9.153	1.011		

The above table reveals that in the first comparisons, since the calculated `t' value (1.29) is less than the standard table value (1.96), there is no significant difference between the mean scores of value conflicts with respect to type of management of schools. In the second comparisons, there is significant difference between the mean scores of value conflicts with respect to type of management of schools. In the third comparisons, there is significant difference between the mean scores of value conflicts with respect to type of management of schools.

Hence, Hypothesis VIII which states that, *"There is no significant difference between the mean scores of "value conflict" of students studying at the higher secondary level with respect to type of management of schools"* is partially accepted.

Influence of Father's Monthly Income on Value Conflicts

The obtained scores of value conflict with respect to father's monthly income have been computed as the difference is tested for significance as shown below.

TABLE. 6.10: Showing the Significant Difference between the Mean Scores of Value Conflicts with Respect to Father's Monthly Income

Group	Number of Students	Mean	Standard Deviation	Standard Error	Critical ratio	Level of Significance
Less than Rs.3,000	87	73.4713	9.417	1.010	0.90	N.S
Above Rs.3,000	215	74.5674	9.969	0.680		

The calculated table value (0.90) is less than the standard table value (1.96) at .05 level, so it is clear that there is no significant difference between the mean scores of value conflicts with respect to father's monthly income.

Hence, Hypothesis IX which states that, «There is no significant difference between the mean scores of «value conflicts» of students studying at higher secondary level with respect to father's monthly income» is accepted.

Influence of Sex on Fortitude

The mean scores of fortitude of boys and girls have been computed and the difference is tested for significance as shown below.

TABLE. 6.11: Showing the Significant Difference between the Mean Scores of Fortitude of Male and Female XI Standard Students

Group	Number of Students	Mean	Standard Deviation	Standard Error	Critical ratio	Level of Significance
Male	145	12.7862	2.366	0.197	2.19	0.05
Female	157	12.1911	2.351	0.188		

The calculated table value (2.19) is greater than the standard table value (1.96), so it is clear that there is significant difference between the mean scores of fortitude of male and female students. Hence, Hypothesis X which states that, «There is no significant difference between the mean scores of «fortitude» of students studying at the higher secondary level with respect to sex» is rejected.

Educational Implications

Mental health is to be assessed by how a person thinks feels and acts, when faded with life's situations. Mental health is how people look at themselves, their lives and the other people in their lives, evaluate their lives, evaluate their challenges and problems and explore choices. This including stress, relating to other people and making decisions. The teachers and parents are responsible for the development of a good mental health.

Family acts as a powerful source of influence on the child's social maturity and other related traits. Social maturity appears to be cumulating and one who is socially adaptive gets greater opportunities to further practice and improve one's social skills. The implications of findings such as those reviewed are that, our education program planned on the theory that there are various stages of development in pupil's social maturity. So, contributing to the social development of pupils and helping them to attain social maturity are important. It is the ability or skill with which an individual maintain order and system in his relation with others in the society.

CONCLUSION

The purpose of the present investigation was to study the relationship among the variables, such as value conflicts, mental health and social maturity. The study is sure to find some usefulness in the field of education and findings of the study can serve as a database for further research.

❐

7

Education and Society in Modern India

Sociology and education go hand in hand. If education goes up, society will improve. If education fails to go up the growth of society will be stunted. Therefore I will concentrate on education in this article.

A country can grow only if it makes the maximum use of its resources. India is blessed with huge population of 1200 million, and children below 7 form the bulk of the population. Unfortunately, the school education in India leaves a lot to be desired. Unfortunately, the education system is controlled by unqualified politicians. And those who participate in the process of education are more interested in financial returns, rather than quality of education. Neither the politicians nor others interested in the education system do not consider it as a service. Given below is a table 1 containing some essential information.

Table. 7.1

S. No.	Country	Literacy Rate	Expenditure on Education (% of GDP)
1	Japan	99%	6.5%
2	South Korea	97.9%	8%
3	China	96.4%	7.4%
4	Russia	95%	4.9%
5	India	74%	6%

The Rational for selecting this group of countries: Except for Russia, the other four countries are South Asian countries. They have very ancient civilizations and they were the last to industrialize. If we look at the condition of these countries, about a century back, the level of education would have been more or less the same. All these countries were devastated in World War 2. In the case of South Korea, it was the war between North and South Koreas in the late 40s and early 50s. The reason for including Russia was just to give an international flair. Russia was devastated in the Bolsheviks revolution. The Russian society was turned topsy-turvy. In 1917, the Czar was over thrown and the communist took over. It was a totally proletarian regime. In the Russia of 1917, teachers were treated as bourgeois and either killed or exiled. Russian education took a long time to recover. But we see that these four countries other than India were quick to recover and they saw to it that literacy rate touched everyone. India failed miserably.

As you can see from the tables that the literacy rate in India is very low compared to the other countries. This is mainly because of the quality of those who control educational decision making process in India. Moreover the percentage of money spent is much lower than the other countries. These countries have been selected because their literacy rate was very low around 50 years back. All the countries except India have managed to make a near total literacy rate of 100%. The only country lagging in literacy rate is India.

Education is a life-long process. In the opinion of many prominent educationalists 'Education is the most powerful weapon in the world which is used for changing the world', Mandela (2003). According to David Archer (2018), 'To build a nation, you need education'. According to one of the topmost expert in children's education, Maria Montessori, 'Early childhood education is the key to the betterment of society'. Coming nearer home the teenage wonder girl, Malala Yousafzai (2013), 'One child, one teacher, one book, one pen can change the life of the child'.

It is no use believing in our political system and bureaucratic system to bring about a change in our education. They are utterly incapable of doing so. The results are there to see (Table No.1).

Objectives

It is up to the educated youth of India to bring about the change we desire. Our aim is two-fold. Number one is the search to find out what are the best ways to bring about quality education. Number two is to find out how we can energize the youth to use the best methods to increase the knowledge of our children.

My effort is to do research on how we can make our objectives into reality. Our endeavor will be to do research on how to increase education through the efforts of youth and not rely on government.

Suggestions

Only the youth of our country can bring forth change in the growth of knowledge to the future citizens of our country. The ideal situation would be for every educated youth to take upon himself to educate at least 5 young people, outside the school system. The children could be their brothers and sisters or children of their friends and relatives. This is an ideal which will be very difficult to bring into practice. It will be my endeavor to bring this into reality. It will need lots of dedication and hard work.

According to my scheme of things we should make full use of technology, internet, and social media. This will be my PhD project.

Many people are of the opinion that this will be a impossible task. In their opinion today's youth are more interested in bettering their future than in making sacrifices for bettering the nation. If we study the history of youth, all over the world, real changes have been brought about only because of the ideological passion of youth for justice and fair play. For example: the Napoleonic revolution in France was because of this youth power. The entrenched dictatorship of Hosni Mubarak in Egypt was toppled by student power. All over the world, dictators are always afraid of students.

I will give a few examples of how vision and determination can work miracles. Mohandas Karamchand Gandhi, with his bare hands could drive away the mighty British Empire from our country and obtained our freedom. Another young man, working in a petrol pump as an assistant, could build up the biggest industrial enterprise in India, Reliance Industries Limited. Another young man studying in a University in US could build up the biggest network of subscribers all over the world, within 20 years. The name of the company is Facebook, and the young man is Mark Zuckerberg. Verghese Kurien was working in a cooperative society in Anand, Gujarat. Because of his vision and dedicated hard work he could bring about a revolution in Gujarat. He has lifted thousands of poor women into self sufficient entrepreneurs. In the process he has made India the milk capital of the World. Mohammed Yunus was a social entrepreneur in Bangladesh. He saw the plight of rural women borrowing money at exorbitant interest rates from money lenders. He decided to do something to help the poor women. He set up the Grameen Bank to lend money to poor women. He was so successful, that he was awarded the Noble Prize for uplifting the women of Bangladesh.

Thus we see that where there is a will and vision and persistent hard work, anything can be achieved.

❐

8

Gender Inequality in Education

Gender inequality in education is a persistent problem in Indian societies, especially for the girls from rural areas and lower socio economic backgrounds. Gender is a social construct that impacts attitudes, roles, responsibilities and behavior patterns of boys and girls, men and women in all societies. Gender relations vary from society to society. It is not only a women's issue but also a people's issue being shaped by power relations in multicultural societies like India. It deals with human concerns encompassing diversities and differences. It has been the most endemic form of discrimination operating across cultures in developed and developing societies. When one analyses the present context of gender discourses, the prime concern is how gender functions as a determinant of politics of knowledge production. Gender issues mean the discussion on both men and women, though women who suffer from gender inequality. From all gender issues, gender inequality is the most prevalent in India. Consideration of gender inequality is now common in Government, Non-Government organizations and in the politics in India. Education has the inbuilt potentials of initiating social change in the context of gender relations.

II. GENDER INEQUALITY

Gender inequality is the idea that women and men are not equal. Gender inequality refers to unequal treatment or perceptions of individuals wholly or partly due to their biological differences and socially constructed roles. Gender inequality acknowledges that men and women are not equal and that gender affects an individual's lived experience. These differences arise from distinctions in biology, psychology and cultural norms. Some of these distinctions are empirically grounded while others appear to be socially constructed. Studies show different live experiences of gender issues across many domains including education, life expectancy, personality, interests, family life, careers and political affiliations. Gender inequality is experienced in societies and communities differently across cultures.

Gender inequality is not perpetuated exclusively through differential access to and control over material resources. While there are very distinct biological differences between boys and girls and these can create different needs and capacities for everyone, these differences do not in them lead to or justify unequal social status or rights. The distinct roles and behaviors that are defined for boys and girls and men and women in a society may give rise to gender inequalities, i.e. differences between men and women that systematically favour one group. Gender can be a key determinant of who does what, who has what, who decides, who has power, and even who gets an education or not.

III. GENDER INEQUALITY IN EDUCATION

All activities of socialization attempted in schools make girls realize that they are not equal to male students. Every time when students are seated in rows or asked to stand in lines, teachers unintentionally exhibit the tendency to differentiate boys and girls. Teachers misunderstand the aim of socialization of girls as preparing them for gender roles of women and act accordingly. Girls are appreciated only if they are neat, quiet, soft spoken and submissive. On the other hand, boys who are very active, independent and talking fluently are encouraged. The attitude of becoming famous is more important than proficiency and achievement in education, is promoted among girls. But in boys, attitude is created to consider acting independently and mastering skills are important.

Sex differences in education are a type of sex discrimination in the education system affecting both men and women during and after their educational experiences. Men are more likely to be literate on a global average, although women are more prevalent at in some countries. Men and women find themselves having gender differences when attaining their educational attainments. Although men and women can have the same level of education, it is more difficult for women to have higher management jobs and future employment and financial worries can intensify. Men tended to receive more education than women in the past, but the gender gap in education has reversed in recent decades in most of the Western countries and many of the non-Western countries also.

IV. ROLE OF SCHOOLS IN DEVELOPING POSITIVE ATTITUDE TOWARDS OPPOSITE GENDER

Schools can play an important role in inculcating gender sensitivity in etiquettes and manners of students. It is necessary to create a gender responsive school in which the academic, social and physical environment and its surrounding community take into account the specific needs of girls and boys. A detailed action plan with a definite road map is required in the school curriculum to achieve gender equality. Teachers play a very important role in the early upbringing of a child. Their idea and beliefs can change the thought processes of young children. Children in the formative years easily nurture values and virtues taught to them. Gender sensitivity training should be mandatory for teachers. The training will enable them to disseminate the desirable attitude based on mutual respect and trust between girls and boys. Teachers and peers directly influence gender differentiation by providing boys and girls with different learning opportunities and feedback. Teachers and peers are also sources of learning about gender. Teachers present curricular materials that contain gender stereotypic behavior, and peers exhibit gender stereotypic attitudes and behavior. Children internalize gender stereotypes and prejudices, which in turn guide their own preferences and behaviors.

Schools are important contexts for the socialization of young children's gender attitudes and behavior. Teachers and classmates shape children's gender attitudes and in turn, gender differences in cognition and behavior. Unfortunately, teachers receive relatively little training in recognizing and combating gender stereotypes and prejudices their own and others and as a consequence, teachers often model, expect, reinforce, and lay the foundation for gender differentiation among their pupils. Thus, most schools create and maintain rather than counteract traditional gender stereotypes, biases, and differences. However, educators who adopt a commitment to gender egalitarianism and thus promote cross gender interaction, expose pupils to counter stereotypic models and discuss and teach challenges to gender stereotyping and harassment optimize their pupils' developmental outcomes.

V. GENDER SENSITIVE CLASSROOMS

Classrooms need to be gender sensitive. We have to take care of few do's and don'ts for making classroom interaction gender sensitive.

1. Encourage both boys and girls to be class leaders (perhaps one of each sex). Appoint two monitors in each classroom, a boy and a girl
2. Address and call on girls and boys equally. Do not segregate boys and girls in the classroom in primary classes
3. Make mixed groups for group activities and games
4. Try to 'switch role' for breaking down gender barriers and stereotyping of gender roles
5. Make both boys and girls share activities like cleaning, moving furniture, to the chalkboard during a lesson.
6. Plan and conduct activities that give opportunity to all children accepting one another as equals.

VI. CAUSES OF GENDER INEQUALITY

Bad Mentality

Women are discriminated to the extent that they are best suited for such jobs like nurturing, housekeeping and service provision, while men are believed to be suited for such careers involving high level of decision making and authority. Most people believe that women cannot rule big organizations. Even the women themselves have the same mentality that they cannot most of top positions.

Education level

Lack of proper education is one of the major causes of gender inequality. This is because nobody can go far without adequate education level in the world of today. Many families do not pay proper attention to girl child. They see them not better as compared to men. In this case, they end up not getting proper education.

Tradition and Culture

Culture and traditions are one of the major reasons which makes female to be regarded as not important in many African countries. Some of the village elders in most communities do not support women leadership.

Religion

Research on gender inequality show that a number of teachings in some of the religions is a great cause of increased pains in the world than peace. Even though religion plays a very important role in every human, there exist some weaknesses in some religions which act as cages to the women.

Empowerment

Women lack enough empowerment in some parts of the world. Understanding the importance of empowerment will motivate women and curb the issue of gender inequality. Gender inequality will lead to violation of rights, sexual violence. This problem can be addressed by empowering women and government may also take specific policies in favour of balancing the genders by educating the women folk.

CONCLUSION

Thus, education became a pre-requisite for the acquisition of knowledge, enhancement of skills, development of attitudes and values, and so forth. It is mainly because big gender inequalities in all stages of education in terms of the gross enrollment ratio; gender differentiation in terms of educational literacy; big gender gap in enrolment in Science and Arts subjects; poor enrollment of girls in higher education; gender bias in curriculum and self-learning material; appointment in certain positions in schools and school committees as well as in higher educational institutes have adversely affected the Indian education system. This situation has made accessibility, equity and quality in education almost a far cry. Research shows gender discrimination mostly in favor of men in many realms including the workplace. Discrimination affects many aspects in the lives of women from career development and progress to mental health disorders.

❒

9

Effectiveness of Computer Assisted Instruction Program (CAI) in Teaching Astrophysics for the Secondary School Students

In the present era Computers are used in the classroom as a support system to improve the teaching learning process. It also possible to use the computers to reach new skills or concepts, give remedial teaching, provide for enrichment of learning, development of habits, promote scientific attitude, creative thinking and problem solving etc. all these aspects together have been emphasized in the National Policy on Education, 1986.There is clear and widespread agreement among the public and educators that all students need to be proficient computer users or "computer literate". However, while Governments are spending great deal of money on technology, there seems to be only a vague notion of what computer well enough to play a game, send e-mail or surfing the Web be considered computer literate? Will a student who uses computers in school only for running tutorials or an integrated learning system have the skills necessary to survive in our society? Will the ability to do basic word processing be sufficient for students entering the workplace or post-secondary education?

Computer-assisted instruction (CAI) is an interactive instructional technique whereby a computer is used to present the instructional material and monitor the learning that takes place. CAI uses a combination of text, graphics, sound and video in enhancing the learning process.

In order to overcome the difficulties faced by the students, teacher should adopt different methodology in teaching of Science like drill method, using different audio visual aids, computer aided instruction, Science club etc. One of the methods is auto-instructional method. It is a method of individualized instruction. One of its forms is CAI (Computer Assisted/Aided Instruction) auto instructional teaching. It is very useful to the teachers and the students as it lessens the burden of teaching and learning and it makes teaching and learning interesting. It also helps the students to learn at their own pace and at their own convenience. It motivates the students and increases the enthusiasm of the students. In this method students read different frames and answer the questions that follow and by this way they learn automatically. Even the learning that takes place through CAI is accurate and untiring. The most beneficial part of CAI is it provides the mixture of wide range of visual, graphics and pictures to make the teaching learning more interesting. Investigators have developed the Computer Assisted Instruction for teaching and learning mathematics for class VIII students in arithmetic portion and tested the effectiveness of the developed CAI.

Objectives of the study

1. To prepare a computer assisted instructional program for Teaching Astrophysics as Secondary level.
2. To compare the effectiveness of Computer Assisted Instructional program in teaching astrophysics with traditional method of teaching science.
3. To compare the mean gain scores of achievement of experimental group and control group in pre test.
4. To compare the mean gain scores of achievement of experimental group and control group in post test.
5. To compare the mean gain scores of achievement of control group in pre test and post test.
6. To compare the mean gain scores of achievement of experimental group in pre test and post test.

Hypothesis of the Study

1. There is no significant difference between the achievements of Pre-test and Post Test Among the students of Experimental group.
2. There is no significant difference between the achievements of Pre-test and Post Test Among the students of Conventional group.
3. There is no significant difference between the achievements of experimental group and conventional group in post-test.

4. There is no significant difference between the achievements of Experimental group and Conventional group in post test.

Significance of the Study

- The teacher can explain the movements of celestial bodies through the animation.
- 3-D diagrams of the planets, galaxies, stars, comets, asteroids and other cosmic matters can be shown to explain them in detail.
- Instead of explaining, the teacher can use audio clips.
- Some Videos related to astrophysics can be shown to students. It will increase their interest in the subject.
- There is an opportunity for the students to interact with the computer.
- Innovations in teaching will help the students to grasp more knowledge about the subject.
- Teachers can cover many points of the concept in less time.
- Teacher can elaborate and explain the concepts in an easy and interesting way.
- Innovations in teaching process develop the interaction between the teachers and taught; hence the teaching will be effective.
- Students will have fun to learn and enjoy the teaching.
- Teacher will get the knowledge regarding the modern technology and its applications in the field of education.
- The utilization of CA1 in education process reduces the work load of the teacher.

Delimitations of the Study

- The research is limited to the Bagalkot city.
- The research is limited to the students studying in 8th standard.
- The research is limited to the concepts of astrophysics.

Design of the Study

The experimental design is employed for the present study. The pre-test is conducted before going to conduct the instructional program. And the pre-test scores are recorded. Based on the marks obtained in pre-test, the experimental research design is divided and equated as two types of groups: 1. Control Group, 2. Experimental group. After the selection of the sample and allocation of the students to the two instructional treatments, the instructional program is conducted.

The instructional treatment is manipulated in the form of Computer Assisted Instruction program setting to the experimental group where as the control group is taught through conventional method.

After the instructional treatment of 30working days, Post-Test is administered to both the groups to know the effect of treatment.

Population of the Study

In this study, one of the English medium secondary schools of Bagalkot city is selected. In that secondary school the students studying science subjects in VIII Standard 40 Students constituted the population of the study.

Nature of the Sample

To achieve the objectives of the study, the researcher uses the experimental method. The sample consists of 40 students from two different schools studying in VIII standard. The sampling is done through Simple Random Sampling method.

The research study is carried out on two groups of Bagalkot city, who are studying in VIII Standard. Each group consists of 20 students. The avg.age of the students is 13 and above.

Tools Used

In order to secure the data, a pre-test and post-test is administered to the experimental group as well as control group; both pre-test and post-test were developed by researcher with the help of experts. The purpose of the pre-test is to equate both the groups, without any significant difference. The purpose of the post-test is to know the Effectiveness of Computer Assisted Instruction program.

Data Collection

There are two different treatment patterns which are applied during the experiment. Both the groups are taught through routine method by the same teacher. The teaching through Computer Assisted instruction is used as the strategy for the experimental group. During the treatment the experimental group received the treatment of independent variable i.e., Computer Assisted Instruction (CAI). The Control group was kept in a Conventional method of Teaching during the treatment.

Before the Treatment Pre-test is administered and after the Treatment Post Test is administered for Both the Groups to collect the data.

Limitations of the Present Study

The present study was limited to Astrophysics of Class VIIIKSSEB text book and therefore whole content of Science textbook was not covered. The duration of the study was one month for each tryout. Data was analyzed using quantitative methods only.

Analysis of Data

The achievement scores of the sample are obtained as a result of both pre-test and post-test. After obtaining the scores, the lists are prepared for each group. The means, standard deviations, standard error of the differences of the two means and t-test are computed. Significance of the difference between the mean scores of both the groups on the pretest scores and post-test scores is tested at 0.05 levels by applying the t-test. To see the effect of the treatment on both the groups the t-test was applied on both pre-test scores and post-test scores.

Figure1: The Factorial Design is Symbolized as Below

	Experimental	Control
Male	CELL1	CELL-2
Female	CELL-3	CELL-4

TABLE. 9.1: Significance if the difference between the mean Scores of Experimental group Students in pre-Test and Post-Test.

Variables	N	df	M	SD	t-Value	Tabled t-value	S/N
Pretest	20	38	6.05	2.889	10.449	2.02	S
Posttest	20		15.75	2.981			

It appears from the above table that mean Scores in the pretest of Experimental group is 6.05 and mean Scores in post test of the experimental group is 15.75. The Difference between the two means was found significant at 0.05 levels. Also table T Value for df 38 at 0.05 level of Significance is 2.02 where as the obtained t value is 10.44. Hence there is a significant difference between the achievements of Experimental group in Pre test and Post test.

TABLE. 9.2: Significance if the Difference between the Mean Scores of Control Group Students in Pre-Test and Post-Test.

Variables	N	df	M	SD	t-Value	Tabled t-value	S/N
Pretest	20	38	6.65	2.593	8.35	2.02	S
Posttest	20		11.15	3.21			

It appears from the above table that mean Scores in the pre-test of Control group is 6.65 and mean Scores in post test of the control group is 11.15. The Difference between the two means was found significant at 0.05 levels. Also table T Value for df 38 at 0.05 level of Significance is 2.02 where as the obtained t value is 8.35. Hence there is a significant difference between the achievements of control group in Pre test and Post test.

TABLE. 9.3: Significance if the Difference between the mean Scores of Experimental Group and Control Group in Pre-Test.

Variables	N	df	M	SD	t-Value	Tabled t-value	S/N
Experimental Group	20	38	6.65	2.593	8.35	2.02	S
Control Group	20		11.15	3.21			

It appears from the above table that mean Scores in the pre-test of Control group is 6.65 and mean Scores in pre test of the Experimental group is 6.05. Also table T Value for df 38 at 0.05 level of Significance is 2.02 where as the obtained t value is 0.69. Hence there is a significant difference between the achievements of control group and Experimental group Pre test.

TABLE. 9.4: Significance if the Difference between the mean Scores of Experimental Group and Control Group in Post Test.

Variables	N	df	M	SD	t-Value	Tabled t-value	S/N
Experimental Group	20	38	15.75	2.981	4.696	2.02	S
Control Group	20		11.15	3.21			

It appears from the above table that mean Scores in the Post Test of Control group is 11.15 and mean Scores in Post Test of the Experimental group is 15.75. Also table T Value for df 38 at 0.05 level of Significance is 2.02 whereas the obtained t value is 4.696. Hence there is a significant difference between the achievements of control group and Experimental group Post Test.

This is because after conducting the pretest researcher taught the content through computer assisted Instruction. So teaching thorough CAI helped students to achieve significantly in post test.

Educational Implication of the Present Study

Students enjoyed learning arithmetic through CAI and it helped students as a supplementary material. Self learning material should be developed in Science where ever possible for all classes and should be used along with the conventional method to make learning an enjoyable and pleasant experience.

10

Educational Innovations in Distance Education

Distance learning is a term that describes instructional systems which allow learners to participate in learning activities from locations other than that of the instructor or other learners. While the term was first used to describe print based courses (also known as correspondence courses), today the term is used as a synonym for online learning. Today, many instructional technologists prefer the term 'distributed learning' over distance learning since the same learning activities work regardless of the physical distance between learners and instructors. Many distance learning courses are combined with classroom-based learning activities. Such courses are typically referred to as blended learning experiences. Distance Education uses all forms of instructional technology, from print to the computer. This range will include radio, television, audio video conferencing, computer aided instruction, e-learning, on-line learning etc.

Open and Distance Learning (ODL)

There is a clear distinction between 'open learning' and 'distance learning'. 'Open education' is the system in which the student is free to choose the time and place, but 'distance education' is a teaching methodology used when the student and teacher are separated by time and place. Thus it follows that not all open-learning institutions come under the purview of distance education and not all organizations that use distance education are open learning institutions.

Indeed there are many cases in which students are in traditional classrooms, connected via a video-conferencing link to a teacher in a distant classroom. This method is typical in geographically dispersed institutions. Conversely, the term virtual university is sometimes used to describe an open-learning institution that uses the Internet to create an imaginary university environment, in which the students, faculty, and staff can communicate and share information at any time, regardless of location.

Historical Development of 'Distance Education'

Distance Education has traversed four to five 'generations' of technology in its history. They include print, audio/video broadcasting, audio/video teleconferencing, computer aided instruction, e-learning, online-learning, computer broadcasting/webcasting etc. Yet the radio remains a very viable form, especially in the developing nations, because of its reach to the common man living in a rural village. In India, the FM Channel is very popular and is being used by universities, to broadcast variety of educational programs in areas such as teacher education, rural development, programmes in agriculture for farmers, science education, creative writing, mass communication etc., apart from traditional courses in liberal arts, science and business administration. The increasing popularity of the iPods, PDA (Personal Digital Assistant) and Smart Phone has provided an additional medium for the distribution of distance education content. Some educational institutions are integrating distance and on-campus students in college courses. Some courses allow distance students to watch on-campus class meetings live via online streaming video, and display real-time comments from distance students on an online chat board displayed during the lecture, making it possible for real-time discussion between on and off-campus students.

Educational Innovations in Distance Education

The UN Millennium Development Goals emphasize on education for sustainable development. In this context, there is a need and demand for innovative methodologies and programmes in the ODL system that would meet the quality requirements of the large and diverse communities of the country, for their overall development. The Indira Gandhi National Open University (IGNOU) is a pioneer in Open and Distance Learning in India and is among the prime educational institutions not only in the country but also in the Indian sub-continent. It has crossed the national boundaries, providing higher education and assisting other developing countries in this regard. It strives to provide cost-effective and quality education to all sections of the society, including those living in remote and far-flung areas through the ODL system.

IGNOU, recognizing the need for such an innovations in the ODL system, established the National Centre for Innovations in Distance Education (NCIDE) with a view to provide a ground for nurturing bright minds whose ideas are expected to revolutionize the ODL system. The aim of the Centre is to develop a culture of constant search for new innovative solutions towards IGNOU's mission of flawless education, cost efficiency and borderless access to qualityeducation. NCIDE promotes, develops and pilots innovations in all aspects of the ODL system and works through the build-operate-transfer (BOT) mechanism. It provides intellectual and technological support to the stakeholders for the growth and development of the ODL system. It acts as a resource centre for prototype development that ensures quality assurance, cost- and learner-related effectiveness, and system efficiency. NCIDE encourages innovations in distance education through collaborations within IGNOU and with other institutes in India and abroad.

Flexibility, cost and convenience are driving more college students to take part in distance learning. The latest report from the Digital Learning Compass says that more than 6 million students across the nation — **nearly 30 percent of all post-secondary learners** — have taken at least one course online. At the same time, the **market for distance learning is becoming even more competitive**. Many schools are adapting innovative ways to enhance student engagement and access to online courses.

The following are some strategies and practices **that institutions can use to increase engagement** of students and teachers for better outcomes in the distance mode of learning.

1. **Instill a Culture of Online Learning Across the Campus**
   The goal of supporting students in online courses starts with institutional leaders and **should be interconnected with all student services**. This covers everything from integrating registration systems for both online and campus courses in providing the same services to both types of learners, including tutoring and library resources.
2. **Increase the Role of Coaches and Mentors**
   Online learners who feel disengaged can regain a sense of belongingness when they have access to staff and faculty who can serve as coaches and mentors. They may assist the learners in more complex and even personal issues.
3. **Tap Instructional Design Specialists to Improve User Experience**
   A list of online learning best practices from Brown University emphasizes partnerships between faculty and instructional design specialists. Faculty members bring their content and teaching mastery to the table, while **the expertise of Instructional Design specialists can be used in**

learning theory, learning management systems and creative online tools. Together, they can develop courses that use varied methods to deepen learning, as well as let the instructor's true voice come through to better connect with students.

4. **Consider High-Tech Innovations for Higher Education**

   Some schools have run successful distance learning programs using technology such as 'predictive analysis' and 'biometrics'. For example, facial recognition software will use real-time feedback to help track students' focus and tailor content to them while they are taking the course.

5. **Use ICT in Distance mode of Instruction**

   Information and Communication Technology (ICT) touches all parts of life including education. The impact of ICT in education can be felt strongly by observing the uses of ICT tools, such as multiple media, in teaching. These ICT tools support the predominant print media being used by the ODL system. The current multiple media being used by the ODL system include audio and video cassette tapes, CD-ROM, interactive radio, television, teleconferencing, video-conferencing, online teaching through multimedia and recently, instruction delivery through iPods.

6. **Use New Techniques in Learner Support System in Admission Procedures**

   The learner support system is overloaded and is slow owing to several factors. An innovative application of technology in admission procedures and practices that is useful and effective can be introduced in place of conducting physical counseling of candidates for admissions. This has the characteristic of user-friendliness and cost effectiveness which are considered highly useful innovative practices. If technology has been used creatively and applied for monitoring the learners' needs and for receiving the feedback from the learners and for dissipating any other learner related dynamic information, it is considered as an innovation which could be a software that can monitor counseling sessions. Further, the feedback from the learners would help in making necessary changes in the system basing on the needs of the learner.

7. **Use Innovative Practices in the Evaluation of Methodologies**

   Monitoring and evaluation are critical elements in managing the system. They provide an evidential base and establish linkages between course structure, instructional delivery and expectations from the students. Evaluation is the most important strategy of the ODL system. The overall aim of the evaluation is to ensure that the programme/course result in the expected outcomes from learners. Evaluation of students in ODL system becomes critical since the learner is not present physically in front of teachers/evaluators as in case of traditional teaching/evaluating mode. The learner in ODL system is generally evaluated by providing self assessment questions in the course book itself, questions at the end of each unit, multiple choice questions, projects, assignments, and through term-end examination. These methods are proved very effective innovative practices in the process of evaluation of the learner under ODL system.

8. **Improve Quality Management and Benchmarking in Distance Education Institutions**

Quality management plays a key role in developing and maintaining quality in distance education institutes. It deals with the quality of the learning experience and the support services. It helps to ensure the completion rates of studies and diminishes dropout figures and results in satisfied students who may in the future be willing to start new studies. Also it ensures that the students are easily accepted in the traditional universities. Benchmarking is one form of monitoring and measurement used in quality management. Benchmarking is being highly used in educational organizations to evaluate various aspects of the teaching-learning processes in relation to best practices or innovations. It provides new methods, ideas and tools to improve the effectiveness of the organization. The ODL system in India needs to improve its quality management and benchmarking mechanisms to develop and establish innovative practices in the system for increasing its efficiency.

CONCLUSION

Open and Distance Learning system would be proved more effective when we introduce the above innovative practices in the system in place of the existing practices.

❐

11

E-Learning in Distance Method

E-learning is commonly referred to the international use of networked information and communication technology in teaching and learning. The number of other terms is also used to describe this mode of teaching and learning. These include online learning virtual learning, distributed learning network and web-based learning. Fundamentally, all these referred to educational processes which utilize information and communication technology to mediate asynchronous as well as synchronous learning and teaching activities. On closer scrutiny, however, it will be clear that these labels refer to slightly different educational processes and as such they cannot be used synonymously with the term e-learning. These comprise lot more than online learning virtual learning, distributed learning, networked or web-based learning.

EVOLUTION OF E-LEARNING

The higher education sector is in the midst of fundamental change. Never before has there been such intense public debate about the place of the university and its role in society. During the 1980s and 1990 there was significant growth in the number of student studying part–time and through distance learning. There has also been a dramatic growth in no-traditional learners, beyond the typical 18-24 year old mainstay of university demand. The growth in and essential of lifelong learning women returning to the workforce after child rearing a burgeoning retirement age population together have dramatically shifted the demographic reality of tertiary education. It is not surprising then that flexible delivery has become something of mantra for tertiary students while also tapping into new national and global opportunities. This appropriate delivery trend has accentuated since the turn of the century with the emergence of new forms of distance delivery that draw upon advances in the various information and communication technologies (ICTs).

NEED oF E-LEARNING

The need for e-learning has as many different answers as the number of different perspectives that people have. E-learning is seen as desirable form of perspectives. The specific need relate to, quite significantly determines approach to e-learning. It is, therefore, important to carefully analyze these and choose a position. Outline some of these below:

Teacher's shortage: In many disciplines, shortage of qualified teachers is a problem plaguing most educational institutions. The quality of the available teaches is another major concern. Given the financially attractive opportunities in the industry and poor academic environment that is seen in most of the educational institutions, teaching jot is among the lowest in the preference list for many.

E-LEARNING AS A PRODUCT IN A CONTEXT

There is an increasing recognition that successful learning required not just quality instructional content but an appropriate context that includes facilitation and an understanding of the learner. The teacher, who supervises the successful deployment an integration of the content into the teaching and learning environment, facilitates this context. The teacher's role is to find, adapt and deliver knowledge using a variety of techniques appropriate to knowledge domain and the needs of the learner. In terms of e-learning, this suggests more away from self-paced instruction and fully online implementation models, toward what is being termed a blended learning approach.

E-learning should not be viewed as just a product, an identifiable artifact of learning objectives, content and interactions. E-learning as a product is a uncertain value until it is deployed in a context that includes its users, technical and organizational attributes the artifact itself has a limited shelf-life and needs to be modifiable, or it will succumb to the pressures of new curricula, changing demographics and favored learning styles and be discarded or completely reworked.

DELIVERY OF E-LEARNING

E-learning may be considered as a backbone for all educational programs, which can be delivered in two platforms. These are:

- **Scheduled Delivery Platform** – Scheduled delivery technology is provided through multicasts, like video broadcast over the network, remote laboratories access, virtual class rooms (live web based classes, access to practical in the labs) etc., can be accessed through a network. Though this method of e-learning creates interaction between the teacher and student, it is restricted by time and place requirements.
- **On Demand Delivery Platform** – The information is provided round the clock and at any place. It includes web based training classes, information resources and interactive CD-ROM services on demand. E-learning can be accessed by a browsing software on any operating system like, WINDOWS, UNIX, MAC, AMIGA etc., over Internet or Intranet environment, by downloading the free web browser software's like Netscape, Telnet etc.

CHALLENGES FACED BY THE E-LEARNERS

The development of E-learning has thrown up new problems focused on the copyright and intellectual property rights implications of electronic text. Students, researchers, staff, employees and other end users affiliated with virtual university or digital libraries should be allowed to print-on-paper excerpts of digitally available works on the same conditions according to which they may make photocopies of print material. The library authority has to discuss seriously with publishers on this aspect in order to evolve some mechanism profitable to users, publishers as well as authors. Users may be charged for each access, downloading from servers and/or each kind of digital library collection. This would provide a reverse for publishers, authors and libraries.

OPPORTUNITIES AND AFFORDANCES OF E-LEARNING

A growing body of literature, learning and teaching is suggesting that learning is greatly enhanced when it is anchored or situated in meaningful and authentic problem-solving activities. This approach to learning and teaching is founded on the principles of learning by donning and experiencing. It places or confronts learners with authentic situations and scenarios which are motivating and which require learners to carry out tasks or solve problems and reflect upon their actions. While such learning designs are suited for any learning and teaching context of media, their effectiveness and efficiency can be somewhat constrained by the fixed time, space and pace limitations of learning and teaching in conventional campus-based classrooms setting. Similarly, printed by their inability to capture and carry much else other than text, picture and illustrations.

ADVANTAGES OF E-LEARNING

E-learning is beneficial to education, corporations and to all types of learners. It is affordable, saves time, and produces measurable results. E-learning is more cost effective than traditional learning because less time and money is spent traveling. Since e-learning can be done in any geographic location and there are no travel expenses, this type of learning is much less costly than doing learning at a traditional institute.

Flexibility is a major benefit of e-learning. E-learning has the advantage of taking class anytime anywhere. Education is available when and where it is needed. E-learning can be done at the office, at home, on the road, 24 hours a day, and seven days a week. E-learning also has measurable assessments which can be created so the both the instructors and students will know what the students have learned, when they've completed courses, and how they have performed.

Students like e-learning because it accommodates different types of learning styles. Students have the advantage of learning at their own pace. Students can also learn through a variety of activities that apply to many different learning styles learners have. Learners can fit e-learning into their busy schedule. If they hold a job, they can still be working with e-learning. If the learner needs to do the learning at night, then this option is available. Learners can sit in their home in their pajamas and do the learning if they desire.

- Self paced
- Time and location flexible
- Cost effective
- Global teaching phenomenon
- Large knowledge domain to choose
- Life time learning options
- More streamlined and focused

MODERATING AND FACILITATING

E-learning requires good moderating and facilitation skills. Moderating involves encouraging students to participate in discussion forums and conferences, ensuring that certain students don't dominate, keeping discussions focused on the topic at hand, and summarizing/ synthesizing the highlights of discussions. Facilitation means providing information that will help students to complete their assignments, suggesting ideas or strategies for them to pursue in their course work, and getting students to reflect on their responses and work

FACULTY COLLABORATION

E-learning offers many opportunities for student interaction and it also provided many possibilities for collaboration among teachers and students. Basically the following kinds of collaborations can be thought of:

- Teacher to teacher collaboration
- Teacher to student collaboration
- Student to student collaboration

There is no face-to-face interaction like traditional classroom hence nobody feels ashamed or hesitation to present his/her opinion. It helps to modify or correct once fault.

CONCLUSION

E-learning refers to learning that is facilitated using digital tools and contents. It involves some form of interactivity, which may include online interaction between the learner and their teacher or peers. According to Kaplan-Leiserson e-learning covers wide set of applications and processes such as web-based learning, computer-based learning, virtual classrooms, and electronic collaboration. It includes the delivery of content via Internet, Intranet/Extranet (LAN/ WAN), audio- and videotape, satellite broadcast, interactive TV, and CD-ROM. In other words, e-learning is concerned with learning facilitated and supported through the use of information and communications technology (ICT). It can cover a spectrum of activities from supported learning, to blended learning (the traditional and e-learning practices), to learning that is entirely online. Whatever the technology, however, learning is the vital element. E-learning is no longer simply associated with distance or remote learning, but forms part of a conscious choice of best and most appropriate ways of promoting effective learning.

❐

12

Women Empowerment throguh Open and Distance Learning in India

Education is the basis for the development of any nation. Education for all is one of the criteria through which the developmental goals of any country could be assessed and evaluated. Open and Distance Learning have been increasingly promoted as a key solution for the historically disadvantaged group i.e. Women. It has emerged as a tool for accessing higher education for women. ODL has been breaking almost all divisions in the education system based on gender, age, race, space, income, time etc.

Open Learning & Distance Learning

The first Open University was established in 1969 in United Kingdom in which first students enrolled in 1971. The idea behind was to bring high quality in learning to the people who had not got the opportunities to study in formally set up universities. Open universities provides diplomas & degrees in education through their open enrollment, distance and internet based education programmes.

Dr. B.R. Ambedkar University was the first Distance Education University established in 1982 in Hyderabad, India. In the present times, open universities have become an invaluable component of National Educational programmes and policies in both developed and developing countries. Information and Communication Technologies (ICTs) plays an important role in empowering women in the developing countries of the world. In present times, Distance education has come out as an advantage to women to furnish them through acquisition of knowledge, leading towards new ways of thinking and to be autonomous and liberated. Education is a fundamental right for all individuals and all the individuals in the society should be benefitted equally without any discrimination based on sex, creed or religion. But according to the data based on literacy levels of the whole world, there is a significance difference between men and women. According to UNESCO, literacy rates of women are very lower than the literacy rate of men particularly in South Asia.

Government explores the use of distance education to provide education at large scale because of expensive conventional educational methods. This also results in excluding of marginalized groups i.e. women who cannot cope up with regular campus based learning because of their productive and reproductive roles. According to Malik, Belawati and Baggaley (2005), Distance education has made possible to impact education at all levels particularly tertiary education can be helpful in maximizing the economic wealth. Open universities are powerful instruments for equalizing opportunities for higher education and also for leveling educational imbalances. Learning takes place outside the schools, colleges and university campuses in Distance Education and communication is provided through Radio, Television, Print Media, Internet, Whats app, Skype etc.

- It is a system of learning which blends:
- Students support
- Makes flexibility in learning provisions
- Removes barriers to access
- Provides curriculum and instruction design
- Gives credit to prior learning
- Provides programme delivery

What is Women Empowerment?

Women Empowerment means strengthening women to resist community, patriarchal forces, biases which are working within the society. This ensures their full participation in all aspects of national development. Empowerment helps women in gaining self-confidence and gives strength to confront gender inequalities in the house, community, national and at international levels. Empowerment is a process of changing the nature and direction of individuals in favour of the marginalized sectors of the society. It is a process to develop autonomy, confidence and self-control in the individuals.

Empowerment means enabling an individual to think, to decide and to take action in an autonomous way. Women Empowerment is process of identifying their strength, their opportunities and their role in molding their own destiny. Now the question arises, how universities can empower marginalized group i.e. women? What can be done to improve women access to education for empowering them? These are the major questions needs to be answered. Women empowerment is a global issue which needs to be addressed.

These barriers have reduced in present times because of open & distance learning provided by various universities. Open and Distance Learning has flexible system and mode of delivery has facilitated a lot in continuing women's education. It has become an ultimate choice for women and also an alternative mode to widen access to higher education. Open and Distance Learning model provided a conducive learning environment to women learners. Delivery of content is also user friendly and self-learning materials are available in printed and electronic modules.

- Benefits of Open and Distance Learning
- Improvement in women's social esteem by earning degree
- Provided second chance to continue their education.
- No requirement to stay on campus to earn degrees.
- Allowed women to study at their own place, time and pace.
- Enhanced the means of empowering women.
- Enabled women to pursue education along with household task.
- Provided flexible system to complete their education.
- Enabled women to earn income.

How Open and Distance Learning (ODL) enhanced Accessible Education for women in India?

ODL has really empowered women by enhancing accessible education to them. The conventional structure of Education was notable to meet the demands of female education, ODL has filled this void. This mode of delivery has provided various opportunities in benefiting the education for women. According to Chaudhary (1995) educated mothers are able to contribute the quality education to their children more efficiently.

There are many groups of women who have not been able to access formal education because of many reasons e.g. women who adhere the religion practice of purdah were not able to access formal education. But Open and Distance Learning mode has empowered these women by allowing them to sit at home and pursue their education without putting risk in their marriages. Other group is of working women. These women were intended to further study after bachelor's degree but due to the marital life and child rearing, they were restricted to continue their study. This hindrance is also covered by Open and Distance Learning mode.

The ODL Potential for Women

A number of Vocational Education Programmes have been designed by various open universities to enhance the knowledge and skills of students for their immediate employment. These need based programmes are delivered through Vocational Programmes Centers. These programmes primarily helpful for the under priviledged section of the country as they have to shoulder many domestic responsibilities.

These days Internet has also become a tool of empowerment of women. There is also growing access of Web these days which has resulted in empowering women by using various tools on the internet. Women have begun to use various social networking sites like Face book, Twitter etc. for Online Activism which has empowered them to organize campaigns and also in voicing their opinions for equality rights. Blogging has also become a powerful tool in recent years for the educational empowerment of women. Electronic Learning (e-learning) has made easy accessibility and affordability for women as they can study from their homes. Information and Communication Technologies (ICTs) has been a most important tool for bridging the gaps in the society.

CONCLUSION

Open and Distance Learning mode of Education has enabled the women to have access of functional training, made them self-reliant and prepared them for the demand of the social system. Distance Education has great potential to equalize opportunities for women and it is an important milestone in the development of Higher Education. Open and Distance Learning is a way of meeting women's educational aspirations to meet obligations of the career and the society.

❒

13

ICT in Education: Its Benefits, Difficulties and Organizational Development Issues

Recently, the development of ICT gradually replaces the traditional teaching pedagogy. Face to face classroom interaction is getting replaced by online communication, traditional white or black board is getting replaced by interactive whiteboard and books or printed resources are getting replaced by online resources. It is believed that technology can bring our education sector from the Dark Age to the light age. This is because the implementation of ICT in college can bring about some potential benefits. However, to obtain those benefits we have to overcome its enormous difficulties. These difficulties may vary from college to college, from region to region, and from country to country. It is frequently firmly believed by the developing countries that the most essential prerequisite of building prosperous nations is technological access, skills, and managements. We often assumed that what makes the developed countries developed is because they have good technological access, skills, and managements. This makes many developing countries see and learn what the developed countries do with their technology. In reality, not only we as the developing countries face difficulties in integrating ICT into our college sector but also the developed countries.

The Potential Benefits of ICT

ICT can provide a considerable benefit in supporting learning. By using technology in their learning, the students can be active learners. They will be aware of what information they need, why they need it, and how they can get that information. This active learning also implies an independent learning. By having access to internet in their college the students will not totally depend on the teachers. They can explore information available in the internet, find information that they need, copy it, and go on to find more and more information. By using this learning system, the students also becomes self-managed in their learning process.

ICT also can provide a way for dynamic and collaborative learning. By using internet our learning is not limited to the college hours, demographically where we are, and who our teachers are. We can access internet anytime and anywhere. As stated e-learning allows the students to get information faster from everywhere and anytime. Technology also enables usto cross the demography limits. Rural students can access information from urban areas, get information and share knowledge with other students or teachers in the same area or even different countries. Besides dynamic learning, ICT allows all the human components of colleges; the principals, administrators, teachers, IT coordinators, and the students to get involved in the collaborative learning and forming learning communities.

Organizational Development Issues for Implementing ICT

Implementing ICT in classroom is not the matter of bringing the most modern technology to the colleges and throwing all of the stuffs into classroom for the teachers to use it. This will not work effectively.

Cosmetic use of ICT happens when teachers feel that they are pressed to use technology in their teaching, even though they believe that using computer for teaching certain lesson is not the best method. They may say to their self I do not usetechnology in my class, others may see me as incompetent teacher. Thus, they are forced to use technology in their class even though it is not really needed. Technological imperative traps colleges when the college community becomes extremely enthusiastic about using technology in colleges, no matter it are really useful or not. Colleges are trapped in romantic vision when the colleges believe that technology is better than teacher. They believe that technology can replace teacher in teaching. Technological competition occurs when a certain college achieves superior status just because it applies the most up-to-date technology without thoughtfully considering the education instructional design. To make the use of ICT in education effective, then we have to consider some organizational aspects. Those are the college's culture, the role of the leaders, the selection of the software/hardware, the college integrity or ethical issue, and college management system.

Many colleges are rejecting the implementation of ICT because there is a mismatch between the college's culture and the introduced software/hardware. "How acceptable a new technology will be in a society depends on how well the proposed innovationist the existing culture." Thus, before introducing the new ICT in particular colleges, we have to understand the college's culture. More importantly we have to understand the intended value which the colleges want to transmit to their students. The college's community will reject the coming of the new technology if the introduced technology is not congruent with the college's value.

The other consideration is getting the support of the leaders. The leaders have power to influence the teachers and other staffs to accept or refuse a certain technology. One who can empower and influence them is the college's leader. The principals also should be willing to learn the introduced software/hardware. They should give examples for the teachers how to accept and learn the new technology. Consideration on the ethical issue relating to the use of technology is also very important. Colleges are regarded as the place to grow moral integrity. The proposed ICT will be clearly rejected if the colleges regard that that ICT will endanger the colleges integrity. For instance, internet access will open up an opportunity for the students to plagiarize or download pornographic sites. Many students do not care how to carefully operate the computers so that it can last longer. Even some of them steal the component of the computers. The colleges should address this problem unless they should spend expensive cost to buy new computers again and again.

The ICT implementation should also be supported by good coordination and management system on the ICT application. Progress of ICT in colleges, or conduct ICT training. This aspect is very important since many teachers are reluctant to use technology in class because they frequently do not get immediate help when they stuck with computers in class. The practical factors include the management and coordination, the time availability of teachers and students, the availability of technology, sufficient training and college support. Attitude and ethos factors cover the perception and belief of each college's member, and the college's characteristics.

They also do not have computing educational background/skills. Secondly, there is insufficient college support. When teachers find problems with the technology in class, they do not get immediate help from the IT-coordinators. This makes many teachers are reluctant to use technology since stuck technology machine can interrupt the teaching-learning process. Thirdly, there is lack involvement of the college leaders. The unsupportive leaders may impede the successful implementation of ICT. Fourthly, frequently, the layout of classroom also can cause difficulty. Using computer/technology in class requires moveable chairs or flexible seat design which allows the students to work in groups and individually. Moreover, computers need to be placed in special class with certain temperature or other special environmental condition to make the computers last longer. Fifthly, the introduced and implemented software frequently is inappropriate to the college's culture, value, and students need.

Difficulties

Causes Technological difficulties

- **Lack of Computer Facilities:** There are some colleges which do not have computer facilities at all.
- **The Colleges only have some old Computers:** These computers frequently work very slowly and the students become impatient and de-motivated in using computers. Moreover it takes long time.
- **There is no Maintenance:** Many of the teachers only know how to operate it. Many of them even do not know how to operate it safely.

Teacher's refusal

- Teachers are afraid of being embarrassed if they do not know how to operate a sudden stuck computer.
- Many senior lecturers will keep their status quo, keep the traditional pedagogy, and influence the junior teachers to reject the implementation of ICT.
- Teachers also may be afraid of being replaced by computers.
- Many public colleges receive only a small amount of subsidy from the government. These colleges are not able to buy computers or run its maintenance.

CONCLUSION

Implementing ICT in colleges/education has many benefits and difficulties. Each college has its own barriers depending on its contextual factors. Generally the Difficulties can be classified into four kinds of barriers. Those are technological barriers, teacher's refusal, student's refusal, and poor college's technological system. To successfully implement ICT in colleges need to consider many aspects. It will waste a lot of time, energy, and money if before implementing it, we do not consider those aspects. Those are the college's culture, leaders, ethics, and technological management system. ❐

14

Innovative Digital Courseware in Distance Learning

In Distance Learning, Innovation is a great force to increase productivity. Innovations in information communication technologies with digital techniques present opportunities to improve teaching and learning in distance Education.

Distance education places learner and instructors in separate locations. in the earlier days of distance learning ,it was most common to see distance learning used for rural learners who were at a distance from an educational institution. using some form of technology to communicate and interact.

PARAMETER OF DIGITAL COURSEWARE

Need Analysis

It is very important to define the needs before developing the digital courseware. Needs can be identified from the perspective of different stakeholders like learners, teachers, subject experts, practitioners, policy makers etc. It can also be based on the findings of primary and secondary research studies and can be inferred from the current scenario of the educational setup.

Context Analysis

It is the collection of data to understand the physical, technical and socio-cultural contexts in which the Digital courseware will be used.

Learner analysis: (Target Audience)It refers to capturing data with respect to the target audience.

Content Analysis Content analysis defines the scope, appropriateness and nature of the Digital courseware. Good content comprehension is required before designing and developing content. It also helps in understanding the purpose and mode of using Digital courseware.(The Department of School Education and Literacy (DSE&L) MHRD, Govt. of India)

Forms of Digital Courseware

Digital courseware is any form of learning material available digitally. it provides flexibility in time, place, and making rich real environment for learner in distance learning.

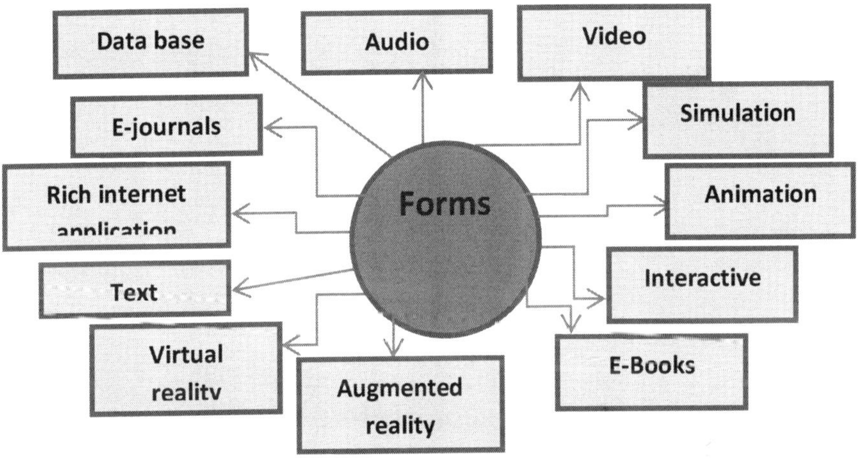

Need of Digital Courseware

- Digital courseware is any form of learning material available digitally which a learner accesses or interacts with so as to achieve related learning outcomes.
- Wide variety of digital courseware is available for free use for teachers, instructors, researchers and students. If used appropriately, digital learning resources can add considerable value to the quality of teaching and to the learners' experience.

Digital Courseware Design Principles

- Align to learning standards or objectives Make the software web based
- and easily accessible.
- Design with the three "i's" in mind: interactive, intuitive, and inquirybased.
- An effective compromise is to engineer an intuitive interactive virtual environment that
- provides students the freedom to explore, yet limits their possible choices. This follows the instructionalstrategy of guided inquiry (National Research Council, 2000).
- Reinforce scientific methodology and critical thinking skillsCreate openended

Process of Developing Digital Courseware

- Digital courseware, development depends upon the nature of the content and its target learners.
- Instructional design is the practice of creating instructional experiences that make the acquisition of knowledge and skill more efficient, effective and appealing.
- The process broadly consists of determining the current status of learners 'understanding, defining the end goal of the instructional material and creating some 'intervention' to assist the transition.
- This systematic approach provides a step by step process for the analysis of the learners' needs, the design and development of the material.
- There are various instructional design models available. Most of the models involve the process of analyzing the learners' needs and goals of the instructional material development, development of a delivery system and content, pilot study of the material developed, implementation, evaluation, refinement of the materials etc.

Digital learning pros

- Using Digital teaching learning process in the classroom allows learner to experiment more in pedagogy and get instant feedback.
- Digital learning environment in the classroom helps ensure full participation.
- There are countless digital resources for enhancing rich education and making learning with conceptual clarity and retention. (Saraswathi.G and Leo Stanly.s)

Implementation Strategy

- Validate in terms of usability, technical features, expected outcome etc.
- Testing the developed digital courseware on a sample of the target group to establish its validity and usability.
- Declaring terms of the compliance of the digital courseware with all standards and requirements.
- Develop feedback mechanism keeping in view various learners and purpose improving digital learning based on the feedback received from various learners.

CONCLUSION

The distance, communication and infrastructure which give rise to major challenges for open and distance learners may be taken care of by experimenting and applying innovations in the field of open and distance education, the majority of which is directed towards optimum utilization of ICT. Some of the solutions to these challenges, in Indian context, are suggested and discussed as optimum utilization of ICT viz.

❐

15

Mobile Learning Technologies for Teaching and Learning

Mobile learning has enhanced upon e-learning by taking it a step further and allowing students to learn virtually anywhere a mobile signal is available. New mobile technology, such as hand-held based devices, is playing a large role in redefining how people receive information. Mobile learning opens up with many doors to new technology and will continue to become more complex as the years go on. So many more opportunities are given to get an education and to expand one's knowledge. This is the only way great way to help people learn better. The recent advances in mobile technology are changing the primary purpose of mobile devices from making or receiving calls to retrieve the latest information on any subject. Mobile devices can be used in brick-and-mortar or online settings to enhance learning experiences. The mobile phone (through text SMS notices) can be used especially for distance education or with students whose courses require them to be highly mobile and in particular to communicate information regarding availability of assignment results, venue changes and cancellations, etc. Mobile devices facilitate online interaction between instructor and student and student to student.

MOBILE LEARNING TECHNOLOGIES

M-learning in the context of work can embrace a variety of different forms of learning. It has been defined as the "processes of coming to know, and of being able to operate successfully in, and across, new and ever changing contexts, including learning for, at and through work, by means of mobile devices". (i) M-learning for work, (ii) M-learning at and through work and (iii) Cross-contextual m-learning.

Learning for work, which could be also described as 'just-in-case' learning, involves classic and formal education activities, such as training courses, that prepare learners for future work-related tasks. A typical, corporate application is the delivery of mobile compliance training, which can be seen as a viable means to reach geographically mobile employees, such as consultants or staff in logistic and transport systems. Another application is mobile simulations that prepare learners for future situations, for example real-time SMS-based simulations for disaster response training.

SPECIAL FEATURES OF M- LEARNING TECHNOLOGIES

Now-a-days, the education system one works in is not always known for its speed at latching on to new ideas and methodologies, but with the mobile learning it is catching up-quickly since the mobile revolution is here. More and more schools are moving toward mobile learning in the classroom as a way to take advantage of a new wave of electronic devices that offer portability and ease of use on a budget. Net books, iPods, cell phones, iPods, e-readers and even PDAs are increasingly becoming the tools of choice for today's educators. Mobile learning technologies offer teachers and students a more flexible approach to learning. Today's students are no longer the people our educational system was designed to teach. "Digital natives" are being exposed to more gadgets and technology than was ever thought possible. This is having a profound effect on the ways in which children learn. They are more engaged in learning when using the latest technological gadgets.

The iPod Touch, for instance, is among the more popular mobile learning devices to hit classrooms across the country. This tactile, touch-screen device is easy for children to use and comes with built-in Wi-Fi to access the Internet. However, it also has the ability to tap into the thousands of apps available at the iTunes store.

MOBILE LEARNING TECHNOLOGIES AND CLASS ROOM PRACTICES

Cell phones traditionally have a bad reputation in schools, but that is starting to change. Instead of banning cell phones, some forward-thinking educators are actively embracing them. But the innovative uses of cell phones in education involve websites like Poll Everywhere and Text the Mob,_which allow a teacher to create a set of questions that the students can respond to with a text message. The results can be displayed instantly as a graph through an LCD projector, or on an interactive whiteboard, and the teacher can gauge the level of student understanding very quickly. A class set of student response systems can be an expensive outlay, but if your students already bring their cell phones to school, why not put them to use in the classroom? Students are more engaged and motivated to learn when they use mobile devices and research shows that academic performances can improve.

For example, the National Council for Curriculum and Assessment in Ireland, for instance, is currently in phase 3 of an interesting experiment with the use of cell phones at a number of Irish schools. Most students speak English as their first language, but Irish language lessons are encouraged to maintain a link to Ireland›s cultural past. The NCCA program aims to increase the level of oral fluency in Irish by providing students with cell phones to support them in language classes. Students are sent text messages with Irish vocabulary words to use during classes and call a number with a voice-response system to leave answers to teacher questions. We as educators need to take note of this and look for safe, productive ways to integrate mobile learning devices into our curricula.

MOBILE LEARNINGFORCHILDREN WITH SPECIAL NEEDS

One example of mobile technology for children with special needs is Proloquo 2go, an assistive technology app available on iTunes. Students with autism spectrum disorders and others who may have difficulty speaking can use the app's library of symbols and text-to-speech conversion to communicate easily and naturally with others. This type of assistive app helps broaden students' horizons both in and out of the classroom. What about e-readers? Is there really a place for these in the classroom? Yes, they are portable, easy to update and cost-effective and can be read on net books, e-readers, laptops and more. It's only a matter of time before other states start to follow and welcome e-books into their own curricula.

VALUESOF MOBILE LEARNING TECHNOLOGIES

- Improving levels of literacy, numerical ability and participation of young adult.
- Using communication features of a mobile phone as part of a larger learning activity, e.g.: sending media or texts into a central portfolio or exporting audio files from a learning platform to your phone.
- Developing workforce skills and readiness among youth and young adults.

- Tutors who have used m-learning programs and techniques have made the following value statements in favour of m-learning:
- It is important to bring new technology into the classroom.
- Devices used are more lightweight than books and PCs.
- Mobile learning can be used to diversify the types of learning activities students partake in (or a blended learning approach).
- Mobile learning supports the learning process rather than being integral to it.
- Mobile learning can be a useful add-on tool for students with special needs. However, for SMS and MMS this might be dependent on the students' specific disabilities or difficulties involved.
- Mobile learning can be used as a 'hook' to re-engage disaffected youth.

BENEFITS OF MOBILE LEARNINTECHNOLOGIES

1. Relatively the cost of mobile devices is significantly less than PCs and laptops.
2. Multimedia content delivery and creation options.
3. Continuous and situated learning support.
4. Decrease in training costs.
5. Potentially a more rewarding learning experience.
6. New opportunities for traditional educational institutions.
7. Readily available a/synchronous learning experience.

CONCLUSION

Mobile learning is a hot new item that continues to gain popularity based on convenience. The fact is that convenience is everything in today's busy society and will continue to be in generations to come. Learning at and through work, which could be labelled as "just-in-time" mobile learning occurs in informal education settings at the workplace. Learning through work also occurs by interacting with distant peers through phone. The aggregation of interests and experiences serves not only as a means to raise awareness but also to help find competent experts on demand, for example with context-sensitive expert location systems.

Cross-contextual learning that bridges the gap between work settings and formal education formats has perhaps the biggest potential for work-based mobile learning, especially with respect to tertiary educational systems.

❐

16

ICT Awareness among Distance Education B.Ed. Students

The aim of this study is to investigate the level of ICT awareness among distance education B.Ed. students. Participants are 100 distance education B.Ed. students. ICT Awareness scale was used for collecting the data. The results revealed that there is distance education B.Ed. students are having an average level of ICT awareness and also Male and female distance educationB.Ed. students havediffered significantly in their awareness about ICT.

Education is a process of human enlighten and empowerment for the achievement of a better and higher quality of life. Teaching is an ever-changing profession. The field of education is expanding each year as advancement is made in technology and brain-based research. To keep pace with the changing world, teachers must have current knowledge and skills of educational technology. Just as technology is influencing and supporting what is being learned in schools and universities, so too is it supporting changes to the way students are learning. Moves from content-centered curricula to competency-based curricula are associated with moves away from teacher-centered forms of delivery to student-centered forms. Through technology-facilitated approaches, contemporary learning settings now encourage students to take responsibility for their own learning. The growing use of ICT as an instructional medium is changing and will likely continue to change many of the strategies employed by both teachers and students in the learning process.

Significance of the Study

The inclusion of ICT in the existing distance educationB.Ed curriculum is very important and its effective integration into the mainstream is absolutely essential. Teachers are being challenged to integrate ICT's into the curriculum and to facilitate new forms of teaching and learning. It is very difficult for them to accept this responsibility before mastering basic computer literacy skills and demonstrating a high degree of confidence in the general use of ICTs. As per the government vision of inclusion of ICT facilities in school, it is the teacher's responsibility to the wellversed in ICT knowledge. To be well versed in ICT the distance educationB.Ed Curriculum should provide adequate ICT facilities and computer education to the future teacher. In the content, there is a need to study some aspects of ICT in distance educationB.Ed. students. The present investigation fulfills the research gap of the study.

Statement of the Problem

ICT in Education is the foundation upon today's development. It is a dynamic force in the life of every individual influencing his physical, mental, emotional, social and ethical developments. It is a complete development of the individuality of a child enabling him to make an original contribution to human life. Exploring the application of ICT in education lies in the hands of teachers i.e. how willingly teachers make use of various technologies to integrate them for making it reachable to the student community. Teachers are no more instructors but a researcher for designing various methods, approaches and models for making a meaningful transaction. All this is possible with appropriate hardware and software technology as it is both and aid for teacher education, enabling educators and trainees to communicate with students enhancing collaborate working among educators. Teachers have the key role to develop the pupils. The teacher must have knowledge of the principles of ICT. Hence thepresent study stated as follows "ICT awareness among distance educationB.Ed. students".

Objectives of the Study

- To find out the level of awareness on ICT of distance education B.Ed. Students.
- To find out whether there is any significant difference between male and female distance educationB.Ed. students with respect to awareness about ICT.

Hypotheses of the Study

- The level of awareness on ICT of distance educationB.Ed. Studentsare average.
- There is no significant difference between male and female distance education B.Ed. students with respect to awareness about ICT.

Methodology

The present study, the investigator applied normative survey as a method. The sample 100 distance education B.Ed. studentswho are studying in the first year of the Bharathidasan University distance education program. The following tool was used for data collection ICT Awareness scale constructed and standardized by Dr. Prabhabati Devi, (2004). The data were analyzed using mean, standard deviation and t-test.

Analysis and Interpretation

Hypothesis No - 1

The level of awareness on ICT of distance educationB.Ed. Students are average.

TABLE. 16.1: Level of ICT Awareness of Distance Education B.Ed Students

Sample	N	Mean	S.D.	Level of ICT awareness
Whole sample	100	84.31	5.207	Average Level

From thetable1, the mean value of the entire sample is 84.31 and S.D is 5.207. The calculated mean value is higher than the percentile 25 (82) but less than percentile 75 (87). Hence, it is inferred that distance educationB.Ed. students are having an average level of ICT awareness. Hence, the framed null hypothesis is accepted. It is inferred that the level of ICT awareness among distance education B.Ed. studentsare average.

Hypothesis No - 2

There is no significant difference between male and female distance educationB.Ed. students with respect to awareness about ICT.

TABLE. 16.2: Male and Female Distance Education B.Ed. Students in their Awareness about ICT

Gender	N	Mean	S.D.	C.R. Value	Level of Significance
Male	47	83.78	5.473	4.38	**Not Significant**
Female	53	84.83	4.900		

From thetable 2, it is found to be critical ratio value 4.38, which is significant at the 0.05 level.Hence, the framed null hypothesis is rejected. It is inferred that male and female distance education B.Ed. studentshave differ significantly in their awareness about ICT. While comparing the mean scores of the male and female distance education B.Ed. students are slightly differing in their level of awareness about ICT.

Major Findings

The level of ICT awareness among distance educationB.Ed. students is average.

Male and female distance educationB.Ed. studentshavediffered significantly in their awareness about ICT.

Recommendations

Based on the study workshops and training programmes should be organized by professionals of ICT to teachingdistance educationB.Ed. Program on modern technology and its uses. To develop steps awareness on ICT should be taken by the government to raise and maintain. All state motive self-employment awareness to ICT in all levels and develop awareness on ICT knowledge, attitude and skills among the distance education B.Ed students.

CONCLUSION

The distance educationB.Ed. students are having an average level of ICT awareness and Male and female distance educationB.Ed. students have differ significantly in theirICT awareness. So the teachers and counselors should maintain the up to date information to the students. The distance educationcurriculum frame workers should consider the above findings while constructing content for distance educationB.Ed students. ICT promote behavioral change through awareness of ICT in education. The findings of the present study provide suggestions to both states administrations and Universities authorities to provide more ICT resource facility in academic programs to promote technological based quality education.

❐

17

Implications for Education in the Era of Knowledge Societies in Uses of ICT

The metaphor of "information society" was first used in Japan by Kohyama (1968) and it was in Japan that this metaphor was first used as a rationale for national policy (Masuda, 1981). In the 1970s, the authors of computer-related texts were not likely to refer to an "information society" but instead used words like "information age" and a "computerized society" (cf. Martin and Norman, 1970; Rothman and Mosmann, 1972). However by the late 1970s and early 1980s, the information society was mentioned so often around the world that many forgot that it was only a metaphor. In fact by the late 1980s, "information society" had become a phrase that captured the essence of a culture inundated by information and dominated by information technology (IT). Daniel Bell's "framework for the information society" spearheaded the movement to legitimize the information society concept (Bell, 1979). He confirmed that a majority of the jobs in the United States were information oriented in that they were structured to produce informational rather than material products. In subsequent years, as global networks became ubiquitous and a global information economy became more obvious, the information society metaphor became even more widely accepted (Webster, 2002).

THE KNOWLEDGE SOCIETY

Ironically, the information society concept was undermined by the emergence of a new metaphor in the 1990s, the "knowledge society." While the information society metaphor was associated with an "explosion" of information and information systems, the knowledge society metaphor primarily referred to economic systems where ideasor knowledge functioned as commodities. Many, if not most, people could not differentiate the two concepts because they tended to largely equate information and knowledge (Allee, 1997). Confusion about the nature of knowledge is still a problem, especially in the field of education. The educational community tends to define knowledge mostly in terms of facts or declarative knowledge, but the field of management defines it much more broadly encompassing insights, values, and other tacit cognitions (Tiwana, 2002). In this chapter, the broader definition of knowledge will be used.

INFORMATION VS KNOWLEDGE

Increasingly, the definitional distinction of information from knowledge is that information consists of intentionally structured and formatted data, but knowledge consists of cognitive states needed to interpret and otherwise process information (cf. David and Foray, 2003). While information can generally be reproduced for minimal costs, knowledge reproduction requires training, apprenticeships, and other more costly forms of transmission. Knowledge that is difficult to codify and reproduce is called "tacit knowledge." Tacit knowledge includes judgment, experience, insights, rules of thumb, and intuition and its retrieval depends upon motivation, attitudes, values, and the social context (cf. Polanyi, 1996; Tiwana, 2002). A knowledge economy necessarily depends upon information as well as the intellectual capital of economic communities. Thus, a knowledge society necessarily presumes an information society, but not the other way around. In this chapter's discussion of education, the rhetoric of the knowledge society will be used, but for the most part it will apply to the information society as well.

KNOWLEDGE SOCIETIES IN EDUCATION

While economists tend to think of "knowledge society" as a global economy, other social scientists tend to think of it as a smaller level social collective. Thus, a knowledge society may exist on at least four levels: a global system, a national or cultural system, a social organization like a professional society, and a smaller community, e.g., the "Dead Poet's Society." A knowledge society is generally defined as an association of people with similar interests who try to make use of their combined knowledge. Of course, knowledge societies are not new, but what is new is that there has been a sharp rise in them and they are much more visible. Their rise follows digital networks that make them possible without members coexisting (do you mean residing?) in the same region and the technology makes accessing and sharing knowledge so much more feasible. On top of that is the pressure to exchange knowledge that emerges from the knowledge economy. Loosely speaking, any educational system is a knowledge society, and that would include schools and classrooms. However, unless the educational unit devotes particular attention to knowledge-related activities, it is not particularly useful to call it a knowledge society. When an educational group invests considerable effort toward sharing and producing new knowledge, then it should be called a knowledge society. Communities of practice, typically groups of teachers that work with each other to improve their teaching, are good examples of knowledge societies, especially those that use all the tools, electronic and otherwise, to facilitate their goals (cf. Hargreaves, 2003). "Knowledge society" in the next section refers to the (global) knowledge society. Later sections of the chapter shift toward smaller scale knowledge societies.

ICT

As noted already, ICT stands for information and communication technology and refers in principle to all technologies used for processing information and communicating. In most educational circles, it means computer technology, multimedia, and networking, especially the Internet. Educators in the United States and a few other countries use the term "technology" or "information technology" instead; however, this appears to be changing to include ICT. In business and industry, the most common label is IT, but sometimes the terms "new media" or "digital media" are used. This semantic diversity derives from the rapidly evolving integration of computers with communications, video, and audio technologies, where the separate technologies become nearly indistinguishable. In this discussion, the acronym ICT is used, recognizing that it means the same as IT or technology to many. Daily invention of new technologies provides a major challenge to implementation of ICT-based educational strategies. Given the skyrocketing pace of new ICT in the past decade, it would not be surprising in the next 5 years to see whole new forms of e-commerce such as Internet auctions or radically new ways to do homework using personal software agents that roam the Internet. It is imperative to track such developments because not only do they change the skill requirements for students, but also they impact society and change research priorities for research on ICT and education internationally.

SOME KNOWLEDGE-BASED MODELS IN EDUCATION

Scardamalia and Bereiter (1996) pioneered various strategies linking educational needs with ICT and knowledge concepts. One strategy is to use software that helps students build new knowledge using scientifically guided experimentation and computer-based tools and resources. Another is to foster and guide knowledge-building communities (Bereiter, 2002). Learning tools are used that assist both with basic skills and with higher-level knowledge. The common element to these strategies is the goal of preparing learners for the knowledge society through exercises in ICT knowledge-based activities. Using a very different rhetoric, Jonassen's (1999) "mindtools" paradigm also seeks to optimize learning using software to augment higher-level knowledge-based functions. Mindtools, which are guided activities utilizing software tools, put the student in the role of designer or partner, as most activities require construction of some type of product, usually knowledge. Other activities facilitate collaborative conversations, cognitive amplification, and reflection aimed to enhance critical thinking skills. The influential "How People Learn" model argues that the last research in the cognitive processes of learning provides a guide for instruction (Bransford et al., 1999; National Research Council, 1999a). Taken as a whole, their synthesis of contemporary research identifies knowledge, assessment, and student-centeredness as major sources for optimizing learning. These educational approaches also offer guidance in designing assessment strategies for measuring knowledge-based skills using ICT. A later section discusses how tasks using mindtools might be adapted for delivery as performance tests.

STUDENT KNOWLEDGE FRAMEWORK

In this section, a conceptual framework will be offered that flows from imperatives inherent in the information and knowledge society visions. The purpose of the framework is to explicate how societal knowledge demands suggest that learning activities and assessment strategies be structured. After a discussion of the framework, there will be discussion of the role of ICT in these learning activities. Ultimately, the argument is made that ICT and knowledge-related learning go hand in hand, helping to identify the desired direction of education in the twenty-first century. Figure 1 shows how knowledge-related skills or capabilities go hand in hand with knowledge-related task phases. Skills are needed to carry out task phases of knowledge related tasks. And completing these task phases helps develop knowledge-relatedskills. We call these tasks "task phases" because to work effectively on such tasks requires a systematic approach consisting of a number of steps within each task, and a sequence of processes or phases. Skills and task phases as illustrated in figure are mutually supportive. Carrying out task phases is only possible with knowledge-based skills, but doing task phases helps to develop knowledge-based skills. Complex tasks tend to require all five of the task phases. A project consists of a collection of tasks or task phases organized to achieve a specific outcome.

CONCULUSION

One should infer from this chapter that progress harnessing of technology for education requires progress in understanding the tools and their context, both educational and social. For that understanding to go forward effectively requires increments in theory and research. The theory part includes refining the concepts and specifying the underlying influences within the overall system. The concepts of the information and knowledge society are central to that understanding. In particular, we need to know much more about knowledge: how best to define it, how to utilize students' prior knowledge in the learning process, how to manage knowledge in organizational environments, how to let it guide the construction of assessments, and so on. In support of this emphasis upon knowledge, Brown and Duguid (2000) argue that learning is the acquisition of knowledge and it "presents knowledge management with its central challenge". Furthermore, they state that learning is social and "it requires developing the disposition, demeanour, and outlook of the practitioners." While this very well captures the process of apprenticeship, professional, and most workplace learning, it also applies to general education.

❐

18

Learning Chemistry at H. Sec. Level through Technology Assisted Courseware

In order to make the computer as assistor, the investigator used and modified the operating system as user friendly. And at the same time, the investigator used texts, video, audio, animation, virtual environment etc to make learning of chemistry enjoyable. This study attempts to explore students' conceptual understanding about chemistry at+2 level. By reviewing all the relevant factors, the investigator aims for the "Learning Chemistry at Higher Secondary level through Technology Assisted Courseware".

NEED AND SIGNIFICANCE OF THE STUDY

In Chemistry there are three branches namely organic, inorganic and Physical. The heart of the subject is the Periodic table which contains 119 elements which occur naturally as well as prepared artificially. But students don't get clear understanding related to those 119 elements. Another important status is the introduction of smart class which has been introduced by the government. Most of the materials are available in the form of CD. But some of the teachers don't use technology to teach in the class and they lack knowledge regarding the usage of computers. The present day teachers lack motivation that they are shaping the pillars which are going to support the future society. Teachers give inadequate explanations and make the students starve more for knowledge. They are not given proper in-service training to use the computer in the class. The above mentioned factors made the researcher to prepare chemistry concepts in the form of courseware for learning chemistry at the higher secondary level. The researcher has produced courseware in learning chemistry by taking two units from +2 chemistry and identified the effectiveness of the courseware for learning chemistry.

OBJECTIVES OF THE STUDY

- To find out the significant difference between pre and post test mean achievement scores of the control group.
- To find out the significant difference between pre and post test mean achievement scores of the experimental group.

TITLE OF THE STUDY

The title of the study is precisely stated as "Learning Chemistry at Higher Secondary level through Technology Assisted Courseware"

HYPOTHESES

- There is no significant difference between pre and post test mean achievement scores of the control group.
- There is no significant difference between pre and post test mean achievement scores of the experimental group.

DESIGN OF THE STUDY

The present study adopted the experimental design with the sample of 40 from XII standard students from Trichy district by using purposive sampling technique.

ANALYSIS AND INTERPRETATIONS OF THE STUDY

Hypothesis: 1

There is no significant difference between pre and post test mean achievement scores of the control group.

TABLE. 18.1: The Pre and Post test Mean Achievement Scores of the Control Group

Test	No of students	Mean	S.D	Mean difference	't' value	Degrees of freedom	Level of significance (0.01 level)
C- group Pre-test	20	21.40	5.75	3.15	1.623	38	Not significant
C- group Post test	20	24.55	6.52				

The mean scores of the pre test scores of the control group through traditional method is found to be 21.40 with SD of 5.75. The mean scores of the post test of the control group through traditional method is found to be 24.55 with SD of 6.52. The mean difference 3.15 is found to be not significant for the‘t’ value of 1.623 for 38 degrees of freedom at 1% level of significance. Therefore, the hypothesis is accepted.

It is concluded that there is no significant difference between pre test and post test mean achievement scores of the control group.

Hypothesis: 2

There is no significant difference between pre and post test mean achievement scores of the experimental group.

TABLE. 18.2: The Pre and Post Test mean Achievement Scores of the Experimental Group

Test	No of students	Mean	S.D	Mean difference	‘t’ value	Degrees of freedom	Level of significance (0.01 level)
E- group Pre test	20	21.45	5.95	17.35	9.16	38	Significant
E- group Post test	20	38.80	6.03				

The mean of the pre test scores of the experimental group through the multimedia courseware is found to be 21.45 with the SD of 5.95. The mean of the post test scores of the experimental group through the multimedia courseware is found to be 38.80 with SD of 6.03. The mean difference 17.35 is found to be significant for the‘t’ value 9.16 for 38 degrees of freedom at 1% level of significance. Therefore, the hypothesis is rejected. Hence,

It is concluded that there is a significant difference between pre and post test mean achievement scores of the experimental group.

FINDINGS OF THE STUDY

- There is no significant difference between pre and post test mean achievement scores of the control group.
- There is a significant difference between progressive and post test mean achievement scores of the experimental group.

EDUCATIONAL IMPLICATIONS

1. The utilization of courseware for learning chemistry enhances the achievement level of higher secondary students.
2. Learning chemistry through technology assisted courseware improves the pass percentage of students at the Higher Secondary classes.

DELIMITATION OF THE STUDY

- The sample is selected for experimentations is from class XII chemistry only.
- The e-content prepared for learning chemistry is based on the state board syllabi prescribed under Uniform System of School Education in Tamil Nadu.

CONCLUSION

The present study was carried out to find out learning chemistry at higher secondary level. As the present learning process at the higher secondary level is rigid, time bound and outmoded, it was planned to device teaching tasks in the form of multimedia courseware for the benefit of the learners so that the learners could attain the mastery of the subject according to their own pace and ability and feel motivated through personal involvement in the process of learning. It is pointed out that the multimedia courseware is user control as the tasks are constructed and offered to each learner through a separate personal computer. The present study clearly demonstrates the effectiveness of multimedia courseware for learning chemistry at higher secondary level.

❐

19

Technological Content Knowldege in Teaching Learning Process

Technology is a body of knowledge devoted to creating tools, processing actions and the extracting of materials. The term 'Technology" is wide, and everyone has their way of understanding its meaning. We use technology to accomplish various tasks in our daily lives, in brief; we can describe technology as products and processes used to simplify our daily lives. We use technology to extend our abilities, making people the most crucial part of any technological system. Technology is also an application of science used to solve problems. But it is vital to know that technology and science are different subjects which work hand-in-hand to accomplish specific tasks or solve problems. Technology is the collection of techniques, skills, methods and processes used in the production of goods or services or in the accomplishment of objectives, such as scientific investigation.

Teaching and Learning Process

Teaching-learning process is the heart of education. On it depends the fulfillment of the aims and objectives of education. It is the most powerful instrument of education to bring about desired changes in the students. Teaching learning are related terms. In teaching - learning process, the teacher, the learner, the curriculum& other variables are organized in a systematic way to attain some pre-determined goal.

Four aspects of the teaching-learning process:

- Discussion between the teacher and learner
- Interaction between the learner and some aspect of the world defined by the teacher
- Adaptation of the world by the teacher and action by the learner
- Reflection on the learner's performance by both teacher and learner.

Technological Knowledge

Technology knowledge (TK): Technology knowledge refers to the knowledge about various technologies, ranging from low-tech technologies such as pencil and paper to digital technologies such as the Internet, digital video, interactive whiteboards, and software programs.

TYPES AND EXAMPLES OF TECHNOLOGY

We use technology to accomplish various tasks, so technology comes in different forms. Below I have listed some of the different types of technology we use on a daily basis and in each kind of technology I have included an example of that particular technology.

Communication Technology

This is a system that uses technical means to transmit information or data from one place to another or from one person to another. Communication is a daily essential for all; it is used to convey ideas, exchange information, and express emotions. Humans use communication technology tools like phones, computers, emails, fax or messaging tools to stay in touch with friends and family.

Assistive Technology

Assistive technology is used by people with disabilities to accomplish specific tasks that are difficult or impossible to perform. The term "Assistive" means helping or providing an extra hand.Due to advancement in technology, we have a variety of assistive technologies that assist many to accomplish tasks that may otherwise be considered impossible.

Information Technology

Information Technology is a set of hardware and software tools used to store, transfer and process information. Information technology tools help in providing the right people with the right information at the right time. Big financial institutions like banks use information technology to operate their entire businesses as well as serve their customers.

Educational Technology

Education technology aims at improving a student's performance by creating and managing various technological processes and resources in or out the classroom. It is an academic discipline which prepares individuals to acquire deeper understanding and knowledge. It helps them learn how to devise solutions to problems through research, design, evaluation, and utilization.

Content knowledge (CK)

Content knowledge (CK) is teachers' knowledge about the subject matter to be learned or taught. The content to be covered in middle school science or history is different from the content to be covered in an undergraduate course on art appreciation or a graduate seminar on astrophysics. Knowledge of content is of critical importance for teachers. As Shulman (1986) noted, this knowledge would include knowledge of concepts, theories, ideas, organizational frameworks, knowledge of evidence and proof, as well as established practices and approaches toward developing such knowledge.

Knowledge and the nature of inquiry differ greatly between fields, and teachers should understand the deeper knowledge fundamentals of the disciplines in which they teach. In the case of art appreciation, such knowledge would include knowledge of art history, famous paintings, sculptures, artists and their historical contexts, as well as knowledge of aesthetic and psychological theories for evaluating art. The term **content knowledge** refers to the body of knowledge and information that teachers teach and that students are expected to learn in a given subject or content area, such as English language arts, mathematics, science, or social studies. Content knowledge generally refers to the facts, concepts, theories, and principles that are taught and learned in specific academic courses, rather than to related skills—such as reading, writing, or researching—that students also learn in school.

Technological Content knowledge (TCK)

Technological content knowledge refers to the knowledge of how technology can create new representations for specific content. It suggests that teachers understand that, by using a specific technology, they can change the way learners practice and understand concepts in a specific content area. Technology and content knowledge have a deep historical relationship progress in fields as diverse as medicine, history, archeology, and physics have coincided with the development of new technologies that afford the representation and manipulation of data in new and fruitful ways. Consider Roentgen's discovery of X-rays or the technique of carbon-14 dating and the influence of these technologies in the fields of medicine and archeology. Consider also how the advent of the digital computer changed the nature of physics and mathematics and placed a greater emphasis on the role of simulation in understanding phenomena.

Technological changes have also offered new metaphors for understanding the world. Viewing the heart as a pump, or the brain as an information-processing machine are just some of the ways in which technologies have provided new perspectives for understanding phenomena. These representational and metaphorical connections are not superficial. They often have led to fundamental changes in the natures of the disciplines. Understanding the impact of technology on the practices and knowledge of a given discipline is critical to developing appropriate technological tools for educational purposes.

CONCLUSION

TCK is an understanding of the manner in which technology and content influence and constrain one another. Teachers need to master more than the subject matter they teach; they must also have a deep understanding of the manner in which the subject matter (or the kinds of representations that can be constructed) can be changed by the application of particular technologies. Teachers need to understand which specific technologies are best suited for addressing subject-matter learning in their domains and how the content dictates or perhaps even changes the technology—or vice versa.

❐

20

Blended Learning in Distance Education: Need and Importance

India is one of the growing economies of the world today; it requires a large knowledge and skill based manpower to sustain the economic growth. The formal system of education is not only enough to meet the need and demand of the Indian economy today. Hence, distance education or open education modes are making their contribution in an effective way and to fill the gap between the expected and existing demand with respect to the educational opportunities and its attainment. Distance Education was initially named as 'Correspondence Education' which was developed in the mid-nineteenth century in Europe and then its limbs spread to the other contents and nations elaborately. When the distance learning started in India, the one the finest technology or medium available at that time is the postal system alone. At that time, distance learning was to open educational prospects to the people who needed to learn but they were not able to attend the regular or traditional school due the following categories and reasons– women, professionals, physically challenged people and people far away from the educational opportunities and availabilities due to geographical issues.

Development of Distance Learning in India

After independence, India has made a great progression in education system and educational process. Education was accessible only to the prestigious class of Indian in the beginning and the remaining people such as poor and middle class peoples were not given or availing the educational opportunities in higher education due to many reasons. Also, educational institutions were limited in numbers with high regulative norms and procedures for admissions in different aspects. The pressure has led to speedy growth of higher education in India in order to increase the number of educational institutions. But, the reality was that the development was quantitative rather than qualitative so as meet the demand of the society. Hence, an alternative mode was needed to ensure the quality of the education and its productive success. Consequently, distance education or distance learning came to exist to meet the demand of the massive people and the society. In India, distance learning was stated in the name of Correspondence Course 1962. The Delhi University established a School of Correspondence Course and Continuing Education (CCCE) in the year 1962. Based on the success of Delhi University, University Grants Commission (UGC) recommended the Correspondence Education expansion for many reasons and UGC framed guidelines for commencing correspondence courses in Indian Universities thereafter for further expansion and development of Distance Education and Distance learning.

Blended Learning

Blended learning is the mix of traditional classroom activities and technology based experiences provided with electronic gadgets. Otherwise, blended learning is a hybrid teaching methodology to make the learning complete and compete. It is a relatively new strategy and it represents a much greater transform in basic technique than simply using computers in the classroom. Hence, this learning is fundamental change in the teachers and learners approach the learning experiences in and out of classroom. No single, reliable definitions for blended learning exist, or even a universal agreement on the term itself. On the other hand, Blended learning sometimes referred as a formal education programme in which a student learns at least in part through delivery of content and instruction via digital and online media with some element of student control over time, place, path, or pace. The meaning of blended learning widely diverged to encompass a wide variety of synthesis in learning methods until 2006, when the first 'Handbook of Blended Learning' by Bonk and Graham was published. Graham challenged the breadth and ambiguity of the term's definition, and defined 'blended learning systems' as learning systems that "combine face-to-face instruction with computer mediated instruction. Currently, use of the term 'blended learning' mostly involves combining Internet and digital media with established classroom forms that require the physical co-presence of teacher and students.

Models of Blended Learning

- **Face-to-face driver** - where the teacher drives the instruction and augments with digital tools
- **Rotation** - students cycle through a schedule of independent online study and face-to-face classroom time
- **Flex** - Most of the curriculum is delivered via a digital platform and teachers are available for face-to-face consultation and support
- **Laboratories** - The entire curriculum is delivered via a digital platform but in a consistent physical location. Students usually take traditional classes in this model as well
- **Self-Blend** - Students choose to augment their traditional learning with online course work
- **Online Driver** - All curriculum and teaching is delivered via a digital platform and face-to-face meetings are scheduled or made available if necessary.

It is observed that these new educational technologies will enrich the distance interaction between teacher and student and the production of highly interactive self-paced learning packages used in the distance learning environment. This will be greatly beneficial to the distance learners who carry out their learning anytime and anywhere.

Blended Learning in Distance Education

In is well known that the mix of traditional and technology based instruction and teaching is noted as blended learning experiences and environment; blended learning in distance education provides space to the teachers and learners for the option of using the most appropriate technology to fit the specific learning situations. In this scenario, teaching may be done with a single technology and the learning activities may not be possible to adopt single technology to meet the specific need of the learners. Here the blended learning provides opportunity to the learner in general and the distance learners in specific to use all available and appropriate technology to understand, interact, submit and get feedback and contact the teaching organization effectively.

Now-a-days, distance education is more dependent on information and communication technologies. Technological advancements especially in the area of ICT allow teachers to employ various strategies in general and providing blended learning environment in particular that could actively engage student's interest throughout without any deviation. Distance Education programmes are delivered through open and flexible study pathways. The programme structure is designed to run in both full-time and part-time modes to cater for working students and high-school / secondary school graduates. Flexible study modes provide an alternative to traditional face-to-face learning and teaching, and allow you to study where ever the learners may be. Blended learning provides a combination of face-to-face tutorials and distance learning which are applied in an interactive learning environment. Blended learning gives students and tutors an environment to learn and teach more effectively. Students can select the best activities to suit their own pace, learning style and level, as well as time and place. Students can also make decisions, think creatively and critically, investigate and explore as well as solve problems they face in learning and real life.

Advantages of Blended Learning

The following items are the benefits of Blended Learning listed by Hijazi, Crowley, Smith and Shaffer (2006);

- Using the World Wide Web resources to support class activities
- Students can participate at any time
- Students can collaborate on their own time
- Supply students with additional learning materials if they need them
- Reduce the instructor's redundant tasks
- Increase the quality of communications between the instructor and learner

Role of Teachers in Implementing Blended Learning

With the advent of information and communication technologies and educational technology, it is important to have great willingness to accept, adopt and utilize new technologies. Simultaneously, it will reflect on blended learning in all mode of learning opportunities without any doubt. Adoption of blended learning is a complex process for higher education institutions and academic staff. Although the move towards blended learning is generally instigated at institutional level, factors determining its success and minimizing resistance of faculty often emerge at delivery level. Factors affecting the integration of blended learning branched from the attitudes and perceptions of academic staff towards new teaching practices and technologies. Availability of resources such as time, technology and support of e-developers also surfaced as determinants of positive attitudes towards adopting new teaching practices. The challenge for institutions implementing blended learning strategies is to build on positive staff attitudes, provide appropriate resources and help staff develop blends of teaching practices and use of technologies that deliver the best outcomes in particular teaching and learning contexts so as to extract the better outcome among the students.

CONCLUSION

The explosion of knowledge on behalf of information and communication technologies and educational technology has been drastically growing without any limit. The aim of education and distance education are being fulfilled to a great with availing all resources and technologies in a productive. In order to ensure the quality of education and the distance education institutions must be careful about the use of proper technologies and media. Effective combination of media and technology is necessary for assuring effectiveness of the distance learning system/ distance education. Blended learning significantly reduces face-to-face instruction by incorporating rich, online learning experiences to the distance learners particularly. Although there are potential benefits, transitioning from traditional face-to-face course to blended learning courses can be challenging for both students and faculty. For instance, students successful in blended learning courses need to be independent learners, have good time management skills, and feel comfortable using technology in formal education in general and in distance education in particular. Faculty teaching blended learning courses must adopt new tools and new mindsets to increase the likelihood of positive outcomes. Considering these potential challenges, transitioning to the blended learning model should be carefully managed to ensure that both students and faculty are ready and receptive to this approach so as realize it apex outcomes to the expected level appropriately.

❐

21

Distance Education in Modern Society

Distance education might have offered valuable contributions to the dissemination of education in the past, but that its future would probably be more modest. At that time middle of an extensive reform period concerning all sectors of the education system. Compulsory education had been extended from seven to nine years, and new lower secondary schools had been established in almost every local community. Upper secondary schools had for a long time been the privilege of the urban population. In the 1960s and 1970s they spread at an extraordinary speed to a great number of small centers in the rural parts of the country as well. And even institutions at the post-secondary level were spread in a very decentralized pattern all over country throughout the 1970s and 1980s.

It was seen as one of the fundamental issues in a modern welfare society that all local communities as far as possible should offer equal educational opportunities. The priority given to the maintenance of a high-quality, decentralized system of primary and secondary education was part of a policy to strengthen and develop local communities. Also the many regional institutions of higher education were based on a concern for local and regional development. At that time we were not talking of distance education, but of correspondence education. The main technologies involved besides print and written communication, were audio cassettes, radio and television.

MEDIA AND TECHNOLOGY IN DISTANCE EDUCATION

Television in particular was regarded as a powerful medium, and most people believed that it had an important role for distance education in filling the gap in educational opportunities between the generations. However, many politicians and educationists thought that in, say 20 years' time, when the school system had expanded and was able to offer equal opportunities at all levels of education and in almost all the local communities, the role of distance education would be a much more limited one. In the future, distance education would be needed to cater for some of the very remote and sparsely inhabited local communities, to serve some groups of disabled persons who could not take part in ordinary school activities, and perhaps also to disseminate the effective updating of knowledge in some particular areas where development would be too fast for the school system to keep up by ordinary measures.

Before leaving the discussion of attitudes to distance education 20 years ago, I would like to mention a couple of driving forces that ought to have given another perspective, but did not change the views of the future of distance education within the education sector at that time.

First, we were in 1970 fully aware of the need for lifelong learning, permanent education or recurrent education - those catch-words propagated by various international organizations at that time. Manifestos and reports were produced, new legislation was introduced and money was set aside for adult education based on this perspective. However, it was either conceptualized as a system of recurrent education where people were supposed to go back to educational institutions for a short period of time, or as a new involvement of public institutions in evening classes for adults.

Secondly, we knew very well that in the future, new exciting technological developments would offer new possibilities of education, and particularly in distance education. But the educational community has always been reluctant to accept new technology, and I do not think that most people would have believed that new ways of handling information and electronic communication would really have much impact on education.

THE 'NEW' ROLE OF DISTANCE EDUCATION

In this situation, it seems to me that both politicians and educators are beginning to look at distance education in a slightly different way. For instance, the Norwegian White Paper on Higher Education states that distance education, based on modern communication technology, will be a central element in the future policy of higher education, and particularly within continuing education. The Industrial Research and Development Advisory Committee of the Commission of the European Communities last year presented a report on skills shortages in Europe, the IRDAC report. This report advocates that 'a large structural effort in distance and flexible learning is required in Europe', in order to improve the productivity of education and training.

These are in my opinion examples of a new appreciation of the role of distance education in modern society - an appreciation which has emerged gradually in many countries over some years. Distance education is no longer looked upon as a vehicle for repairing some shortcomings of the education system at a particular stage of development. It is now conceived as a regular and necessary element of the education system - and not only for some particular and rather marginal target groups, but for quite central functions within the education system, serving considerable parts of the adult population.

Distance education has in fact had such a role for most of the time since it started, about 100 years ago. But it has taken a century for the educational and political establishment to realize what roles there are for distance education to play in a modern society.

CHALLENGES FOR EDUCATION IN A MODERN SOCIETY

Two fundamental characteristics of a modern society are complexity and change. Together these characteristics put increasing demands on the education needed for the citizens to cope with their life in the society. I will mention three fundamental demands:

GENERAL LEVEL AND QUALITY

There are increasing demands on the general level and quality of education. This is not only a question of the number of years spent in the initial education system, or the number of graduates in relation to the population. The initial education must establish a broad and general level of competence, relevant to modern society and sufficient to form the necessary basis for continuing learning activities during the whole life-span.

UPDATING AND RETRAINING

Since modern societies require adaptability in many dimensions, education and training must develop ways to cope with the increasing needs of updating and retraining, as well as the need of mastering completely new situations and developments. These needs will concern people regardless of previous education, age, job, and social situation. In particular, many occupations will require increasingly specialized training and more frequent updating and retraining than before. This also means that training will have to be close to work, both in content and in pattern of organization. This development brings forward a need for closer links between educational institutions and industry and business, both to match market demands and to keep teachers in touch with developments outside schools and universities.

Multiple competences and careers People increasingly tend to develop multiple competences across traditional subject oriented or occupational border-lines. Multiple careers also become usual and increase the demand of education regardless of age. In almost all modern societies there is a tendency that the average age of the student population in higher education is rising, and so is the proportion of part-time students with work experience. These students have more autonomous study habits, and require other forms of teaching than younger students. There is also a need for more flexibility and alternative organization of study programs.

DISTANCE LEARNING AND MODERN TECHNOLOGY

I have already suggested that one of the driving forces behind the expanded role of distance education in modern society is technological development. I stress this point with a certain hesitation, because there is a tendency to associate distance education only with the more advanced types of technology. In my opinion, this is a dangerous tendency. Our fascination with technological visions may prevent us designing distance education systems and programs in a way that can enable distance education to play its fundamental role. In distance education, as in other sectors, we need appropriate technology more than visions of the future.

On the other hand, modern information and communication technologies have given us a broader range of options than we had some years ago, and new options will certainly arrive in the future. But this fact does not always make the old technologies obsolete. Books, correspondence tuition, radio and television, audio cassettes, telephone - they are all quite old media, but will nevertheless survive into the next century. Telefax, video cassettes, optical storing media, electronic mail, computer conferencing and video teleconferencing - they are all here at the moment, but they will need many years yet to attain a dominant position in distance education, if they ever do. Most of them will not replace the old media, but supplement them and enrich the total range of information and communication media available in distance education. Every time we introduce a new technology in a distance education system, we run the risk of introducing a new barrier to participation and learning. Therefore, we often have to wait for years while the technology penetrates society and spreads to all the working places and homes where distance learning programmers must be available for individual use.

CONCLUSION

I have argued that in modern society, characterized above all by change and complexity, distance education has several particular roles to play. I have not said much about the organization of distance education systems and their relation to the conventional education system. That is an issue in itself, and it is difficult to discuss it appropriately without reference to the particular educational traditions of the society in question.

❒

22

Open Educational Resources-Global Challenges to Distance Education in the Present Scenario

OPEN EDUCATIONAL RESOURCES

The term "Open Educational Resources"-was first introduced at a conference hosted byUNESCO in 2000 and was promoted in the context of providing free access to educationalresources on a global scale. The most often used definition of Open Educational Resources is, "digitized materials offered freely andopenly for educators, students and self-learners to use and reuse for teaching, learning andresearch". With regard to this working definition, it is important to note that"resources" are not limited to content but comprise three areas. They are learningcontent, tools and implementation resources.

- **Learning Content:** Full courses, courseware, content modules, learning objects,collections and journals.
- **Tools:** Software to support the development, use, reuse and delivery of learningcontent, including searching and organization of content, content and learningmanagement systems, content development tools, and online learning communities.
- **Implementation Resources:** Intellectual property licenses to promote openpublishing of materials, design principles of best practice and localize content.

A wide variety of initiatives in higher education have crystallized around the above threeareas - from institutions that publish the materials they use in their own teaching (e.g. syllabi,lecture notes, reading lists etc.), to projects that support the creation, provision and sharing ofopen content through developing software, standards and licensing tools or buildingcommunities of use.

MAJOR CHALLENGES

Open Educational Resources programmes and projects have generated considerable enthusiasm from governments,funding bodies, institutions, organizations and individuals. The spread of Open EducationalResources creates substantial educational opportunities, but also reveals challenges thatrequire further work in order to reach their full potential.

SUSTAINABILITY

As with any fixed-term, externally funded initiative, the maintenance and sustainability ofOpen Educational Resources is becoming a significant challenge. According to Wiley (2006), the sustainability ofOpen Educational Resources initiatives must be considered in two parts: the sustainable production of Open Educational Resources and thesustainable sharing of resources. The sustainability of any Open Educational Resources initiative is influenced by thesize of the operation (small or large), the type of provider (institution or community) and thelevel of integration of users in the production process (co-production or producer-consumermodel). There are many funding models in the different institutional contexts; however, everyinitiative will have different goals so no single model will fit every project. Atkins (2007) hasidentified a number of approaches to sustainability which should be considered and need tobe explored:

- Encourage institutions, rather than just individual pioneer-faculty, to buy into theOpen Educational Resources movement so that institutional resources will be committed to sustain it.
- Situate Open Educational Resources collections not as distinct from the courseware environment for theformally enrolled students but as a low marginal cost derivative of the routinely usedcourse preparation and management systems.
- Encourage membership-based consortia to share cost and expertise.
- Explore roles for students in creating, enhancing and adopting OER.
- Consider a voluntary (or mix of voluntary and paid) wiki-like model, in which OER isthe object of micro-contributions from many.
- Examine ways that social software can be used to capture and structure usercommentaries on the material.

INTELLECTUAL PROPERTY

Intellectual property issues are at the heart of Open Educational Resources. It was suggested that the issue ofcopyright and ownership of material is "the root cause of slow development in this field,"inhibiting some faculty members and institutions from making more educational contentavailable to the online community. Before publishing educational resources that make use ofthird-party materials on the Internet, the author, or the publisher, must ensure they have theright to use these materials. There are several barriers raised by copyright to the use andproduction of open educational resources as follows.

Practical difficulties for obtaining rights, such as whether a license is applicable ornot, sometimes requires sophisticated legal analysis; it is not always easy to locate theappropriate license holder, which can be very expensive for the Open Educational Resources initiative. Thedifficulties and costs related to rights clearance for use of third-party content areconsiderable, in some cases almost half of the cost of the whole initiative.

The issue of unintended incompatibility between materials or tools licensed underdifferent licenses, or different versions of the same licenses, is becoming a key issue.Like technical interoperability, increased legal interoperability is of fundamentalimportance for the growth of the Open Educational Resources movement.

Low awareness among teachers and researchers producing learning resources ofpermit controlled sharing, with some rights reserved to the author. Although manyacademics are willing to share their work, they often hesitate to do so in this newenvironment for fear of losing their rights to their work. The opposite of retainingcopyright is to release work into the public domain, in which case the author retainsno rights and anyone can use the material in any way and for any purpose.

QUALITY ASSESSMENT AND ENHANCEMENT

There are severalalternative ways of approaching quality management issues which have been used:

- **Institution-Based Approach:** This is to use the brand or reputation of the institution topersuade the user that the materials on the website are of good quality. Themajor challenge here is how the use of open educational material might constantlyimprove the material through reflected use.
- **Peer Review Approach:** This is one of the most used quality assurance processes inacademia. As well as being well-known and well-used in Open source softwareprojects and Open accessjournals, it could also be used for OERto guarantee the quality of a repository's resources. It is

necessary to make reviewdecisions credible, and peer review according to agreed criteria is well suited to thatpurpose.

- **Open Users Review Approach:** This is a kind of low-level or bottom-up approach,letting individual users decide on whatever grounds they like whether a learningresource is of high quality, useful or good in any other respect. This can be done byhaving users rate or comment on the resource or describe how they have used it.

Now, the quality of Open Educational resources can be improved through a centrally designed ordecentralized process and the process may be open or closed. All these approaches can beused separately or dominated, depending on which kind of OER initiative or programme isbeing considered.

CONCLUSION

With tremendous developments in information and communication technology, the education system of today has been enriched by various open educational resources. The optimal utilization of opportunities provided by the technological developments presents a profound challenge for education systems and has serious implications involving cost, access, equity, pedagogy and quality. The paper discusses various opportunities and challenges presented by the use of Open Educational Resources in the distance education scenario of today.

❐

23

Open and Distance Learning and its Influence in Higher Education with Reference to Indira Gandhi National Open University

With expanding base at the elementary and secondary education levels, the demand for higher education has increased. In 1956-1960, UGC had proposed for evening colleges, correspondence course and award of external degrees. Planning Commission in its third five year plan mentioned the need for the introduction of correspondence education in the country. Further the Central Advisory Board for education recommended to set up the Expert Committee under the chairmanship of Dr D.S Kothari, the then Chairman of UGC to look into this proposal. In 1962, the University of Delhi introduced the correspondence course. In 1970, further more convention Universities made an option to open the correspondence courses. Subsequently, renamed as the Directorates of Distance Education. In the year 1980, the Govt. introduced the Open University system with an objective of democratize opportunities for higher education for large segment of Indian population. This particularly reached out the disadvantaged groups such as those for whom access was difficult or impossible. Those living in remote and rural areas, working people, women and other adults who wish to acquire and upgrade their knowledge and skill through studies.

The Andhra Pradesh Open University was established in the 1982 and later it was renamed as Dr. B. R Ambedkar Open University. In 1985, IGNOU was established at the National levels by the act of parliament of India. IGNOU besides offering several programmes also acts as a Promoter & Coordinator for the open and distance education system in the country and Distance Education Council (DEC) was setup by IGNOU for the same 1991. In 2013, DEC was shifted to UGC. IGNOU has achieved steady growth of admission since its inception, indicates the recognition of wide acceptance of the programmes not only amongst the citizens of India but also those from SAAR, Middle East and African Countries. Currently the University having 3 million students role. It clearly indicates the success of university to reach its goal in higher education. The ODL accounts for about 12% of total enrolment in the segment of higher education, and as contributed substantially to the raise of GER of India which is 24.5%. (Ritimoni Bordoloi 2018)

Objective of the Studies

- Current status of Higher education in India
- Influence of IGNOU as ODL leader and its Enrollment in Higher Education

Methodology and Source of Data

Descriptive research methodology has been used, and data has been analyzed from the secondary source of information.

Current Status of Higher Education

India being a developing country with a huge population of more than 1.24 billion the supply and demand for higher education there is a wide gap . On 13th June, 2005 government of India constituted a high level advisory body known as National Knowledge Commission (NKC) to advise the PM about the status of education in India and measures needed to reform this sector. It was headed by Sam Pitroda and submitted its report in November 2007. NKC recommended setting up of 1500 universities by 2015. (Mukesh Chahal 2015). India to achieve a goal in the list of developed nation country requires to increase its higher education , and skilled human resource therefore it will be helpful became a knowledgeable society and in turn will help for national development includes social, economical and cultural society. The concept of human capital is linked with the growth and development of a nation and education would play an important role in producing the human capital for both present and future development (Ritimoni bordoloi, 2018)

Higher education is defined as the education which is obtained after completing 12 years of in the age group of 18- 23 years varies from seven in

Bihar to 51 in Karnataka and Telangana, as compared to all India average of 28.

Influence of IGNOU as ODL leader and its Enrollment in Higher Education

The Indira Gandhi National Open University (IGNOU) was established by an Act of Parliament in 1985, to advance and disseminate learning and knowledge by a diversity of means, including the use of information communication technology, to provide opportunities for higher education to a larger segment of the population and to promote the educational well being of the community, The university began by offering two academic programmes in 1987 ie Diploma in Management and Diploma in Distance Education, with a strength of 4528 students. With steady increase in the enrolment for instance the total enrolment of Fresh and Re- registration of learners in 2016-17 was 821658. IGNOU offers 239 academic programmes through its 21 schools of studies and network of 67 regional centres and over 3000 learner support centres. The university currently has a cumulative student strength of over 3.0 million leaner's. (IGNOU profile 2017). The university has 130, SITs (Satellite Interactive Terminals) across the country to facilitate two –way video conferencing. The university has been identified at the national coordinator for developing Massive Open Online Courses (MOOCs) at certificate and Diploma levels.

Instructional System of IGNOU: The university provides multi- channel, multiple media teaching / learning packages for instruction and self-learning. The different components used for teaching and learning include self- instructional print and audio-video materials, radio and television broadcasts, face –to face counseling/ tutoring, laboratory and hands –on experience, teleconferencing video conferencing, interactive radio counseling interactive multimedia CD-ROM and internet based learning, and the use of mobile phones for instant messaging etc

The learner profile of The University includes, diverse range like, Urban, rural, tribal areas, employed unemployed, disabled, jail-inmates, personnel from government and non-government sectors, defense personnel and paramilitary forces. Etc. Also emphasis towards socially and economically disadvantaged groups. Table 5 shows enrolement growth in total for UG and PG.Programme. Talbe 6 shows the SC and ST enrolment .

Table 5. Shows : Total Enrollment UG and PG Programme in IGNOU

Discussions

There is momentous changes in education, there was a time when education was considered as privilege but now this has changed as education as a right, convention mode of education is based on teacher cantered, institution based education now the time has emerged as education became learner cantered based and workplace based education.

The most significant contribution of ODL in higher education is that it provides a wider opportunities to the female. For instance women enrolment in higher education through distance mode is 46.03% (AISHE, 2016). Because of Open and distance learning Education is no longer considered as one time activity it become life time activity. In India the school dropout 16 % at primary level and 32% at upper primary level (Subhash C Khuntia 2017). Open university education in India is playing a vital role in respect of huge number of enrolled students in higher Education from disadvantaged group of the society (Santi Kundu , 2014). Students hold part time jobs in order to pay for the educational expenses and should divide their attention between a job and college / University education, nearly about seventy five percent of the total students community today have been facing financial problem (Mukesh Chahal 2015) Open and distance learning can be raised as an alternative way for making education as accessible and possible and for providing scope to get skill based education at minimum cost (Ritimoni Bordoloi, 2018). IGNOU securing top position enrolling 7000 students per year from 36 countries around the world (Santi Kundu 2014). ODL is the only way to accommodate those who have dropout from school level, college level and those who are aspiring for higher education who have missed the opportunities to achieve the same for various reason.

CONCLUSION

IGNOU as National Open university for distance education contributed enormously in education, currently it offers more than 239 programme for 40 disciplines. For example students registered in 2016-2017 (fresh and registration) were 8,21, 658 (More than 8 lakh). It has student on roll about 3,032,448 (above 3 million). Degree / Diploma/ Certificates were awarded to the students in the 30th convocation including Ph. D and M.Phil (2,10,811 students) more than 2 lakh students includes the student community from employed , unemployed, urban, rural, tribal, SC/ST, physically challenged , defense personnel, jail inmates, house wife etc. IGNOU has a world leader in the Distance Education has been conferred with the award of Excellence by Common Wealth of Learning (COL) Canada in March 2013. UNESCO declared IGNOU as the largest Open University in the world. IGNOU is emerging as training hub for taking up capacity building interventions in the country particularly in the field of teacher training. Massive teacher training programme under which 24,000 teachers of Kendriya Vidyalaya Sangatan and 36,000 teachers from 5 north-eastern states are trained. IGNOU making sustained to reach out to jail inmates and provided them free education. Till 2015, 96 jails have IGNOU centers across the country.

❐

24

E-Learning a Boon for Distance Education

E-learning is a part of new dynamics that characterises the educational system. It has become an important part of the society, comprising an extensive array of digitalization approaches, components and delivery methods. The use of information and communication technologies(ICT) for educational purpose has increased, & the spread of network technologies has caused e-learning practices to evolve significantly. Education through internet, network is E-Learning. It is the network based transfer of skills & knowledge. E-learning refers to use of electronic applications and processes to learn. The e-learning applications and processes are the web-based learning, computer based learning, virtual classrooms and digital collaboration.

The contents are delivered through the internet, local intranet/extranet, audio or video tape, satellite TV & CD-ROM. E-learning is used by learners and educators in homes, schools, higher education, business and others. In the early days, e-learning received a bad impression, as many people thought bringing computers into the classroom would remove that human element that some learners need, but as time has progressed technology has developed, and now we embrace smart phones and tablets in the classroom and office, as well as using a wealth of interactive designs that makes e-learning not only engaging for the users, but valuable as a lesson delivery medium. The use of e-learning is seen at all levels of educational system.

E-learning has Web-based training (WBT), also known as e-learning and on-line learning, is training that resides on a server or host computer that is connected to the World Wide Web. Distance learning provides "access to learning when the source of information and the learners are separated by time and distance, or both." Distance education courses that require a physical onsite presence for any reason (including taking examinations) have been referred to as hybrid or blended courses of study.

Distance education is institution based, formal education where the learning group is separated, and where interactive telecommunications systems are used to connect learners, resources and instructors. Distance education has two major components, distance teaching and distance learning. Distance teaching is the effort of an educational institution to design, develop and deliver instructional experiences to the distant student so that learning may occur. Education and distance education is comprised of teaching and learning. This task force concentrated on distance teaching.

ASPECTS OF E-LEARNING

There is live instruction where specialized instructors can remain in their own/one locations and provide instructions to many students in other locations. Video content delivery where pre-recorded content is provided as material that can be viewed when needed. Student to student interactions is an aspect where students learn as much from each other as they do from teachers. Up-to-date materials are provided through digital delivery for e-readers where textbooks are expensive to purchase, maintain and deliver. Another aspect is Self-learning which is common in higher education which is done by computer based training.

STRENGTHS OF DISTANCE EDUCATION SYSTEM

The term open and distance learning and its definition are relatively new in the field of education, having gained prominence only in the past 15 to 20 years. The language and terms used to describe distance learning activities can still be confusing, and geographical differences in usage - for example, between North America and Europe - can add to the confusion. Among the more commonly used terms related to open and distance learning are the following: correspondence education, home study, independent study, external studies, continuing education, distance teaching, self-instruction, adult education, technology-based or mediated education, learner-centred education, open learning, open access, flexible learning and distributed learning. Therefore let us be aware the strengths of distance education, though the nomenclature are been used differently.

E-LEARNING-A BOON TO DISTANCE EDUCATION SYSTEM

The use of e-learning is seen at all levels of educational system. E-Learning is visualised as the India's license for boosting up distance education system. The increasing fusion of the online education companies and organisations, it is strongly believed that India shall finally cope with the lag in its higher education system. The only way to bridge the growing division in public and private education in India can be tackled by utilizing ELearning and online learning. A website provides such online courses through collaborations with various well recognised and National level Universities and Institutes all across. E-Learning/ teaching covers a wide set of applications of Computer Assisted Instruction, Computer Based Learning, Web-based learning, Virtual Classroom and On-line Learning. E-Learning/teaching is an interactive learning experience with the access to online tutors which can be made available from any computer, once the user has the access through web browsers. It permits the delivery of knowledge and information to learners at an accelerated pace, opening up new vistas of knowledge transfer. The biggest advantages of E-Learning/teaching lie in its ability to cover distances. It is self-paced, and learning is done at the learners' pace.

E-Learning/teaching involves delivery of content and resources for teaching and learning via different communication protocols. The one such very popular open online course in India is MOOCs which collaborates with National level Institutes as IITs and brings in these online courses. The courses are all free and provide free certificates of completion who are done and have completed all the quizzes and peer evaluation assignments in the respective courses. One can find online courses for various fields like Professional Marketing, Digital Pedagogies, International Business, Forensic Sciences and several MBA courses in the form of distance education. Moreover, even the state universities in India have started their wing of graduate and post-graduate programmes in the form of online education.

ROLE OF TECHNOLOGY IN DISTANCE EDUCATION

Although the expansion of the Internet blurs the boundaries, distance education technologies are divided into two modes of delivery namely synchronous learning and asynchronous learning. In synchronous learning, all participants are present at the same time. In this regard, it resembles traditional classroom teaching methods despite the participants being located remotely. It needs a scheduled timetable to be organized and displayed. Few examples of synchronous technology as Web conferencing, videoconferencing, educational television, instructional television are examples of, as internet radio, live streaming, telephone, and web based.

In asynchronous learning, participants access course materials flexibly on their own schedule. Students are not required to be together at the same time. Mail correspondence, which is the oldest form of distance education, is an asynchronous delivery technology as are message board forums, e-mail, video and audio recordings, print materials, voicemail and fax.

The two methods can be combined. Many courses offered by the distance training use periodic sessions of residential or day teaching to supplement the remote teaching. The Distance Education System uses a blend of technologies and a blend of learning modalities like face-to-face, distance and mixed. Distance learning can use, online interactive faculty chat sessions (OFI), online virtual classes, quiz, and webinars.

CONCLUSION

E-Learning has become extremely popular. The rise in Internet users and the revolutionary changes that have happened in education have created a fertile environment for E-Learning to grow. The face of higher education has experienced a sea change over the decades. Once characterized by the traditional classroom model, higher education today has changed into learning that is instant, online, self-driven and on the go. The journey of higher education in India has been marked with innumerable milestones – most recently, E-Learning. The Government of India is strong supporter of E-learning and the Department of Electronics and Information Technology have been actively developing tools and technologies to promote it.

These are content development, R&D technology initiatives, human resource development projects, and faculty training initiatives to improve through E-learning. The only way to sustain a better future is by educating the younger generation with effective and efficient education methodologies. It optimistic to expose students to the latest technology so that they are not left clueless while they reach the stage at which they will contribute to society. The study shows the positive effects of E-Learning for the higher education system in India. In the country like India it is very essential that the ELearning reaches the lowest sections of the society so that in the near future, we have strong and stable labour force in services and agriculture sector.

❐

25

Utilizing Web-Based Technology on Distance Education

Technological advances have created a paradigm shift in education and the definition of distance learning, as described by James Morrison (1996), who states that telecommunications, software, and the Internet eliminate walls and boundaries. The pervasiveness of the Internet has provided the opportunity to expand the capabilities of conducting instruction outside the classroom. According to the United States Distance Learning Association, «distance learning is the application of electronic means to education in all areas: K-12, higher education, continuing education, corporate training, and military and government training, telemedicine and those devoted to the pursuit of lifelong learning» (USDLA, 1996). Due to the technological advances of the recent past, a great deal of excitement and hope has been generated for the use of distance learning in education. Rapid advances in computer and telecommunications capabilities have made possible the development of learning modules that include elements such as video transmission and the World Wide Web. The users, who are interested in some specific information available in the web page of a website, may then access them on net by using Web browser. The development of a Web site on the Internet is carried out by a vast number of individuals or organisations for serving their purposes from one or the other angles like commercial, professional, social or academic etc.

Web-Based Instructional Approaches in Distance Education

Distance education is becoming a common practice as evidenced by the number of universities that offer distance education programs, the number of businesses offering distance learning and training programs are currently in use. As distance learning continues to expand, educators must be ready to examine the issues generated by this paradigm shift. In the years since the introduction of the World Wide Web in 1993, the use of the Web to deliver instruction has increased immensely. In 1997, Khan first defined web-based instruction (WBI) as "a hypermedia-based instructional program which utilizes the attributes and resources of the World Wide Web to create a meaningful learning environment where learning is fostered and supported" (Khan 1997). However, it may be useful to review where WBI came from in relation to other concepts that preceded it. There are a number of different broad categories that can be considered in discussions of web-based instruction approaches. And the choice of approaches certainly isn't between just face-to-face and distance learning. The common thread among the categories is that computer-based technologies play a central role. The three broad categories to consider are augmented, blended (distributed, hybrid), and online (distance) (Siemens and Tittenberger 2009).

Augmented

In the "augmented" category, web-based instruction is used to extend the physical classroom in order to supplement face-to-face instruction. The online component may be incorporated into activities during class time or used to accomplish assignments outside of scheduled class periods. In this model, students meet with instructors in classrooms on a regular schedule. Some common tools used in this category are online discussion forums, Web Quests, blogs, group work in wikis, and online quizzes.

Blended Learning

The different terms for the second category: blended, distributed, and hybrid learning are used interchangeably. Blended learning is a method of instructional delivery that includes a mix of web-based instruction, streaming video conferencing, face-to-face classroom time, distance learning through television or video, or other combinations of electronic and traditional educational models. Although blended learning can be implemented in a combination of ways, it always accommodates a separation of geographical locations for part (or all) of the instruction and focuses on learner-to-learner as well as instructor-to-learner interaction. A typical model for blended learning might involve an initial face-to-face orientation followed by a period of online classes and then a face-to-face wrap-up class.

Online Learning

In the "online" category, all instruction takes place remotely, either synchronously or asynchronously. Distance learning is often associated with adult learning because it is a model that has the flexibility to fit into busy lives better than traditional models of instruction. For those people with full-time careers and families, there are real benefits to educational opportunities that they can adapt to daily responsibilities. Adults also tend to adapt more readily to the independent structure of distance education and the self-motivation it requires.

Understanding on Web-Based Instruction

Web-based classroom is no longer focused on the teacher, but rather, it is very much learner-centric. This is a risky type of strategy if the teacher is not able to relinquish some control. It also dictates a responsibility change - from the teacher to the learner. While it is student centred, there is still much work to be done by teacher, teaching skills such as time management with students, planning, and organization. Web-based instruction allows for students to progress at a pace they feel comfortable with - within certain constraints of the course such as progress deadlines. As McCormack and Jones (1998) suggest, "the trend in Web-based classrooms is away from the student as a passive recipient of knowledge toward the student involved in the learning process as an active, self-directed participant. Both educators and students with experience on traditional didactic methods may have problems adapting to this new approach". A Web-based classroom is a very active classroom, and students quickly become spread out over a variety of projects.

Benefits of Web-Based Instruction

Distance learning has the capacity to reach many more people in a more cost-effective manner than traditional classroom instruction. As resources shrink and learning requirements expand, many educational institutions are relying on communication technologies, such as distance learning, to enhance the effectiveness and efficiency of education (Ameritech, 1996), there may be a contradiction to their acknowledgment of the educational challenge as the technological infrastructure, human resources, and training which are essential to effective distance learning do not come without expense. In the Web-based classroom, collaboration occurs on a daily basis without having to create collaborative projects or group work for students. It is natural for students to help each other with problems they may encounter as they progress through the course content.

There are other teacher benefits of the Web-based classroom, as well. One of the benefits is that repetitive teaching tasks are reduced. For example, students who miss a class can visit the Web site and "pick up" their assignments at any time, and the teacher need not re-teach the lesson. Because Web-based instruction does not use paper, the management tasks involved with preparing, duplicating, filing, and cleaning up paper-based classes is non-existent. Changes and revisions to curriculum materials are efficient and easy with Web-based instruction as the teacher can revise the materials, publish them to the Web, and the materials are immediately available to the students.

CONCLUSION

The future of distance learning technologies in education will be most influenced by the manner in which educational administrators handle the change process. Administrators must take into consideration the needs and attitudes of the school that is considering distance learning technologies. Each school has a unique set of problems, concerns, and assets which are reflected in the staff and community and which contribute to the culture and climate of the school. By understanding the culture, educators validate the unique nature of each school and its needs. Teachers are at the core of the success of distance learning technologies. Any reform effort should value the experience and professionalism of educators. The growth of distance learning technologies will be dependent upon training and professional development being offered to educators. Educators, in turn, will have the resources to manage and to embrace the changes brought about by distance learning.

❐

26

The Significance of MOOCs in the Domain of Distance Education

Distance education is the delivery of useful learning opportunities at a convenient place and time for learners. It is the education of students who may not always be physically present in an educational institution. The old concept of distance education was exclusively associated with print materials, whereas the new concept of distance education includes supplementary material being used through non-print media such as television, computers, laptops, recorded lectures in CDs and DVDs, video conferencing and interactive session between students and faculties via the Internet. Online platforms have the capability to take higher education to millions of deserving students in far-flung areas who would otherwise have no access to quality education from a recognized university.

WHAT IS MOOC?

A MOOC (Massive Open Online Course) is a course or unit accessible, usually with no prerequisites, to anyone who wishes to enrol, usually for free, and with self-assessment or peer assessment along the way. It is a flexible and open form of self-directed, online learning designed for mass participation. Many now are being offered by household name universities. These may not offer any formal academic credit, but will often award certificates of participation, or even a grade. Most MOOCs are now delivered by acknowledged experts and outstanding teachers.

While access to the course material is free, MOOC platform providers often offer certificates of completion at a cost. MOOC platforms provide institutions with cloud-based hosting environments for delivering courses, offering scale and functionality while the institution provides the course material and reputational value.

MOOCs IN INDIA

The initial objective of digital learning by the Indian government was to provide open resources in the form of e-books, libraries, media files, etc. These are mainly available in National Digital Library of India by MHRD, National Digital Repository by IGNOU, Sakshat by MHRD, eCBSE by CBSE Board, e-PG Pathshala by UGC, and much more. These initiatives focused on making education reachable to as many learners as possible.

The government started offering online courses recently through the following platforms:

Initiative	Year of Launch	Institution Behind Platform	Website Link
National Programme in Technology Enhanced Learning (NPTEL)	2003	All seven IITs and IISc.	https://www.nptel.ac.in
mooKIT	2012	IIT Kanpur	https://www.mookit.co
IITBombayX	2014	IIT Bombay	https://www. iitbombayx.in//
Swayam	2016	MHRD and Microsoft	https://www.swayam. gov.in/

EMPLOYMENT OPPORTUNITIES:

The fundamental point of concern is the credibility of MOOCs and certificates, and whether these are taken seriously by employers or not. The MOOC providers' answer to this has been ID verification methods such as webcams, keystroke analysis, valid photo identification, and in-person test centres in order to verify the identity of participants and confirm that they have completed the work submitted in their name. In addition, employers are able to verify the authenticity of an ID verified certificate using a unique verification URL printed on the certificate itself.

However, being able to prove that a certificate is genuine doesn't help with verifying the actual course content and the level of education acquired through taking a MOOC. From an employer's perspective, interpreting MOOCs on a CV is complicated further if the recruiter is not familiar with this form of education. It is perhaps the lack of awareness from recruiters that represents the biggest employability hurdle for MOOC students.

Although the traditional degree certificate is still the more valued credential among employers in general, employers in today's job market are looking for technically skilled, job-ready candidates, which a traditional degree doesn't always guarantee. Being able to show physical evidence of your abilities are becoming increasingly important in recruitment, and MOOCs can play a key role in this with many MOOC programs culminating in a practical capstone project, giving employers a clear picture of a candidate's abilities.

Moreover, having a transcript of MOOC certificates issued by some of the world's most elite universities demonstrates in itself motivation, perseverance, dedication, and entrepreneurship – traits that all employers will be looking for in a candidate. It is then up to the candidate to show tangible proof of the hard skills he or she has acquired through course certificates and transcripts as well as any evidence of completed project work.

CONCLUSION

While students are travelling more to foreign countries to study, the borderless worldwide web is increasingly able to bring ideas to people, wherever they may be. In markets such as India, where online learners constitute over 20%, there is a great potential for providing international online education. Implementing a national approach to online education strategy would bring challenges in system adaptability and differentiation, credit transfer and credential recognition between schools, by creating a coordinated system reduces redundancies and provides a more seamless, intuitive online education process for lifelong learning.

There is still some way to go before recruiters fully recognise the value of MOOCs on a CV. With MOOCs allowing for greater flexibility compared to traditional education to provide training in the most contemporary fields and conquer the skills gap, these courses hold a promising future for prospective employees.

❒

27

Climate Change and Distance Education

Vast majority of the human beings across planet earth agree that global climate change is the greatest environmental menace humankind has ever faced and it remains as the biggest challenge to be tackled. Intergovernmental Panel on Climate Change (IPCC)'s Special Report on 1.5 °C (SR 1.5 °C) released in 2018 says that the impact of a 1.5C increase in global temperatures will "disproportionately affect disadvantaged and vulnerable populations through food insecurity, higher food prices, income losses, lost livelihood opportunities, adverse health impacts, and population displacements". India is among the countries most vulnerable to climate change. According to World Bank, India has one of the highest densities of economic activity in the world, and very large numbers of poor people who rely on the natural resource base for their livelihoods, with a high dependence on rainfall. *By 2020, pressure on India's water, air, soil, and forests is expected to become the highest in the world.*

Everyone including macro players (Governments, Industries, Media, NGOs, Religion etc.) and micro players (individuals) have to play a vital role in addressing the menace of climate change. For this to happen there is a strong need for in depth understanding of climate change science, which can lead to development and practicing of adaptations and mitigation possibilities by all players. Education is an indispensable element of the universal response to climate change. It increases climate literacy and there by enables the people to understand and address climate change, encourages changes in their attitudes and behaviour and helps them adapt and mitigate to climate change.

DISTANCE EDUCATION

Distance education is the education of students (who are called as distance learners) who may not always be physically present at a campus. Conventionally, this usually involved correspondence courses wherein the distance learners corresponded with the institution via post. Today distance education also involves online education. Massive open online courses (MOOCs), offering large-scale interactive participation and open access through the World Wide Web or other network technologies, are recent developments in distance education. A number of other terms such as e-learning, online learning, virtual classroom etc. are used roughly synonymously with distance education.

CLIMATE CHANGE AND DISTANCE EDUCATION

As human induced factors play a prominent role in the production of green house gases and ensuing climate change, there is a growing need for imparting awareness to all sections of the society. Climate change, though studied under science discipline is essentially interdisciplinary as its impacts cross its boundaries to other disciplines.

Distance education has the potential to expand access to education for different sections of general public. It has overcomes many of the barriers like distance, cost, age etc. Further it has flexible scheduling structure which lessens the effects of the many time-constraints imposed by personal responsibilities and commitments. Not only this open and distance learning mode is also proves to be effective way of spreading the information on any pressing problems and challenges. Thus considering the threat of climate change on world and inadequacy of formal education in addressing the menace of climate change, open and distance education has taken many initiatives to address climate change mainly by offering specialized courses on it for different sections of society.

OPEN AND DISTANCE EDUCATION COURSES ON CLIMATE CHANGE IN INDIA

Some of the open universities and conventional universities (through distance mode) in India have taken initiatives address the menace of climate change by means of launching courses on it in order to equip different target groups. Following are details about a few such open universities and conventional universities (through distance mode).

Post Graduate Certificate in Climate Change and Sustainable Development (PGCCCSD)

IGNOU, New Delhi through its School of Agriculture offers six months Online Course on Post Graduate Certificate in Climate Change and Sustainable Development. It includes two sessions in an academic year i.e. January and July sessions. The course intends to provide the knowledge and equip the learners with appropriate tools and techniques for interpreting the impacts of climate change, and evaluating & implementing adaptive and mitigation measures that reduce vulnerability of systems. Graduates from any discipline are eligible for this course. The course is wide open to scientists and educational functionaries, agricultural graduates and science graduates, school and college level teachers, NGOs, professional, environmental executives, policy makers, journalists

Certificate in Climate Change and Environmental Management (CCCEM)

Mahatma Gandhi University, Kottayam, Kerala offers this six months programme by taking the academic support from Advanced Centre of Environmental Studies and Sustainable Development (ACESSD). It aims to provide basic knowledge on the science of climate change, its impact and mitigation would give a better understanding of the problem and the possible management measures to be evolved. All management strategies primarily focus on the conservation of natural resources that are under threat in the changing scenario of climate change. The prospective target group of learners includes undergraduates, postgraduates, researchers and the general public.

UNITED NATIONS (UN) CLIMATE CHANGE (CC): E–LEARN

United Nations (UN) is always at forefront to address the global issues and challenges. It has been tackling climate change through its own agencies and also in collaboration with countries and other organizations at various levels. As education remains the most powerful tool to awaken the people on climate change, United Nations has started offering simple and effective on-line courses through distance mode through its UN CC: E-Learn, which is a joint initiative of more than 30 multilateral organizations helping countries to achieve climate change action both through general climate literacy and applied skills development. It provides strategic advice and quality learning resources to help people, governments and businesses to understand, adapt, and build resilience to climate change. It is supported by the Swiss Agency for Development and Cooperation (SDC). Following are a few courses by offered it:

Introductory E-course on Climate Change

This e-course provides "everything one needs to know" about the basics of climate change. It is divided into six modules, each taking an average of 2 hours to complete. Each has 4 to 5 learning objectives. A short quiz at the end of each module allows the learners to verify if they have achieved these learning objectives. They have three attempts to try each quiz. Once all 6 modules are completed with above 70% of passing scores individually, they will receive a certificate of completion. The certificate will be automatically available on the 'achievement' section under the course page. One can decide to take all modules or choose to select those that most interest. All modules are available as PDF and PowerPoint Presentation for offline study or training purposes. The modules also include links to other UN resources on climate change, which provides a gateway to more in-depth and specific information.

Children and Climate Change

This course presents how children and youth can be impacted by climate change, how their resilience can be strengthened, and how they can act to address this challenge. It consists of a module divided into five sections and takes around 2 hours to complete. A short quiz at the end allows the learners to test their knowledge. Once completed with at least 70% of correct answers, they will receive a certificate of completion. They have a maximum of three attempts. This module is available as PDF and PowerPoint presentation for offline study or training purposes. The module also includes links to other UN resources on climate change, which provides a gateway to more in-depth and specific information.

Cities and Climate Change

This course focuses on climate change in urban areas, covering how cities are affected by climate change, how they contribute to it, as well as how they plan for it. It includes one module divided into 6 sections, and takes around 2 hours to complete. Once the quiz is completed with above 70% of passing scores, learners will receive a certificate of completion from UN-Habitat and UNITAR (United Nations Institute for Training and Research). They have three attempts to try the quiz. This module is available as PDF and PowerPoint Presentation for offline study or training purposes. The modules also include links to other UN resources on climate change, which provides a gateway to more in-depth and specific information.

Human Heath and Climate Change

This course provides an introduction to the health challenges, as well as the opportunities, that can by associated to climate change. It includes one module divided into 3 sections, and takes around 2 hours to complete. Once the quiz is completed with above 70% of passing scores, the learners will receive a certificate of completion from WHO and UNITAR. They have three attempts to try the quiz. This module is available as PDF and PowerPoint

Presentation for offline study or training purposes. The modules also include links to other UN resources on climate change, which provides a gateway to more in-depth and specific information.

Climate Change–From Learning to Action (Coming up in spring 2019)

The course helps the learners understand what climate change is, how it affects one and all, and what can be done to address it. Learners have to develop a concrete action or project to tackle climate change. Once the learners have completed 70% of the activities (including video lectures and exercises) and have uploaded climate change project, they will receive a certificate of completion.

CONCLUSION

Climate change is a big challenge for the planet earth, and it requires immediate action at a large scale at all levels. **Intergovernmental Panel on Climate Change (IPCC) Special Report on** 1.5 °C **(SR** 1.5 °C) **released in 2018 warns that there is no room for complacency.** Given its unique features, open and distance education has a high potential to develop holistic view about climate change and related issues among different sections of society across world. It is high time that people are sensitized about the availability of such simple, low cost and effective courses on climate change offered through distance education at different levels say at local, regional, national and international. These courses have the potentiality to develop holistic view on climate change among every section of the society. Further these courses offered through open and distance education goes a long way in strengthening the efforts of macro players in addressing climate change through adaptation and mitigation.

❐

28

Challenges in English Learning and Teaching in Distance Education

Education plays imperative role in national development. The increasing rate of population, rapid growth of poverty, vulnerability, unemployment, stratification, unequal opportunity, drop outs, depreciation of money value and mounting needs of education initiated different approaches to education. So, regular education is unavailable to many. Consequently, distance education was an approach under the umbrella of non-formal mode of education which contributed much in the expansion of education. Distance education has become more popular and time-honored approach for education in the modern period. The challenges in both distance education and learning and teaching English is inevitable. The classifications of challenges cater to drive them out. This study focuses to make out the challenges in learning and teaching English in distance education.

CHALLENGES IN DISTANCE EDUCATION

Academic Standard

The main challenge faced by the distance education in all over the world relates to the maintenance of standards. In the absence of formal teaching and education process, understanding the capacity of learner, innovative method of teaching, face to face interaction of teacher and learner and at the spot guidance are very less in non- formal education. There are other factors like choice of materials, lack of enough and well structured study centers and selection of teaching staff, etc., posing more challenge.

Finance

Finance in distance education is paramount challenge especially in developing countries. The cost of distance education programs differ a lot from one program to another. Cost-saving purpose is also one of the reasons for students select distance education. However, there are many cost-savings possibilities in comparison to those of formal education but the problem is that keeping high effective program is at the sky. The main issues concerning resources are how to get more of them from formal and unconventional sources and how best to deploy whatever resources are available to distance education as a whole.

Study Centers

Distance education institution has one main campus and few sub-campuses in its control, while its learners are spread in all over the country. In this way, it is impossible to build own study centers in all of the towns and cities of the country. Therefore, to meet the objective, the university hires the buildings of formal institutions or private management institutions to establish study centers to facilitate its learners.

Assignments

The component of assignments is obligatory one in distance education system. Its obligation is due to its worth and substance. It must be planned cautiously, guided appropriately by the tutors, written seriously, evaluated and then returned particularly well in time to the students. In black and white comments by the tutor on students assignment work has an effect on very much the performance of learner and through this comments they can augment their education.

Uses of Technology

It seems to be self evident that tutors need to be trained to use distance education technology, but too often they are not. According to Greenberg, 1998, the excellent distance education lies on the creative, well-informed tutors. The tutors must be trained "not only to use technology, but also to shift the way in which they organize and deliver material" (Palloff & Pratt, 2000). Bates (1995) suggest that advanced technologies are not innately better than old ones and many of the lessons learned from the application of older technologies will still be relevant to any newer technology. The tutor should be trained to take benefit of both their experience and being able to acclimatize that skill to the new environment of distance education.

Performance of the Administration

Administrators appointed on behalf of that distance education agency are only interested in providing them good education. Weekend classes are offered to them on a regular basis and an assortment of facilities which are offered. These study centers should be regularly inspected by officials from time to time.

Students

The system offers education to the adults, married; working people and people who are not economically vibrant. To impart education to such students we require appropriate planning and motivation to evaluate their ability. We have to bridge the gap between age and time in the field of education so that best learning is delivered to them.

Faculty

The achievement of education program depends on its faculty. Distance education is not an exception to it. In a traditional classroom setting, the faculties duties go around the students' development but in distance education faculty have to face many challenges in teaching.

Interaction and Motivation

The most important challenges in front of distance education are interactivity with the students. In the formal teaching method there is interaction between the leaner and teacher. The teachers can get the actual feedback of their lecture at the learning place not only through the verbal communication but also through the non verbal communication of the learner (body language, gestures & facial expressions). The teacher can openly interact and motivate their students for their learning .

Learning Material

The learning material used in distance education is also a paramount concern. The print material used in distance education is called self learning material. This material is dissimilar from text books used by learners in formal education. The print material used in distance education should be self motivating, self instructive and self learning. The challenge comes in front of the distance education especially in development of this material due to various reasons.

CHALLENGES IN ENGLISH LEARNING AND TEACHING

Students encounter many obstacles in their efforts to become proficient in the English language. They often come to realize that in order to be fully accepted, they must abandon their native language, surrendering an aspect of their identity.

Cognitive Factor

It denotes the number of new perceptions embedded in a lesson. It is learnt that we time and again assess prior knowledge of all students to recognize the concepts and skills they do and do not have. We must then fill in any conceptual gaps by trying to relate new concepts to life experiences of ESL students. Thus, in distance education, it grows to be more difficult to get to know and understand these students.

Cultural Factor

The interlace of language and culture plays vital role in English learning and the amount of cultural knowledge required to figure out meaning in an activity. Meanings of words and the usage of words are mostly determined within linguistic and cultural settings, and they vary from culture to culture. Most of the times culture, social settings, economic background cultivate interest and formulate the mind set of learners. In addition, the details conveyed in our textbooks and lessons are culturally embedded. Culture factor facilitate teachers to interact with students and make them to comprehend the tactics that includes when and what to speak, when to stay silent, when and what to respond and when to write. Language is therefore a "powerful and transformative tool of culture. Like culture, language is learned, it is shared, and it evolves and changes over time (Banks, 2001)". English learners are often expected to determine the classroom behavioral norms independently. In distance education, the culture factor is imperative to bring out effective result because the students from different culture, demography, ethnic groups and linguistic groups gather in one classroom and their expectation and their comprehension capacity vary from person to person. But these cultural factors are not considered due to lack of time and facilities.

Language Factor

It refers to the number of unknown words come across as an English learner reads a text or listens to teacher. A second language is a language studied in a setting where that language is the main vehicle of everyday communication and where abundant input exists in that language. A foreign language is a language studied in an environment where it is not the primary vehicle for daily interaction and where input in that language is restricted. So, teachers have to assimilate the learning capacity of students accordingly must explain text material, for example, if students are not able to understand complex sentences then the sentences can be broken down into comprehensible parts. Teachers' low proficiency levels, or their lack of confidence in their ability, are consistently identified in the literature (see, e.g., Ahn, 2011; Ghatage, 2009; Kuchah, 2009; Little wood, 2007). In distance education, language factor is not considered due to lack of staff.

Learning Factor

It deals about what teachers look forward to students to do with English in the learning activities. An example is brainstorming, an activity that is oral and fast-paced, with few visual examples and nominal explanation in the early stages. An English learner would have complexity following such an activity, let alone participating. Thus, teachers must cautiously consider the learning factor of all activities concerning English learners, making absorption and providing supports accordingly. Teachers are expected to introduce innovative strategies like attention seeking methodologies, task-based learning teaching, etc. because English is alien to the learners who are from rural areas, the poor, marginalized, etc. Therefore, teachers should model both academic and social language and scaffold its appropriate use to help the learner acquire it.

Classroom Factor

In many parts of the world, large classes are a common challenge (Ho, 2003; Shamim, 2012; Wedgwood, 2007), causing teachers to believe it is hard or unfeasible to initiate learner-centered teaching because, for example, they cannot intimately observe students' language use (Li, 1998) or set up pair-work and group-work (Hoque, 2009). A connected issue is the problem of control and discipline (Butler, 2005; Little wood, 2007); Carless (2004) argues that the noise created at some stage in speaking activities can be difficult when the local preference is for quiet and orderly classrooms. It can also be not easy to motivate learners. In many areas, particularly in rural areas, students may struggle to comprehend the significance of learning English as they have little contact with speakers of the language (Ho, 2003; Li, 1998).

CONCLUSION

Education should be effective whether the mode of imparting education is formal or non-formal. The poor, marginalized, vulnerable, interested married people choose this non-formal method of education due to socio economic, cultural conditions. Considering all these factors and challenges, the educational agency has to come forward to surmount by providing basic facilities and teaching strategies, interested and well qualified staff. The barriers which are in the mind of students should be wiped out. The government policies and grand in aid should be conducive to both agencies and students. The students are to involve themselves in learning as formal learning students. In the advanced technology era, learning language is very paramount to the placement, jobs and communications. This study has identified the challenges in both distance education and in English learning and teaching. To meet out the challenges both students and educational agency should work together.

❐

29

Health Education

Health through education had been of great concern during ancient times and so also in modern times in all the civilized nations of the world. Health is very important for human life. Wealth without health is of no use in our life; life is miserable and painful for an individual with ill-health. Though modern man could enjoy all sorts of materialistic comforts in life, thanks to the advancements of science and technology yet he falls often sick due to highly polluted environment in which he lives and works. This study focuses on 'Health Education' and the related issues like 'Malnutrition', 'Communicable Diseases and their Prevention', Safety and First-aid' Personal Hygiene etc.

Meaning and Definition of 'Health Education'

Health education like general education is concerned with changes in knowledge, feeling and behavior of people. It is concerned with developing such health practices as are believed to bring about the best possible state of well-being.-Report of WHO.

Health education is transmission of what is known about health into desirable individual, family and community behavior patterns by means of educational processes. (Dr.V.Ramkrishna and K.S. Krishnaswamy).

Objectives of Health Education

World Health Organization (W.H.O. 1974) had pointed out three important objectives for providing health education. They are:

- To make an individual learn the habits and practices that promote health and follow them throughout his life faithfully.
- To enable everyone to make use of all available community facilities and resources to preserve and improve health.
- An individual/community refrains from doing anything that may be injurious to the health of any other individual or community.
- Importance of Health Education
- Health education be acquired by people's own efforts and cannot be imposed upon them.
- Prejudices, ignorance and other social and cultural factors endanger health.

Nutrition and Health

Nourishment, haven and garments are imperative for man' s presence, of which sustenance involves the primary spot. Nourishment is fundamental for the physical development of our body, reestablishment of body tissues, supply of vitality of imperative calories for undertaking day by day differential exercises of life. The sustenance we devour ought to be sufficiently nutritious to offer us satisfactory vitality to do work, grow substantially obstruction offering invulnerability against illnesses. Nourishment is an imperative part of wellbeing that directs the prosperity of the person. It is essential for the upkeep of wellbeing and effectiveness of the person.

Meaning of 'Nutrition'

Food substances which offer us high calories of energy and stimulate the body growth are called 'nutrition'. It is categorized into five essential types- (1). Carbohydrates, (2). Protein, (3). Fat, (4). Minerals and (5). Vitamins and the deficiency of any one causes malnutrition which ultimately affects our health and make us vulnerable against diseases.

Health Habits

Teachers should emphasise personal hygiene and habits among the students. Of these, three are most important ones- (1). Cleanliness,(2). Diet Habits, (3). Physical Exercise.

Physical Education

Co-operation and guarantee better social alteration and vanity. Physical instruction and wellbeing training are identified with one another. Physical instruction grants preparing in citizenship and investing energy conveniently in beneficial leisure activities. In physical instruction classes each understudy is offered chances to create physical aptitudes as indicated by his/her advantage and capacities by taking an interest in individual amusements, bunch recreations, drill, or athletic rivalries. In physical training, understudies could get quick criticism without even a second's pause regarding their dimension of execution and the level of accomplishment accomplished. This fulfills them and animates them for further practice and interest.

Safety and First-aid

Meaning of 'First-aid'

First-aid refers to the basic help given to any person as an emergency measure, who met with an accident and got injured or immobilized or suddenly fell sick, before taking the affected individual to a regular doctor for proper medical care and treatment. First aid does not mean medical treatment, but refers to safety measures undertaken so that the condition of the patient/victim does not deteriorate further before the arrival of the doctor. First-aid should not be viewed lightly; it is a very responsible job.

CONCLUSION

Anyway much an individual is financially prosperous or accomplished, he is viewed as a crushed man on the off chance that he isn't fruitful in his family life. In this manner family welfare training is an unquestionable requirement for all. Understudies are to be instructed at the school level itself, the distinctive parts of family welfare training viz. Physical instruction, wellbeing training, sex instruction, security and medical aid measures and so forth. The available resources of accomplishing this, have been examined in this exercise. Instructors have incredible job in executing these measures wholeheartedly and make their understudies fruitful in having an upbeat family life.

❒

30

Reading Disorder of Children at Various School Levels

Slow learners are a part of regular schools, thus only proving that they are not physically or mentally disabled but only pace disabled. The only problem with them is that they learn concepts and achieve developmental milestones at a pace slower than their peers. They are not always learning disabled, and may have ordinary lives outside of the classroom. However, academic subjects are a challenge for them.

Reading Disorder

Reading program can alter a child's brain activity, increasing the parts of the left hemisphere used for reading. Children with dyslexia show different levels of functioning in parts of the brain as well as a decreased connectivity between the left and right hemispheres.

In reading disorder, there is a significant gap between the expected level of performance and actual achievement. Difficulties in reading can occur on many levels, and reading disorder may have several causes that manifest in different ways. Common problems in people with reading disorder include:

- Slow reading speed.
- Poor comprehension when reading material either aloud or silently.
- Omission of words while reading.

- Reversal of words or letters while reading.
- Difficulty decoding syllables or single words and associating them with specific sounds.
- Limited sight word vocabulary.

Specific Learning Disabilities

- Auditory processing disorder.
- Dyscalculia.
- Dysgraphia.
- Dyslexia.
- Language processing disorder.
- Non-verbal learning disabilities.
- Visual perceptual/visual motor deficit.
- Genetics.
- Factors during birth.
- In early childhood brain trauma or tumors.

Reading Trouble in Preschool or Kindergarten

- Struggles to recognize letters, match letters to sounds and blend sounds into speech.
- Has difficulty pronouncing words, for example, saying mawn lower instead of lawn mower.
- May have a smaller vocabulary than kids the same age and take longer to master of the alphabet, basic math and days the week.
- Has trouble making rhymes.

Reading Trouble in Primary School or Middle School

- Spells poorly.
- Has difficulty recalling facts and numbers.
- Has trouble learning new skills.
- Frequently reverses letters or puts them in the wrong order.
- Has trouble following directions.
- Struggles with word problems in math.

Teach Reading Skills

- Encourage struggling readers to follow the words with their finger across the page as they read.
- Teach students to recognize phonemes and to sound-out unfamiliar words.
- Help your students with reading comprehension by training them to ask questions, such as “How does this character feel?” “Why did the characters make this decision?” “What could happen next?”

- Older students who are slow learners may also be helped by learning how to summarize chapters and otherwise annotate their reading.

Class Lessons on Study Skills

- Teach students to break down big tasks into small pieces so they aren't overwhelming.
- Teach them how to memorize using mnemonic devices. For instance, "Never Eat Shredded Wheat" is a way to remember the directions "North, East, South, and West."

Individualized Education Plan (IEP) for Children

While IEPs are normally designed for children with learning disabilities, slow learners have also been shown to benefit academically and emotionally from individualized education.

- To get an IEP, schedule a conference with your child's teacher.
- Together, arrange to have your child assessed by the school system at no cost to you.
- After assessment, meet with your child's teacher and all relevant staff at your child's school and design an IEP. Before the meeting, make a list of things you want to include.

CONCLUSION

Learning disabilities are neurologically-based processing problems. These processing problems can interfere with learning basic skills such as reading, writing and/or math. They can also interfere with higher level skills such as organization, time planning, abstract reasoning, long or short term memory and attention. It is important to realize that learning disabilities can affect an individual's life beyond academics and can impact relationships with family, friends and in the workplace.

❐

31

Utilization of Online Programmes by Sec.Level T. in Teaching Learning Process

Teaching is not a mechanical process. It is an intricate, exacting and very challenging one. The demand of new technology and uninterrupted global environment could not be met with the only source of classroom instruction. Blended Lcarning is a formal education program in which a student learns at least in part through delivery of educational content with the best features of classroom instruction via digital and online media to personalize learning and to facilitate some element of student control over time, place, path, or pace. Educational methods have become advanced and changed dramatically in the last decade. The revolution in communication technologies, especially after the invention of the Internet, has introduced new methods of teaching and new ways of managing education. The availability of Learning Management Systems has enabled stakeholders in creating a platform that aids in web-based teaching in a convenient and flexible manner.

E-Teaching – Learning Process

The advert of on-line technologies coupled with an emerging recognition of the importance of effective teaching in university settings are acting together as catalysts to change the face and not we of university teaching and learning. Through on-line technologies, we finally we have the means to create the forms learning environments that we know work best. The classroom for tomorrow is starting to emerge and it is quite different to the classroom to which many are accustomed perhaps the most noticeable difference is in the roles of the participants. Everyone seems to be doing things a bit different.

This differs from face to-face classes where, because of time constraints a relatively small percentage of the students can participate in the discussions during one class session. Because of the lack of physical presence and absence of many of the usual in-person ones to personality, there is an initial feeling of anonymity which allows students who are usually shy in face-to-face classroom to participate in the online classroom. Therefore is possible and quite typical for all the students to participate in the threaded discussions common to web-based classes.

Review of Literature

De Vries (2016) conducted a study on "Significance of Online Teaching Vs Face to Face Similarities and Difference". This study on aims of comparing the two modes of teaching the similarities and differences. It is noted that many principles of teaching, which are used in face-to-face can be applied in online setting with a better understanding of both modes of teaching, the authors hope to encourage colleagues who are uncomfortable with teaching online to decide better when to use face-to-face or online teaching or a mix of both, within educational settings.

Objectives

To find out the significant difference between the different groups of biographical variables such as sex, educational qualifications, and faculty regarding process at secondary level.

Hypotheses

There exists significance different between different groups of biographical variables such as sex, educational qualification and faculty online programmed used in teaching learning process.

Methodology

The investigator preferred normative survey for identifying the utility level of teachers on on-line programmed enhancing the teaching-learning process, (Normative survey studied focuses it is important on focus on what is going on in the present situation. In this study, the level of utilization of on-line programmed in teaching-learning process). It clearly revealed by the selected method of normative survey. The tool sample of the study comprised of 240 secondary level school teachers in Karur district.

Analysis and Interpretation

TABLE. 31.1: Significant Difference between the Mean Scores of Male and Female Teachers and their Utilization of Online Programmes.

S.No	Sex	Mean	SD	N	't' Value	Significance (0.01 level)
1	Male	26.34	6.05	112	2.74	Significant
2.	Female	28.54	6.06	128		

TABLE. 31.2: Significant Difference between the Mean Scores Undergraduate and Postgraduate Degree Holders of Teachers' Utilization of Online Programmes.

S.No	Educational Qualification	Mean	SD	N	't' Value	Significance (0.01 level)
1	Under graduate	27.76	5.96	106	1.38	Not Significant
2.	Post graduate	28.82	5.73	134		

TABLE. 31.3: Significant Difference between the Mean Scores of Arts and Science Teachers' Utilization of Online Programmes.

S.No	Faculty	Mean	SD	N	't' Value	Significance (0.01 level)
1	Arts	27.96	6.02	137	1.34	Not Significant
2.	Science	28.97	5.48	103		

Their exist significance difference between male and female teachers who are working at secondary level in utilizing online programmes that are essential for teaching learning Process. Female teachers who are working in secondary schools utilized the online programmes better than male teachers. Hence the research hypothesis is accepted.

There exist no significance differences between under graduate and post graduate degree holder's teachers who are working at secondary level in utilizing online programmes that are essential for teaching learning process. Utilization of online programme by post graduate and under graduate degree holders working at secondary level are found to be same. Hence the research hypothesis is not accepted.

There exist no significance difference between arts and science teacher who are working at secondary level in utilizing online programmes. Utilization of online programme by arts and science teachers are found to be same. Hence the research hypothesis is not accepted.

Findings

Utilization of online programmes by the female teachers more than the male teachers.PG Degree holder and UG degree holder utilize online programmes in higher secondary schools are found to be same. Arts and Science teacher's utilization the online programmes in various secondary schools are found to be same.

CONCLUSION

The present study reveals that the teachers who are working at secondary level have high level of utilization of on-line programmes in teaching learning process. Eventhough, they have practical skill and knowledge, their skill based and knowledge based activities are not utilized fully in the field on on-line programmes. At the same time, they must also improve their subject knowledge based on the recent ides and those ideas may be complemented while preparing on-line programmes for teaching learning process. The teachers should come forward to teach through computer and they should help computer technicians to prepare a valuable software (knowledge enriched) for on-line programmes so that the learners may get benefited out of it. Hence, it is an essential factor for the teachers and students to adopt this technology to face the challenges in the emerging knowledge-based society. Therefore teachers and students must work together to enhance the level of utilization of online programmes in the teaching-learning process.

❐

32

Use of Brain-Based Teaching for Second Language Learning Through Distance Mode

The teacher is not a technician who implement the different approaches, techniques and educational ideas of others, but rather professionals able to think about and look for solutions when they face new problems. To think about the relations of teaching-learning process around natural learning inclinations like creativity, play, collaboration, emotions, and inquiry, our innovative clusters consciously support the engagement of student and match the basics of learning to better understand how students learn best.

It provides the essential scaffolding structures to make teachers integrate, rather than assimilate, innovative practices into their selection of teaching tools and designs. (Suryakumari M. and Leo Stanly, 2019)

Distance Education

According to Holmberg (1989), people prefer distance education for "the convenience, flexibility, and adaptability of this mode of education to suit individual students' needs". Learners are self-directed, unsupervised, expected and independent to be more autonomous.

Brain-Based Teaching and Learning in Educational Settings

Learners' participation and engagement in materials taught is a direct result of meaningful learning techniques teachers adopts. According to Thoms and Swamy (2014) state that significant learning occurs when faculty convey from teacher-centered educational settings to one is a learner-centered environment. Learners' roles in the learner-centered approach are maximized through the minimization of teachers' dominance. In learner-centered approach, teachers must develop learners' understanding of course content through classroom environment enrichment, this type of environments include emotional, physical, and social aspects that invert the classroom situation from teaching setting to learning field (Kaufman et al., 2008).

Developing meaningful learning experiences can be achieved through integrating the enriched environments, engagement of emotions, music, movement. Meaning making and the lack of pressure maximizes learners' participation and engagement involvement that leads to better understanding and academic achievement (Sousa, 2004, Luna, 2004). Brain-Based Learning Approach helps to facilitate meaningful language learning through the natural way brain work to help learners to use language in a meaningful context. Using such a brain Based teaching approach definitely follows the natural techniques learners use their brains. Natural learning experiences maximize learning opportunities and make learning last longer.

Wolfe (2001) states, Brain-based teaching is relevant and meaningful to previous mentally, emotionally, and physically experiences strengthen memory. Caine and Caine (2006) view that each brain system within the whole brain seems to work collaboratively to provide meaningful learning. It admits the brains' roles in meaningful learning and adapting teaching with the brains' roles. According to Springer (2010) states that students find new information presented more meaningful if it relates to personal life. Therefore, the materials used should inseparable from daily life to be meaningful.

How Distance learning use for language learning

The purpose is to offer courses in languages to schools where it would not otherwise be possible for learners to study them. The potential for providing instruction in the less usually taught languages is particularly improved by distance technology. The guiding rule is for distance learning courses not to become eternal, but to provide as a stepping stone to hiring a normal classroom teacher by laying the basis for a possible language program, particularly in the less commonly taught languages (Kataoka, 1987).

Distance learning Provides the Interaction for Developing language Skills

The achievement of distance learning in increasing students' Second language skills depends on the capability of the teaching program to provide language learning in face-to-face settings. This ability can now be provided through two-way satellite communications that permit teachers to communicate with the learner at each site and to present the interaction required for the development of second language skills. (Clifford, Ray 1990)

Some Successful Distance learning Programs for language learning

English language Courses at fit

The FIT curriculum specifies three English courses, English 1, 2 and 3, in three semesters, respectively. These courses are the combination of English for special purposes and general English (ESP for IT), with ESP content progressively increasing to 80% in English 3. In initial stage is intermediate, the final is upper-intermediate with elements of advanced ESP for IT. The aim of these courses, specified by the faculty authorities, on the basis of IEEE recommendations, is to train the learners for oral and written communication in professional and academic settings. The instructional goals, defined in this way, suggested as the best choice the task-based and Learner-centered teaching approach instead of the text-based or teacher-oriented one.

Hybrid Courses

In current literature on CALL (Computer Assisted Language Learning) is suggested as the optimal solution – "in order to be efficient, Web-based courses should be blended or hybrid", (Wolff, 2003). In hybrid course, all the classes are planned in great detail in advance, carried out and recorded in PowerPoint as slides and as narration. Everything that the instructor says, asks, or explains in the classroom she/he anticipates and records in the PowerPoint presentation. Having the narrated recording, which is comfortable than just the text on the slides, is very essential for some reasons. It gives the learner the sense of a 'real' teaching session. For language teaching, in particular, this is important because the learner both hears the pronunciation and sees the text which is not possible if lectures are given only in the written pdf. or ppt. format.

If the learners need or want to, they can always check their answers with the instructor, through e-mail. A pupil can also record her/his comments and send them through e-mail as the audio file. What is particularly important and needs special prominence is the fact that there is a very strong support segment for the e-learning learner from the teacher, who repeatedly communicates with them through e-mail, mostly in the second language, but if necessary also in their mother tongue. Moreover, the students can also communicate among themselves, via e-mail, forum or chat. (Miroslav Trajanovic1, Dragan Domazet1, Biljana Misic-Ilic2 -, 2010)

How the Brain Makes way for a Second Language

Learning involving complicated brain imaging technologies known as functional magnetic resonance imaging, and also exposed some interesting patterns in the means of our brains process mother tongue and second languages. Joy Hirsch used fMRI to find out how multiple languages are represented in the human brain. They found that mother tongue and second languages are spatially alienated in Broca's area, which is an area in the frontal lobe of the brain that is in charge for the motor parts of language-movement of the tongue, mouth, and palate. The two languages show very little disconnection in the activation of Wernicke's area, an area of the brain in the posterior part of the temporal lobe, which is accountable for an understanding of language.

The fMRI studies advocate that the complexity adult learners of a second language may have is not with considerate the words of the second language, but with the motor skills of forming the words with the and tongue mouth. This may give details why students of a second language can oftentimes understand a question raised in the new language but are not always able to form a quick response.

Thus, for adult English language learners, techniques that stress speaking may be more successful than methods that focus more on listening and reading. For example, rather than lecturing to a class about vocabulary and grammar, a teacher perhaps should motivate their adult students to have conversations in the second language, or to act out short skits incorporating the day's lesson, which would more closely link the learner' abilities to understand and speak the new language. Speaking would thus equal understanding.

These different neuroscience studies inform us that the brain is a really plastic entity. A combination of vocalization listening and seems to be the most biologically beneficial method of acquiring a second language for both adults and children. Incorporating what we know about the way the brain processes language into the way languages is taught will benefit not only learner who want to learner second language, but also all those who hope to extend their linguistic range.

CONCLUSION

It is measured that presenting and integrating language skills in face-to-face language courses needs to be planned well. In distance language learning courses, it is more difficult. The negative perceptions of learner about effective teaching of language skills may be recognized to this challenge Assignments, grading techniques and clarity of learner' responsibilities are also criticized. In fact, it seems to be complex to classify assignments in distance language courses, but when it is planned well, the reactions will be probably better.

❐

33

Computer Skills of National Institute of Open Schooling (NIOS) Diploma in Elementary Education (D.El.Ed) Students

Teachers are expected to develop their students as citizens for the knowledge society; they have to be prepared for this role, throughout their career and also through the various education programmes. As suggested by Hargreaves (2003), we can promote an educational system with highly skilled teachers, capable of generating ingenuity and creativity in children, provided they experience creativity and flexibility and are themselves developed as knowledge society professionals. Therefore, teachers need to be computer skills for their teaching process.

Need and Significance of the Study

The rapidly changing nature of computer technology continues to expand the range of resources available for any subject in specific learning. Education must reflect the influence of technology. Education on the internet is easy, comfortable, trendy and interactive. The learner can go ahead and acquire computer knowledge and skills and adapt the concept of learning by doing. It encourages both independent and collaborative learning while extending and supporting the learning process. Appropriate computer technology places users in control of their own learning. Today, any person with an information requirement may want to use the internet, Students invariably require access to all sorts of information during their studies and the computer and the internet can be used for just this purpose. Students may want to use the network to browse online databases or to search libraries for a book or other published works. The computer and internet also breaks down campus boundaries and allows students access to other academic institutions. A student can get enormous information from all through the world, just sitting before the computer. Computer and internet are being widely used in all walks of life without any disparities. Hence the researcher is interested in studying basic computer knowledge and skills among NIOS Diploma in Elementary Education Students.

Statement of the Problem

Human has always needed to perform arithmetic like counting and adding. During the pre-historic period, they counted either on their fingers or by scratching marks on the bones and then with the help of stone, pebble and beads. The early civilization had witnessed men develop number systems to keep track of the astronomical cycles, businesses, etc. The word computing means 'an act of calculating'. Therefore the basic knowledge about computer is must for us, irrespective of the disciplines in which we are. Elementary education teachers are the vital role of our education system so the present situation they need technical skills. Hence, the statement of problem entitled "Computer Skills of National Institute of Open Schooling(NIOS) Diplomain Elementary Education Students".

Objectives of the Study

- To assess the computer skills of the NIOS Diploma in Elementary Education Students.
- To find out the computer skills of NIOS Diploma in Elementary Education Students with respect to gender.

Hypotheses of the Study

- The level of Computer Skill ofNIOS Diploma in Elementary Education Students is average.
- There is no significant difference between male and female NIOS Diploma in Elementary Education Studentsin their computer skills.

Methodology

The present study, the investigator applied normative survey as a method. The sample 91 NIOS Diploma in Elementary Education Students. The following tool was used for data collection Computer Knowledge and Skill Questionnaire constructed and standardized by Amutha. S(2008). The data were analyzed using mean, standard deviation,t-test.

Analysis and Interpretation

Hypothesis No – 1

The level of Computer skills of NIOS Diploma in Elementary Education Studentsis average.

TABLE. 33.1: Level of Computer Skills of NIOS Diploma in Elementary Education Students

Sample	N	Mean	S.D.	Level of ICT awareness
Whole sample	91	228.95	58.11	Average Level

From the above tablethe mean value of the entire sample is 228.95and S.D is 58.11. The calculated mean value is higher than the percentile 25 (201) but less than percentile 75 (230). Hence, it is inferred that NIOS Diploma in Elementary Education Studentsare having an average level of Computer skills. Hence, the framed null hypothesis (1) is accepted. It is inferred that the level of Computer skills of NIOS Diploma in Elementary Education Student is average.

Hypothesis No - 2

The male and female NIOS Diploma in Elementary Education Student do not differ in their Computer skills.

TABLE. 33.2: Difference between Mean Scores of Gender-based on NIOS Diploma in Elementary Education Students Computer Skills.

Gender	N	Mean	SD	't' value	Level of Significance
Male	42	226.95	58.11	11.80	Significant
Female	49	250.45	70.35		

From the above table,The't' value obtained for the difference between mean scores of male and female NIOS Diploma in Elementary Education Students 11.80. This 't' value is greater than the table value 1.96 at the 0.05 level. Hence the null hypothesis is rejected that there is a significant difference in the Computer skills between the male and female NIOS Diploma in Elementary Education Students. The female NIOS Diploma in Elementary Education Studentsmeansthe score is higher than the male NIOS Diploma in Elementary Education Studentsmean scores in Computer skills. This indicates that the hands-on practice on Computer skills may be strengthened for the male and female NIOS Diploma in Elementary Education Students.

Major Findings

- The level Computerskills of NIOS Diploma in Elementary Education Studentsare average.
- The male and female NIOS Diploma in Elementary Education Studentsdiffers in their Computer knowledge.

Recommendations

Based on the study necessary recommendations are also made for policy making and implementation. The findings of the present study throw light on the dismal state of affair with regard to the Computer skills of NIOS Diploma in Elementary Education Students. The government should encourage and put in incentive to attract state, local, international bodies and non-governmental organizations to invest inComputer related projects in schools.Also, in the NIOS Diploma in Elementary Education curriculum morecomputer-relatedtrainings are added.

CONCLUSION

The problem of technology illiteracy was a serious one among teachers in the country as it cuts across tertiary institutions. Many teachers in the country did not have basic computer skills. Nowadays teaching and learning process needs special attention, as the intersection of all disciplines with Computer skills will be at the core of educational systems. Today teachers have to improve themselves in their Computer skills. So as to be a technology proficient teacher this is the urgent need of today. The present investigation points out the reference toComputer usage by the NIOS Diploma in Elementary Education Students. Definitely, this research is an eye opener for the Elementary Education students to become technology proficient Teachers.

❐

34

The Development of Critical thinking as Primary Goal of Educational Process

As long as people have purposes in mind and wish to judge how to accomplish them, as long as people wonder what is true and what is not, what to believe and what to reject, strong critical thinking is going to be necessary. Dewey even feared textbooks could do a disservice to critical thinking. Dewey said, "The child approaches the book without intellectual hunger, without alertness, without a questioning attitude, and the result is the one so deplorably common: such abject dependence upon books as weakens and cripples vigour of thought and inquiry." Critical thinking refers to the ability to analyze information objectively and make a reasoned judgment. Critical thinking involves the evaluation of sources such as data, facts, observable phenomenon, and research findings. Good critical thinkers can draw reasonable conclusions from a set of information and discriminate between useful and less useful details to solve a problem or make a decision. In learning scenarios that promote and foster problem solving and critical thinking skills, it is much more difficult for the student to simply adhere to the role of the passive student; rather, this type of learning prompts the student to assume the role of a self-reliant thinker and researcher

Characteristics of Critical Thinking

- **Interpretation:** to comprehend and express the meaning or significance of a wide variety of experiences, situations, data, events, judgments, conventions, beliefs, rules, procedures, or criteria.
- **Analysis:** to identify the intended and actual inferential relationships among statements, questions, concepts, descriptions, or other forms of representation.
- **Evaluation:** to assess the credibility of statements or other representations and to assess the logical strength of the actual or intended inferential relationships among statements, descriptions, questions or other forms of representation.
- **Inference:** to identify and secure elements needed to draw reasonable conclusions; to form conjectures and hypotheses; to consider relevant information and to reduce the consequences flowing from data, statements, principles, evidence, judgments, beliefs, opinions, concepts, descriptions, questions, or other forms of representation.
- **Explanation:** Being able to present in a cogent and coherent way the results of one's reasoning.
- **Self-Regulation:** You can monitor and correct an interpretation you offered. You can examine and correct an inference you have drawn. You can review and reformulate one of your own explanations.

The importance of Critical Thinking

Critical thinking is very important in the new knowledge economy:

- **The Global knowledge Economy is Driven by Information and Technology**
- **One has to be Able to Deal with Changes Quickly and Effectively**
  The new economy places increasing demands on flexible intellectual skills, and the ability to analyse information and integrate diverse sources of knowledge in solving problems. Good critical thinking promotes such thinking skills, and is very important in the fast-changing workplace.
- **Critical thinking Enhances language and Presentation Skills**
  Thinking clearly and systematically can improve the way we express our ideas. In learning how to analyse the logical structure of texts, critical thinking also improves comprehension abilities.
- **Critical Thinking Promotes Creativity**
  To come up with a creative solution to a problem involves not just having new ideas. It must also be the case that the new ideas being generated are useful and relevant to the task at hand. Critical thinking

plays a crucial role in evaluating new ideas, selecting the best ones and modifying them if necessary

- **Critical Thinking is Crucial for Self-Reflection**
  In order to live a meaningful life and to structure our lives accordingly, we need to justify and reflect on our values and decisions. Critical thinking provides the tools for this process of self-evaluation.
- **Good Critical Thinking is the Foundation of Science and Democracy**
  Science requires the critical use of reason in experimentation and theory confirmation. The proper functioning of a liberal democracy requires citizens who can think critically about social issues to inform their judgments about proper governance and to overcome biases and prejudice.

Strategies for Developing Critical Thinking:

Thinking through inquiry

Asking questions and using the answers to understand the world around us is what drives critical thinking. In inquiry-based instruction, the teacher asks students leading questions to draw from them information, inferences, and predictions about a topic. If we want students to generate good questions on their own, we need to teach them how to do so by providing them with the structure and guidance of example questions, whether in written form, or by our use of questions in the classroom.

Critical thinking through Writing

Another essential ingredient in critical thinking instruction is the use of writing. Writing converts students from passive to active learners and requires them to identify issues and formulate hypotheses and arguments. The act of writing requires students to focus and clarify their thoughts before putting them down on paper, hence taking them through the critical thinking process.

Critical thinking through Group Collaboration

Opportunities for group collaboration could include discussions, case studies, task-related group work, peer review, or debates. Group collaboration is effective for promoting critical thought because:

Make Connections

Encouraging students to make connections to a real-life situation and identify patterns is a great way to practice their critical thinking skills. Ask students to always be on the look for these connections, and when they find one to make sure they tell you

Reflection

Reflection is a lost art. With the push to cover more content and standards, teachers often make a choice between coverage or pausing for reflection. Reflection comes in many forms: reflective journals, group work, whole class, silent reflection, reviewing yesterday's work, reflecting on an essential question, or creating a product that shows your thoughts about a previous lesson or understanding.

CONCLUSION

The essential critical thinking skills are developed in order to address the challenges of modern education, global competition, and democratic life. Therefore it is necessary to create an atmosphere of learning that allows students to be able to think critically. The ability to think critically and creatively is tools for students to learn independently for life. So the critical thinking skills in education are important because it can determine the quality of the school, and students' behavior that all depends on students' ability to solve problems and make decisions.

❐

35

Techniques and Methods of Teaching, Learning Process in Pondicherry during the 18th and 19th Century

In the field of education and culture the French had a real "mission civilisatrice". Like their counter-parts in British India, it is true, the French needed a host of men to run the Company Administration men who could speak and write their language with fluency. Clerks, doctors, engineers, lawyers and teachers were all needed to keep the administration going. Education under the French was, as it should be under any civilized Government, the chief concern of the State. Whereas in British India, Primary and Secondary Education entirely and Collegiate Education largely was relegated to private effort. Did not the British lightly club education with the Transferred subjects' under Diarchy (1919)-all stages of education were manned and run directly by the French regime. Its chief characteristic was that it was at once secular "Laique". Non-denominational and free "Gratuit" was up to secondary stage. It was perfectly democratic and within the reach of all sections of society as the fees for English and under graduate studies as well as for various examinations was but nominal. Besides, poor but promising bright students were encouraged with scholarships, "Bourses", on the strength of competitive examination to pursue their studies unhindered here as well as abroad.

The attempts made by the French for the promotion of education since their arrival in Pondicherry in the year 1674. It must be noted at the very outset that the French had actually come to Pondicherry not in accordance with any pre-conceived plan, but only at the specific invitation of Shan Khan Lodi, and that too, to serve as a counter poise, vis-vis the growing influence of the Dutch gaining control over the textile trade in the region. Hence their first and primary objective was to consolidate their position in Pondicherry through the promotion of trade. It therefore took some years for the French even to consider the need to evince any special interest either in the education of the French settlers then known as colons or the local population.

The growth of education in Pondicherry in those twilight years has therefore to be explored in the light of this historical perspective. Pondicherry and its surroundings were not just barren lands without population although it was not considerable. But its location close to the estuary of the river sengi, served as a kind of meeting place or a point of anchorage, in the age of sailing vessels, for traders from Greece, Rome and China etc, with peninsular India since time immemorial. So, it would be appropriate to present a brief survey of the political, socio-economic, and culture status and conditions which prevailed in Pondicherry before the arrival of the French in order to identify the factors which ultimately prompted the French turning their attention to the promotion of education among the population under their protection. The denomination 'French' used here includes, besides the French administration, the missionaries as well as company and its servants.

Education in Pondicherry

The legacies of the Church centered education, managed by the missionaries of various priestly orders and the Congregations of sisters were still very strong because the new spirit of Republicanism, born out of the Revolution of 1789, had much of its glow, and was not very much perceptible in the far away colonies. Among the French Colonies, the establishments in India came to enjoy a better status under the Third Republic and a Senator and depute came to represent French India in the French Parliament. Moreover the development in the field of education, the haphazard growth of schools and the languishing state of education called for a general reform.

In these circumstances, Gramboulan, la Inspectuer d'academie was sent on a mission to Pondicherry by the Ministre de la Marine et des Colonies in 1879 to study the situation first hand. He visited Pondicherry and two other establishments. All aspects of school education came under the sweep of his zealous probe. Education in the French medium was made free at all levels during this period. It was free for girls at all levels for any type of education.

French or Indian, Private and Government schools were imparting education according to the Indian system charged fees for boys at all levels. The facility for providing midday meal for poor school children was first made available to the children in Ecole des filles in rue Dumas, ecole de la rue Surcoufand ecole des fillers de la rue des missions even prior to the year 1938. From 1938 onwards, the scheme was gradually extended to other schools. The expenditure was met from the funds of comite de blenfaisance.

Education Pattern

The Education pattern, in the main, was something like this: Primary 4 years, Middle 3 years; Secondary 4 years; and Undergraduate 3 years. Five+ was the age of admission. Monkeying with Nativity and date of birth, like official and astrological age as elsewhere, was impossibility, as the Etat-Civil code enjoined fool-proof registration of births and deaths. A child entering "Ecole Primaire" normally came out of "Ecole Centrale" at 12+ or 13 and was awarded the Middle School "Certificat" after common examination. "Brevet de l'Enseignement Primaire Supericure" capped the emergence from Secondary stage at 16+ or 17 One was crowned with "Baccalaureat de l'Enseignement Scondaire" at 19+ or 20 the highest educational qualification open to the elite of educational youth in French India. For further higher studies, degree level-Licencie es Lettres, Cs Sciences, etc, one had to go to Metropolitan France.

School System

One could pursue undergraduate studies for Baccalaureat only at College Francais in Pondicherry. Secondary schools preparing for Brevet were located in Karaikal, Mahe, Yanam and Chandernagore. Each "commune" had an "Ecole Centrale". The outlying villages, even the remotest, had primary schools of varying sizes with a single, double or treble-teacher-strength, as feeders for 'Ecole Central". Thus the numerous "Ecoles Primaires" dotted over the rural parts, formed the base, the "Ecoles Centrales" in "commune" towns the middle and the Secondary schools the apex of the pyramid with "College Francais" making up the coping-stone".

Curricula and Medium

The curricula and syllabus was largely those followed in France; and, of course French was the medium of instruction right from the infant stage. The method of teaching was 'direct' especially through "language en action". The foreign medium, however, entailed a good deal of learning by rote. In fact, French education stressed repetition, rote and discipline. 'Ecriture' or handwriting was cultivated with great care. We were given the motto: a good handwriting is like a good friend. The Indian language formed the second language from the very beginning and the textbooks, too, were those printed and published in France for French children. History, Geography, Science, Maths, etc, were all taught in French. But history and geography were entirely those of France. So the absurdity ludicrous practice prevailed. The Indian child started reading history, calling France "La mere Patrie", Mother land and Geography all about France and little about India.

As a result of the impact of the freedom movement in the sub-continent spear-headed by Mahatma Gandhi and of periodical constitutional reforms-Minto-Morley 1910, Montage-Chelmsford 1919, Government of India Act, 1935-conceded by the British, the French Educational/Political system also underwent slight modification and adaptation to suit the rising national aspirations of the people. The regional languages acquired an added importance. In order to assist the D.P.I. (French man) inspect Primary School language teachers the senior most Director of Ecole Primaire was nominated Delegate to D.P.I. “”Langue Indigene" gave place to "Langue Indienne".

Language-English

It was but natural that French was encouraged. But Tamil, Telugu, Malayalam and English were not neglected. The regional languages could be studied separately up to the "Certificat" and "Brevet"standards. Tamil "Brevet" diploma holders were qualified to teach Tamil in schools.

English, like Tamil, continued as Second Language for Baccalaureate. But there was no separate school for English. To fill this lacuna, Pondicherry owes a deep debt of gratitude to the foresight and munificence of that great merchant-prince Calve Subbaraya Chettiar, the founder-patron of Calve College (1877), Pondicherry. The foundation was meant for Secondary Education-in three language-French, Tamil, and English: Brevet Francais, Brevet Tamoul and Matriculation. The first two were free; the last had to be paid for. And it may be obvious that English was there on sufferance. Thus, the English section of Calve College came to be affiliated to Madras University and continues to render yeoman service till the present day.

Examinations

A word about the examination system: Public examinations were conducted for the Middle and Secondary stages of Education. Examiners were appointed by the D.P.I. and approved by the Head of the Colony. Such work was purely honorary; Examinations were done in one or two days usually in Pondicherry under the Presidentship and immediate surveillance of the D.P.I. Sub-Committees of two members each valued the answer papers, conducted viva-voce tests and proclaimed the results on the spot. Yes, Viva-voce tests were a common feature to all examination. They were not formal tests, but deciders of the candidate's ability to pass. Hand-writing and drawing (sewing and stitching for girls) had marks, too. A minimum of 50% (Moyenne) was required for a pass. A candidate who passed the written, but failed the oral test was declared to have failed. In the Brevet and Baccalaureate Examinations not infrequently only two or three candidates passed the written part but failed the oral test. The result, then, was "Neant". This helped maintain the high standard of French educational qualifications.

Drawbacks

Excellent as this Educational system sounds its chief drawback, in my opinion, was that it was bookish, theoretical and intra-mural. Audio-visual aids like charts, maps, blackboards were used no doubt, But in science teaching, it was strange that the land of Lavoisier, Louid Pateur, Madame and Monsieur Curie should be blind' to laboratories and experiments. I mean, they were too inadequate in this Age of Science. And the few experiments in the only Lab, were more symbolic than real, as they were performed by teachers rather than by pupils, originally of thinking and doing was at a discount. The British Indian Education produced at least once C.V. Raman Physicist Nobel Laureate.

Again, extra-curricular activities like library, debating-society, games and sports were conspicuous by their absence. And when I went to Annamalai University (1932) from Calve College, I was at bay, that I had missed much at the high school by way of co-curricular activities came to me with a thud. It was like a Martian landed on Earth. Slowly I shook off my shyness and got into the stride. For much of this, the French Metropolitan Educational system had itself to thank. That it was as outmoded as the Napoleonic Code was shown in lurid light by the terrific student upheaval of May 1968 which convulsed France and which almost shook that imperious General de Gaulle out of the presidency. It is far from my intention to weary you all with tiresome details and test you patience. Let me state at once that the secret of success of the French Educational system was due partly (a) to the French Administration system, but largely (b) to the method of recruitment of teachers.

The Education system introduced in India by the French after their arrival had now come under a solid footing. It has nurtured and grown up in die, peaceful atmosphere taking into account the needs and aspirations of the local people. The French republication ideas had been transplanted into the Indian soil by now. Along with the teaching of French language in the colony, the teaching of English and Tamil had also been taken into account. Their efforts were successful in the colony. All these indicate the benevolent measures of the French administration towards their subjects in the French Indian establishments.

❒

36

Effective Role of Science Education in the Society

One of the key themes in the discussion on the modern university is the question "why do we need science? The answer to this question is essential in the function and operation of the university as a centre for science. Generally, supporters of the independence of the university take the position that science should be conducted for its own sake, and for the pleasure of learning, in order to widen human knowledge, discover the world around us and learn more about it. According to this concept, modern academics are the priests of knowledge, who should be totally independent, so that nobody can in any way attempt to in uence the results of their research. In this case, utility is secondary, because autonomy and freedom of research has a greater signi cance. The supporters of such an approach are obviously mainly academics themselves, who would like to carry out their research in a comfortable atmosphere, without pressure, on the principle that "nobody can tell me what I should research".

Fundamental Values of Education

Respect and mutual acknowledgement are the fundamental values onwhich inter-personal contact should be based. In the case of "corruption" by power, especially when it comes to weakness of character, there is a whole range of determinants which work against effective contact. For example – an overblown ego, labelling, a conviction of one's own infallibility, a tendency tothe achievements of others, self-conceit and arrogance.

Respect for colleagues, as well as for the institution itself, is the mark of an ability to work with others. If we are not convinced that the other party is capable of logical reasoning and taking rational decisions, we will be reluctant to engage in forced co-operation which may lead to sham and simulation. From observa-tion of the scienti c community, it is precisely this lack of conviction in the other party's awareness and causative abilities which often precludes any kind of rela-tionship. And if a professor, locked in his or her silent study, has no contact with reality either as creator or co-creator, then his or her lectures will contain inaccu-racies, distortions and sterotypes. He or she then becomes a purveyor of rubbish. Respect creates the appropriate emotional atmosphere, enabling partnercommunication. Academics have to give up being a law-maker and become a "translator", a person who can transform the slightest nuances into simple lan-guage which an average person can understand. On the other hand, the extra-mural world cannot treat the universe of science as something perfect and irrefu-table. Effective partner communication should include criticism, discussion, and an exchange of visions and ideas. Respect cannot eliminate intellectual discus-sion and turn a dialogue into a "monologue of the wisest". Proper communica-tion depends on all sides being engaged in reaching the truth, setting parameters, understanding and agreement. At the same time, academic titles often bedazzle and invoke blind obedience among those who do not possess them.

This means that to ensure proper communication between academic institu-tions and those practicing science in action, there is a need for a well-prepared scienti c staff comprising people, for example, with the title of doctor. Some-times they lack the required communication skills to reach out to lay people, so Ph.D. students and doctors could become "translators" of science and facilitate understanding.More important than language skills, which most academics possess, are undoubtedly psychological skills, such as empathy and the ability to listen attentively.

Importance of Science Education

Opponents of this approach point out that science conducted in this way rarely leads to the development and improvement of living conditions. Placing independence above all else means that we can conduct research for years without any concrete results. There is also the temptation to falsify research results and generally waste funds.

Utilitarian's see the university as a tool, and the conduct of science as a means of solving the specific problems1 which our culture, civilization and modern society are faced with. According to them, the limits of autonomy should be denied by effectiveness and need, and with it funding in the form of grants. This does not mean, of course, that scientists should be restricted in their activity and told what to do. Competitions and grant programmes are rather a form of stimulation and sponsor-ship, an indication of what is of priority in the research process. Apart from these two positions, there are those who treat science as a hobby, for the sheer pleasure of learning, and they should be able to conduct research, but on their own account by seeking sponsors and without incurring any cost.

Competitions and grants can only fulfil their role if applications are assessed impartially. Participants in this kind of scientific rat-race frequently complain that the rules of such competitions are unclear, and that those who assess applications are more guided by their own preferences rather than clearly designed assessment criteria. There are also sometimes scandals, involving accusations of nepotism, collusion or the introduction of additional irrelevant conditions, such as membership in a particular organization or the use of a particular methodology.

It seems that discussion is too focussed on one single chosen aspect, despite the fact that there are numerous monographs dealing with the role of science and the mission of the university. The way to the essence of this problem and ending a satisfactory solution, and at the same time putting an end to these endless discussions, is through recognizing and accepting that the intra- and extra-mural worlds are parallel and of equal status in reality, and that the one cannot exist without the other. They should be treated equally, and science can be the bridge between them. In order to achieve this, it is necessary to eliminate the limitations and barriers which from the outset have the borders of the space in which these two worlds might meet.

Effective Cooperation for Science Education in the Society

The next condition for using knowledge as a platform for understand-ing between the communities is effective cooperation. A space for common activity could be scientific practical projects, in which both those conducting research and those using the science to increase their effectiveness take part. In order for such an effective co-operation to exist, a further range of skills, such as project management, planning and organization, is necessary.

Effective co-operation begins with presenting the needs of the partner organi-zation and the research possibilities of the institute and then forming a joint pro-ject of operation. Just as in the case of communication, there is a temptation for the partner with the greater prestige to push their own opinion and solutions. Such a situation, unfortunately, cannot be described as co-operation between partners, because it is the subjugation of one side by the other. Generally, it is the business partners and institutions operating outside the academic circle who have a better understanding of the needs and are able to correctly de ne the problems. Therefore, it is they who ought to have the most say when it comes to priorities.

Effective co-operation also requires a different approach to the conduct of science. It is essential to put aside the construction of cold, elegant theories in favour of "dabbling" in practical matters, creating something along the lines of science in action, analogous to action science, with which such a method of con-ducting science should be closely connected. The concept of science in action is the close cooperation between researchers and practitioners – academics, vol-unteers, workers in the organization and representatives of the local communitywho are able to build an effective co-operative network for real and speci c problems. Such dedicated teams are able to solve complex problems within the education environment. While academics are able to supply the most up-to-date knowledge, researchers take care of the research methodology and practitionerscan act as scouts, identifying future.

I think that for many academics the concept of the exact sciences co-operat-ing with business, local councils and communities, non-governmental organi-zations and ordinary people who are not part of any institution, is dif cult to comprehend and even shocking, especially for those whose standard bears the motto of independence of science and the university as their primary value. Very often they have lost the sense of this value long ago, and consider that contact between the independent academic and the outside world is the definition of subjugation and a descent into dependency. Here it is worth remembering that respect and partnership are the corner stones of co-operation between communities on the principle of science in action. And if we have this respect, there is no place for some kind of feudal subjugation.

Effective cooperation on a partnership basis can bring many benefits for both sides. Practitioners receive better diagnostic tools, monitoring and support from the academics – experts whose everyday job is analyzing problems in a wider context, possessing the apparatus for this task, as well as up-to-date information. On the other hand, researchers receive inspiration for their explorations, the possibility of testing theory in real situations, occasionally the possibility of discovering something completely unexpected, as well as nancial support within the framework of scienti c research programmes.

In this context, there appears to be only one answer to the question posed at the beginning. Science should of course be conducted for learning and development. However, it is not worth wasting our time on abstract problems, when all around us there are concrete dif culties as well as the consequent possibilities of supporting society through scienti c research.

For some years I have observed a kind of dance among academics, sleep-walking without inspiration, while tackling futile problems already long played-out, inventing ever more scientific problems in the name of research, which do not bring us a step nearer any new knowledge or develop-ment. With a few published articles containing few citations, and without any serious research or inspiration, they climb the career ladder, criticizing the work of others upon a whim". Isolated from reality, after some time they are not even able to distinguish good from bad in science, because they have no such competence, even though the system has elevated them to the top. They make decisions only because they have authority, even though they have no esteem in the local scienti c community, and they are invisible in global science. This sleep dance can be partly interrupted by reaching out to the once in need and supporting local community activities in resolving their burning issues.

CONCLUSION

Education is the manifestation of human behaviour in the society. Education alone especially science education can inculcate and transform the effective awareness and divine realisation among the society.

❐

37

ICT Enabled Education in India

Information and Communication Technology (ICT) in education to converse, generate, circulate, stock up, and administer information. In some context, ICT has also become important to the teaching-learning communication, throughout such approach as replace chalkboards with interactive digital whiteboards, using students' have possession of smart phones or other plans for learning through group of students point in time, and the "flipped classroom" replica where students watch lecture at home on the processor and use classroom time for more interactive movements. When teachers are digitally knowledgeable and train to use ICT, these approach can lead to higher order thinking skills, give innovative and individualized option for students to communicate their understanding, and go away students better ready to arrangement with continuing technological transform in the world and the place of work. As the lead joint Nations Organization for education, UNESCO guides international efforts to help countries appreciate the role such technology can play to increase speed progress toward Sustainable Development Goals. UNESCO shares information about the many ways technology can make possible universal access to education, connection learning divides, support the development of teachers, enhance the quality and significance of learning, strengthen inclusion, and improve education administration and domination.

Various Devices / Technology In ICT Includes

- Access of course materials through remote devices,
- Online digital repositories for lectures, course materials, and digital library,
- Online/ cloud based academic management systems,
- Employing the flipped classroom concept,
- Making use of handheld computers, tablet computers, audio players, projector devices etc.

Objectives of ICT In Education:

- Enhancing learning experiences and providing new sets of skills,
- Reaching more students with Massive Open Online Courses(MOOCs),
- Facilitating the training of faculties,
- Minimizing costs and saving time associated with information delivery and automating regular day-to-day tasks,
- Improving the administration of institutions to enhance the quality and efficiency of service delivery.

Effectiveness of ICT in Education

Being aware of the significant role of ICT in our life, especially in the educational activities, education authorities should be wise enough in implementing the strategies to empower ICT in supporting the teaching and learning process in the classroom. Nowadays the role of Information and Communication Technology (ICT), in the education sector plays an important role, especially in the process of empowering the technology into the educational activities. Education sector can be the most effective sector to anticipate and eliminate the negative impact of ICT. Technology in another side can be the most effective way to increase the student's knowledge. The use of ICT in education adds value to teaching and learning, by enhancing the effectiveness of learning. It added a dimension to learning that was not previously available. After the inception of ICT in schools, students found learning in a technology.

Need and Importance of ICT Education In India

"Smart technology" is the familiar terminology that is widely being used in every being's life. Smartphone's, tablets, gadgets, smart televisions, etc., are the products of smart technology that have made human life smarter, easier and accessible. Smart technology has not only enhanced the way of living but also became an integrated part of everyone's life. The Information and Communication technology to be precise has become a driving force behind economic growth and a developmental tool as well. ICT is an extended term for Information technology which is a technological source to make information available at the right time, right place in the right form to the right user. Earlier, one had to wait for the newspapers to get the information across the world. Now with the smarter technology, information can be accessed from anywhere using smart phones and gadgets. All this is made possible with the help of Information and Communication Technology. Information technology has been influencing our lives in the recent years in the fields of education, healthcare, and business. So in the Modern India we must have the modern era ICT Education.

Computer-Based learning

Computer-based learning is one of the modules of school communication tool that helps students to enhance their learning skills through computer aided education. It imparts computer knowledge in students and enables them to obtain large amounts of information from various websites. After two decades of introducing computers to schools, education has been revolutionized ever since then. It reduces time spent on mechanical tasks such as rewriting, producing graphs and increases the scope of searching. It not only helps in finding information but also in organizing information making it easier to share with others.

Internet

Internet tools like Email, social networks, newsgroups and video transmission have connected the world like never before. Students can now communicate using emails and social networking groups that provide knowledge based information. Distance learning, online learning is also enabled through the internet. Students can learn online and also talk to experts online. Notes, readings, tutorials, assignments can be received by students from anywhere. The Internet provides major information in texts, audios, videos and graphics which can be accessed by the individual. Online learning allows students to interact with each other and faculty to interact with students.

Classroom Learning

With the introduction of ICT in education, classroom learning is one attribute that makes learning experiential and experimental to students. Students can listen to the instructor or teacher, receive visual cues through PowerPoint images, handouts or whiteboard lists and participate actively. This helps in immediate interaction and students have opportunities to ask questions and participate in live discussions. This school communication software module further benefits in building and maintaining personal and professional relationships as classrooms offer greater personal contact with other students and teachers.

Video Conferencing

This is yet another medium of communication wherein students can communicate with other students or instructors online. It enables students to become active participants in their own learning. Video Conferencing is a powerful communication tool that has the potential to change the way we deliver information to students. It is just one of the today's integrative technologies that empower students to prepare for a better future.

CONCLUSIONS

The timing has never been better for using technology to enable and improve learning at all levels, in all places, and for people of all backgrounds. From the modernization of E-rate to the proliferation and adoption of openly licensed educational resources, the key pieces necessary to realize best the transformations made possible by technology in education are in place. Educators, administrators, and teacher preparation and professional development programs now should embed these tools and resources into their practices. Working in collaboration with families, researchers, cultural institutions, and all other stakeholders, these groups can eliminate inefficiencies, reach beyond the walls of traditional classrooms, and form strong partnerships to support everywhere, all-the-time learning. Although the presence of technology does not ensure equity and accessibility in learning, it has the power to lower barriers to both in ways previously impossible. No matter their perceived abilities or geographic locations, all learners can access resources, experiences, planning tools, and information that can set them on a path to acquiring expertise unimaginable a generation ago.

All of this can work to augment the knowledge, skills, and competencies of educators. Tools and data systems can be integrated seamlessly to provide information on student learning progress beyond the static and dated scores of traditional assessments. Learning dashboards and collaboration and communication tools can help connect teachers and families with instantaneous ease. This all is made more likely with the guidance of strong vision and leadership at all levels from teacher-leaders to school, district, and state administrators. For these roles, too, technology allows greater communication, resource sharing, and improved practice so that the vision is owned by all and dedicated to helping every individual in the system improve learning for students.

❒

38

Blended Learning in Teaching Mathematics

E-materials are part of a new trend, the so called blended learning, i.e. a new teaching method combining physical and virtual sources. Besides the classical presentation of the material, the students have access to electronic materials such as videos, presentations, electronic worksheets, java applets, e-tests and educational software's like Geo Gebra. These materials can be attained through web-applications accessible not only through a computer but also through tablets and smart phones. The presence of tablets, smart phones and net books grows in direct proportion to their price. Now days, almost every student owns a smart phone with an internet connection which allows an individual approach to electronic materials. Teachers can thus exploit the potential of ICT in the teaching of mathematics.

TEACHING MATHEMATICS IN AN ICT ENVIRONMENT

- **Direct teaching (face to face)** - both teachers and students have access to ICT and use it actively
- **E-learning** - learning and teaching only in electronic form
- **Blended learning** - a combination of contact teaching and integrating ICT means while actively using e-learning.
- To make the teaching more effective teachers can now use electronic materials:

- videos, presentations (created in MS PowerPoint, interactive boards), concept maps, electronic texts - these materials are used for self-study or as course material for students who need an individual approach (physically, mentally or socially disadvantaged groups of students or vice versa, gifted students) or can be also used in new methods of learning (constructivism in the digital environment, the Flipped Classroom method)
- Electronic worksheets, e-tests that are used to practice the curriculum, mathematical Java applets, educational software such as GeoGebra and the like.
- Electronic tests to evaluate

ADVANTAGES OF ELECTRONIC MATERIALS FOR BLENDED LEARNING

There are many websites and recently even applications for smart phones which are used to teach mathematics in the form of blended learning. It's quite popular among teachers and contains a lot of material made by the teachers themselves. Some of the websites of the teachers are also suitable collections of electronic materials. Websites that contains many fine "HotPotatoes" tests and other various materials for teachers of mathematics in elementary or secondary schools:

The use of digital environment for developing the creativity of mathematically gifted students. Accelerated cognitive growth is typical for gifted students, which can be developed under sufficient motivation and creativity using proper didactic environment. Other typical characteristics of gifted students involve curiosity, joy from discovering, asking uncommon questions and a good ability to argue. Therefore a constructivist approach in teaching is very appropriate for developing the creativity of mathematically gifted students.

The theory of constructivist learning, which was developed by the Swiss psychologist Jean Piaget, is based on the assumption, that a student while actively interacting with his environment gradually constructs an inner system of understanding. The whole process of learning should be done in a simulative educational environment, which inspires students to explore. By such environment we mean digital environment, taking advantage of ICT, computers, tablets, interactive whiteboards, software, etc. This kind of environment is close to the students, it is their work aday reality.

Constructivism in pedagogy requires that the following should be included into teaching: real-life (authentic) problem solving, creative thinking, group work, object manipulation, visual teaching aids, e.g. interactive computer software. An excellent stimulative digital educational environment for all the methods of constructivist approach is the open-source software Geo Gebra. Geo Gebra as a tool for a stimulative digital environment. In such digital environment and using constructivist approach in teaching, we can develop the creativity of students. Students have the possibility to create hypotheses, verify and solve new problems. They can extend their curiosity, tendency to ask, independent thinking and the ability to observe. It helps and improve the students' creativity.

BLENDED LEARNING CLASSROOM

The look of a Blended Learning math classroom can vary from teacher to teacher, and from school to school. Here are some examples of a Blended Learning classroom in action:

- **Student Centers:** Student centers (yes, even at the middle school level) can enhance differentiation through Blended Learning. At some centers, struggling students strengthen their content knowledge by working with a teacher or using an Internet site tailored to instructional videos. Other centers have students work individually on an interactive learning program, in small groups on enrichment projects, or receive peer tutoring.
- **Flipping the Classroom:** This involves students watching a video of a teacher-instructed class and working on example problems as a homework assignment. Watching the video and completing the problems before attending class allows more class time to focus on practicing and enhancing knowledge of the skill. If a teacher is not comfortable using video, they can use a Smart Pen or a note-taking app such as ShowMe. These tools allow students to see what a teacher is writing during the verbal instruction without seeing an image of the teacher. This method can lead to more effective note-taking, it can increase the background on a content area before beginning a lesson the next day, and it can help with the remediation of a missing foundational skill.

Seek Continuous Improvement

Having a policy of open communication and providing education about the digital tools being used will assist in smoothing the transition as teacher transform class into a Blended Learning environment. Helping parents understand Blended Learning should be a combined effort between school and home, and the knowledge that students are becoming more active in their learning process should help ease some fears. If students who do not have access to a computer or device at home and cannot go to the public library to use a computer, offer a way to support them at school. Options include access to devices or computers during homeroom or a working lunch period, or offer before-school or after-school hours for those students. If teacher have been using Blended Learning in classroom, take a step back and evaluate it. Consider what is working well and what needs revision, and share that knowledge with others. Collaboration and peer support will make teachers even more successful on their teaching process.

SOME SCENARIOS FOR TEACHING MATHEMATICS

1. **Videos Introducing the Content**
   Depending on the size of the lesson, Teacher chooses two to four videos that deliver the necessary information. Most come from YouTube, although teachers can also make their own. For each lesson, Teacher aims to:
   - Limit each video to five minutes or less.
   - Choose a variety of videos that address the content in different ways.
   - Include at least one entertaining, high-energy video, such as a rap.
2. **Quick Check to Sssess learning:** After watching the content, students must complete an online quick check before they can move on. This consists of four questions that give the teacher immediate feedback as to whether they understood the material. From there, Teacher might instruct students to revisit the videos, or Teacher might work with them individually until they've mastered the content.
3. **Independent Practice to Apply learning:** Once they get the green light on their quick check, students choose from a handful of activities that allow them to work directly with the concepts they've learned. Options might include working through written problems, building models, creating drawings on the computer or using toothpicks to demonstrate angles.

Once the unit begins, students tackle the checklists one at a time, working through them independently or in small groups. Each day when it's time for math, they pick right up where they left off the day before.

"This opens the door so they know it's OK if they're not on the same lesson as everyone else," Teacher says. "That way, you're also not leaving out the high flyers that also need to be pushed. When they finish that checklist, there's always something at the end so you're not leaving them out or holding them back. You're still pushing them forward."

CONCLUSION

Blended learning is defined as a formal education program in which a student learns, at least in part, through delivery of content and instruction via digital and online media with some element of student control. Although it may be a big step for some teachers, underneath all of the hype is a strong concept that gives students some control over their learning environment and can promote student engagement. Remember, Blended Learning is not simply scanning a worksheet into a device or computer. It consists of content material relevant to students, where they can, in part, self-pace their learning. Technology is not replacing teachers or direct instruction, because both are still very valuable instead, it is enhancing the education experience and turning at least some control over to the student.

❒

39

Internet Use of Learning in Distance Education

Computer-based training, Web-based training, Internet based training, online training, e-learning (electronic learning), m-learning (mobile learning), computer-aided distance education - online education goes by many names and comes in a variety of styles, but at its core: "Online education is electronically supported learning that relies on the Internet for teacher/student interaction and the distribution of class materials."

From this simple dentition comes an almost infinite number of ways to teach and learn outside of traditional classrooms and away from college campuses. With online education, students can turn anywhere with Internet access and electricity into a classroom. It can include audio, video, text, animations, virtual training environments and live chats with professors. It's a rich learning environment with much more flexibility than a traditional classroom. When used to its full potential, online education has been shown to be more effective than pure face-to-face instruction. It can be engaging, fun and tailored to fit almost anyone's schedule.

Significance of Education

Some sites like these contain valuable tools and accessories to aid in the learning process. As well as notes and multimedia displays, they may include things like hypertext chapters. In the future, there may not even be a need for paper textbooks. The Internet has also enabled teachers to teach a class from thousands of miles away. With video conferencing, a professor in Guam can teach a class in Michigan in close to real-time. Virtually all libraries are now connected over the Internet. At Lake Superior State University you can check the catalogs of almost any library and even check out books from nearby libraries.

The Internet

The Internet has made it easy for researchers to obtain information. No longer do you have to travel to get rare documents they are now just a few clicks away. The corresponding Internet site for this textbook greatly improves the overall effect on the education of students. Students have quick access to any part of the text. They also receive visual and audio stimulation, which has been proven to increase the amount of information the student remembers. Some students are simply not strictly audio learners. Listening to a professor or teacher lecture sometimes just isn't enough for students. With the site they can review material quickly and easily and see the multimedia imagery at their own pace. Students can even take practice tests to see if they have learned the material.

Global Nomads Group

Perhaps one of the most impressive things that the Internet has done to improve education is videoconference teaching. Not only can this connect the teacher to a class thousands of miles away; it can also connect a class with other groups or events such as a city council meeting. Different classes can interact and discuss topics, or perhaps sit in on a discussion of experts. Some sites such as Global Nomads Group offer assistants to educators when it comes to videoconferences. Global Nomads Group is a non-profit organization dedicated to promoting global education through videoconferencing and interactive broadcasting. We partner with educators to conduct collaborative learning projects that encourage ross-cultural dialogue and reflections on the global issues that affect our lives.

Libraries and Internet

This site provides all kinds of help and ideas when it come videoconference education. One of the best ideas on this site is the "Times of disaster" program which brings kids who have gone through a tragedy together. "The first session was between youth who were close to the Oklahoma City bombing and those affected by the September 11th terrorist acts in New York City. Footage of the 2.5 hour video conference was aired by NBC's Today Show on October 5, 2001." These days the Internet is making it easy to find the things you need to research a topic or to simply browse through material. Most University Libraries are connected to the Internet.

Some of the many features of this site include online searches using various methods and engines. You can search the catalog on-line and even read some full text documents. Finding the material you need for a research paper or project is easy. No more are the days of spending hours flipping through the card catalog trying to find something that has to do with your topic. There are even on-line books; these are actual full-length books that you can read over the Internet. With a generic username and password you can read a book from almost anywhere

Memory Technology and Multimedia

The growth of Internet has accelerated the growth of many technologies. One of them is the memory of technology. Compact Disk Read only memory (CD-ROM) and Digital Versatile Disk (DVD) are two popular media used in the e-education system. Enormous amount of data 640 MB on CD-ROM on a DVD can be stored and this compact disk can be physically transported to any school. The multimedia contents of these CDs can then be presented to the students thereby giving them the benefit of best education. Another advantage of the virtual school is that it caters to the requirements of the not so well gifted" or the under achievers. The basic concept is that all pupils in the same age group are capable of reaching the same academic achievements, if provided appropriate education. E-education systems are being implemented in schools all over the world in early 1996. The then President of U.S.A. Bill Clinton wanted every class room in America to be connected to the information super highway thus creating world class room. In England 10,000 schools has been linkedto internet on the "National Grid for Learning".

Online Education Programs

- **100% Online Education** - Fully-online degrees are earned from the comfort of your own home with no required visits to your college or university campus.
- **Hybrid Education** - Hybrid education allows students to pursue a combination of online and on-campus courses.
- **Online Courses** - While online courses may be part of a degree program, they can also be taken on their own in order to master a certain subject or learn a specific skill.
- **MOOCs** - MOOCs, or massive open online courses, are usually delivered in lecture form to online "classrooms" with as many as 10,000 people.

Computer Education in India

In India the government has announced "Operation Knowledge" "Bidyarti Computer Scheme" "Shikshak Computer Scheme" and School Computer Scheme. They are the schemes for penetration of computers in schools. Internet connectivity in all schools will convert them into smart school which has been conceptualized as places where the emphasis is not only on 77 but also use of skills and values that will be important in the new millennium. E-education at higher institutions has become an entirely different phenomenon. Unfathomable oceans of knowledge are being generated and are becoming accessible through innumerable servers of the Internet. Students can apply for a course through e-mail, receive instructions material on Internet receive consultation, receive question paper, send the answer sheets and finally get a degree certificate through e-mail. It will be only necessary to take a print out if hard copy is necessary for compilation of the process. Digital libraries have appeared on the scene, which are very useful in the areas of research. Today, communicating with a friend in china has become as easy and cheaper as communicating with a friend in a neighboring town since individuals nowadays use internet as a quicker and easier means of communication.

CONCLUSION

Information technology has created a new class of professionals. There are knowledge workers and knowledge managers in the society today then there are the knowledge users. To derive benefit of the technology in his day-to-day life, every person should be able to operate the spacing computer and the Internet. In addition to this the knowledge workers and knowledge managers are to be prepared by the education system. One more class of students created by e-education system is the technicians and technologists, who can develop the technology, realize it and then operate the systems for the user. The Internet technology has thus made the best teaching material and best education technology available to all students irrespective of their geographical location and political affiliations.

❐

40

Education and Society

Instruction is a noteworthy establishment in many social orders. Training is a long nonstop procedure of learning and modification of association between the individual and his condition and instruction might be characterized as the progressions achieved the person because of the cooperation. In an expansive sense all life is training and the individual proceed so learn through tout his life. Training is development and advancement. It is a procedure in which, and by which the learning character and conduct of the youthful are formed and merged. It shows him acceptable behavior evenhandedly and appropriately. It drives him to understand the genuine noteworthiness of life. Human science is a restrained eye that both looks at how we jump on in our every day lives and finds these subtleties onto a 'map' that stretches out past those prompt encounters'.

1. **CLIMATIC VARIABLES**

   Climatic conditions comprise an essential reason for destitution. The hot atmosphere of India decreases the limit of individuals particularly the ruralites to work for which generation seriously endures. Visit flood, starvation, seismic tremor and typhoon cause overwhelming harm to agribusiness. Besides, nonattendance of convenient downpour, exorbitant or insufficient downpour influence seriously nation's horticultural creation.

2. **STATISTIC FACTORS**

The accompanying statistic factors are responsible for destitution in India.

(i) **Rapid Development of Populace**

Quick development of populace bothers the destitution of the general population. The development of populace surpasses the rate of development in national pay. Populace development not just makes troubles in the evacuation of destitution yet additionally brings down the per capita pay which will in general increment neediness. The weight of this decrease in per capita salary is borne intensely by the destitute individuals. Populace development at a quicker rate expands work supply which will in general lower the pay rate.

(ii) **Size of Family**

Size of the family has significant bearing on rural poverty. The larger the size of family, the lower is the per capita income, and the lower is the standard of living. The persistence of the joint family system has contributed to the health and earning capacity of the realties.

3. **PERSONAL CAUSES**

(i) **Absence of Inspiration**

Absence of inspiration is a vital reason for country destitution. Some realties don't have a thought process to buckle down or even to acquire something. These records for the destitution of the realties.

(ii) **Idleness**

Most of the rural people are lazy, dull and reluctant to work. Hence they rot in poverty.

4. **MONETARY CAUSES**

(i) **Low Farming Efficiency**

Destitution and genuine salary are especially interrelated. Increment in genuine salary prompts decrease of the extent of destitution. So far as horticultural area is concerned, the ranchers even today are following the customary strategy for development. Thus there is low farming profitability bringing about rustic neediness.

(ii) **Unequal Dispersion of land and Different Resources**

Land and different types of benefits comprise wellsprings of pay for the ruralites. Yet, shockingly, there has been unequal dispersion of land and different resources in our economy. The size-wise dissemination of operational property shows a high level of fixation in the hands of a couple of ranchers prompting destitution of numerous in the rustic part.

(iii) Decline of Town Enterprises

At present subsequent upon industrialization new processing plants and businesses are being set up in country territories. Town ventures neglect to contend with them as far as quality and cost. Thus they are shut down. The laborers are tossed out of work and lead a real existence of neediness.

(iv) Immobility of Work

Fixed status of work likewise accounts, for provincial destitution. Regardless of whether higher wages are offered, workers are not willing to leave their homes. The joint family framework makes individuals lazy and stay-at home. The ruralites are for the most part unskilled, insensible, preservationist, superstitious and fatalistic. Destitution is considered as inherent, something predetermined. Every one of these variables lead to horrifying destitution in country India.

(v) Lack of Work Openings

Joblessness is the impression of neediness. As a result of absence of business openings, individuals remain either jobless or underemployed. The greater part of these jobless and underemployed specialists are the little and minor ranchers

5. SOCIAL CAUSES

(i) Education

Training is a specialist of social change and libertarianism. Neediness is likewise said to be firmly identified with the dimensions of tutoring and these two have a round relationship.

(ii) Caste Framework

Position framework in India has dependably been in charge of rustic neediness. The subjection of the low rank individuals by the high position individuals caused the neediness of the previous «Station framework went about as a springboard for class misuse with the outcome that the partner of the destitution of the many is the plushness of the few. The second is the reason for the first"

(iii) Joint Family Framework

The joint family framework gives government managed savings to its individuals. A few people exploit it. They live upon the salary of others.

(iv) **Social Traditions**

The ruralites spend a substantial level of yearly profit on social functions like marriage, passing gala and so on. Subsequently, they stay under water and destitution.

(v) **Growing Obligation**

In the rustic part the greater part of the rurality's rely upon borrowings from the cash banks and landowners to meet even their utilization costs.

CONCLUSION

We talk about on training and society, destitution in India, social causes, individual causes and financial causes.

❐

41

Educational Innovations in Distance Education

The world shrewd pattern in the foundation of a deep rooted learning framework and development of a learning society , current separation instruction is getting to be a standout amongst the best learning stages for the individuals who wish to seek after their further examination. The middle for separation Learning and Innovation or CDLI is a part of the Newfoundland and Labrador branch of training in charge of giving proficient instruction chances to understudies living in remote zones .

DISTANCE EDUCTION HISTORY

Separation instruction was established in December 2000 after the suggestions of the 1999 flashes – Williams pastoral board on instructive conveyance. Beginning in the 2002 school year many school made e – courses as accessible through the inside. These courses utilize a similar educational programs as study hall – based training however are accessible to understudies whose schools may not offer courses they wish to tae or are required to specific callings.

INNOVATION

Development in its cutting edge importance is a « new thought , innovative musings, new creative impulses in type of gadget or strategy» . Advancement is frequently additionally seen as the use of better arrangements that meet new necessity , unstated needs, or existing business sector needs. The inverse of advancement is exnovation.

DEFINATION OF INNOVATION

All around just put, advancement is tied in with remaining significant we are in a period of exceptional change. Therefore, what may have helped an association be effective in the past could conceivably be the reason for their disappointment later on organizations need to adjust and advance to meet the consistently changing necessities of their constituents.

EDUCATION INNOVATION IN THE TECHNOLOGY

- The essential mechanical asset of separation training is the web which encourages its different angles.
- Headsets are utilized for vocal correspondence.
- Webcams are utilized for visual educating.
- Tablets are utilized to impart composing.
- Desire2learn is utilized for nonconcurrent correspondence.
- Eliminate live is utilized for synchronous correspondence through lea web conferencing.
- Polycoms are currently being acquainted into certain schools with give the separation instruction instructor a way to outwardly screen their understudies while in class.
- Mostly restrictive programming is utilized, albeit some product depends on the GNU GPL.

THE BASIC OBJECTIVES OF DE INCLUDE

- Providing scholarly, money related and Technological help to stake framework.
- Encouraging developments in separation instruction through gather India and abroad for
- re – designing and continuing the open and separation instruction.
- Development of advancement programs, rules instrument training for consistent access.
- Developing a system of creative people, foundations.

DISTANCE EDUCATION ADVANTAGE

- Study from anywhere, anytime.
- Flexibility of time.
- No commuting.
- Plethora of schools and colleges to choose.
- Lower costs.
- Learn while working.

DISTANCE EDUCATION DISADVANTAGE

- No Interaction with teachers and professors.
- Lack of seriousness, competition and learning environment.
- Job markets do not accept online degrees.
- Not all courses are available and can be learned through distance education.
- Format of courses not suitable or everyone.
- Internet availability and affordability.

CONCLUSION

In spite of the fact that removes training is anything but another pattern, however has a gigantic increment because of creating innovation. Separation training conveyance will at long last rise as solid instruction approach with use off telephone, work area and TV at an equivalent time in future. That has now drastically changed. Furthermore, innovation is by and large very much utilized in video, sound content, illustrations, movement, and recreation.

❒

42

Implications for Education Knowledge of Societies in Uses of ICT on Globalization Based on Education

Communities of practice, typically groups of teachers that work with each other to improve their teaching, are good examples of knowledge societies, especially those that use all the tools, electronic and otherwise, to facilitate their goals (cf. Hargreaves, 2003).. Daniel Bell's "framework for the information society" spearheaded the movement to legitimize the information society concept (Bell, 1979). He confirmed that a majority of the jobs in the United States were information oriented in that they were structured to produce informational rather than material products. In subsequent years, as global networks became ubiquitous and a global information economy became more obvious, the information society metaphor became even more widely accepted.

THE KNOWLEDGE SOCIETY

Ironically, the information society concept was undermined by the emergence of a new metaphor in the 1990s, the "knowledge society." While the information society metaphor was associated with an "explosion" of information and information systems, the knowledge society metaphor primarily referred to economic systems where ideas or knowledge functioned as commodities. Many, if not most, people could not differentiate the two concepts because they tended to largely equate information and knowledge (Alee, 1997). Confusion about the nature of knowledge is still a problem, especially in the field of education. The educational community tends to define knowledge mostly in terms of facts or declarative knowledge, but the field of management defines it much more broadly encompassing insights, values, and other tacit cognitions (Taiwan, 2002). In this chapter, the broader definition of knowledge will be used.

INFORMATION VS. KNOWLEDGE

Increasingly, the definitional distinction of information from knowledge is that information consists of intentionally structured and formatted data, but knowledge consists of cognitive states needed to interpret and otherwise process information (cf. David and Foray, 2003). While information can generally be reproduced for minimal costs, knowledge reproduction requires training, apprenticeships, and other more costly forms of transmission. Knowledge that is difficult to codify and reproduce is called "tacit knowledge." Tacit knowledge includes judgment, experience, insights, rules of thumb, and intuition and its retrieval depends upon motivation, attitudes, values, and the social context (cf. Polanyi, 1996; Taiwan, 2002). A knowledge economy necessarily depends upon information as well as the intellectual capital of economic communities. Thus, a knowledge society necessarily presumes an information society, but not the other way around. In this chapter's discussion of education, the rhetoric of the knowledge society will be used, but for the most part it will apply to the information society as well.

KNOWLEDGE SOCIETIES IN EDUCATION

While economists tend to think of "knowledge society" as a global economy, other social scientists tend to think of it as a smaller level social collective. Thus, a knowledge society may exist on at least four levels: a global system, a national or cultural system, a social organization like a professional society, and a smaller community, e.g., the "Dead Poet's Society." A knowledge society is generally defined as an association of people with similar interests who try to make use of their combined knowledge. Of course, knowledge societies are not new, but what is new is that there has been a sharp rise in them and they are much more visible. Their rise follows digital networks that make them possible without members coexisting (do you mean residing?) in the same region and the technology makes accessing and sharing knowledge so much more feasible. On top of that is the pressure to exchange knowledge that emerges from the knowledge economy. Loosely speaking, any educational system is a knowledge society, and that would include schools and classrooms. However, unless the educational unit devotes particular attention to knowledge-related activities, it is not particularly useful to call it a knowledge society. When an educational group invests considerable effort toward sharing and producing new knowledge, then it should be called a knowledge society. "Knowledge society" in the next section refers to the (global) knowledge society. Later sections of the chapter shift toward smaller scale knowledge societies.

ICT

As noted already, ICT stands for information and communication technology and refers in principle to all technologies used for processing information and communicating. In most educational circles, it means computer technology, multimedia, and networking, especially the Internet. Educators in the United States and a few other countries use the term "technology" or "information technology" instead; however, this appears to be changing to include ICT. In business and industry, the most common label is IT, but sometimes the terms "new media" or "digital media" are used. This semantic diversity derives from the rapidly evolving integration of computers with communications, video, and audio technologies, where the separate technologies become nearly indistinguishable. In this discussion, the acronym ICT is used, recognizing that it means the same as IT or technology to many. The scope of ICT is dynamic and continuously changes with the creation of new technologies. At one time, technology referred only to hardware, now it includes software techniques as well. Daily invention of new technologies provides a major challenge to implementation of ICT-based educational strategies. Given the skyrocketing pace of new ICT in the past decade, it would not be surprising in the next 5 years to see whole new forms of e-commerce such as Internet auctions or radically new ways to do homework using personal software agents that roam the Internet. It is imperative to track such developments because not only do they change the skill requirements for students, but also they impact society and change research priorities for research on ICT and education internationally.

SOME KNOWLEDGE BASED IN EDUCATION

Scardamalia and Bereiter (1996) pioneered various strategies linking educational needs with ICT and knowledge concepts. One strategy is to use software that helps students build new knowledge using scientifically guided experimentation and computer-based tools and resources. Another is to foster and guide knowledge-building communities (Bereiter, 2002). Learning tools are used that assist both with basic skills and with higher-level knowledge. The common element to these strategies is the goal of preparing learners for the knowledge society through exercises in ICT knowledge-based activities. Using a very different rhetoric, Jonassen's (1999) "mindtools" paradigm also seeks to optimize learning using software to augment higher-level knowledge-based functions. Mindtools, which are guided activities utilizing software tools, put the student in the role of designer or partner, as most activities require construction of some type of product, usually knowledge. Other activities facilitate collaborative conversations, cognitive amplification, and reflection aimed to enhance critical thinking skills. The influential "How People Learn" model argues that the last research in the cognitive processes of learning provides a guide for instruction (Bransford et al., 1999; National Research Council, 1999a). Taken as a whole, their synthesis of contemporary research identifies knowledge, assessment, and student-centeredness as major sources for optimizing learning. These educational approaches also offer guidance in designing assessment strategies for measuring knowledge-based skills using ICT. A later section discusses how tasks using mindtools might be adapted for delivery as performance tests.

STUDENT KNOWLEDGE

In this section, a conceptual framework will be offered that flows from imperatives inherent in the information and knowledge society visions. The purpose of the framework is to explicate how societal knowledge demands suggest that learning activities and assessment strategies be structured. After a discussion of the framework, there will be discussion of the role of ICT in these learning activities. Ultimately, the argument is made that ICT and knowledge-related learning go hand in hand, helping to identify the desired direction of education in the twenty-first century. Figure 1 shows how knowledge-related skills or capabilities go hand in hand with knowledge-related task phases. Skills are needed to carry out task phases of knowledge related tasks. And completing these task phases helps develop knowledge-relatedskills. We call these tasks "task phases" because to work effectively on such tasks requires a systematic approach consisting of a number of steps within each task, and a sequence of processes or phases. Skills and task phases as illustrated in figure are mutually supportive.

CONCULUSION

Carrying out task phases is only possible with knowledge-based skills, but doing task phases helps to develop knowledge-based skills. Complex tasks tend to require all five of the task phases. A project consists of a collection of tasks or task phases organized to achieve a specific outcome. One should infer from this chapter that progress harnessing of technology for education requires progress in understanding the tools and their context, both educational and social. For that understanding to go forward effectively requires increments in theory and research. The theory part includes refining the concepts and specifying the underlying influences within the overall system. The concepts of the information and knowledge society are central to that understanding. In particular, we need to know much more about knowledge: how best to define it, how to utilize students' prior knowledge in the learning process, how to manage knowledge in organizational environments, how to let it guide the construction of assessments, and so on. In support of this emphasis upon knowledge, Brown and Duguid (2000) argue that learning is the acquisition of knowledge and it "presents knowledge management with its central challenge". Furthermore, they state that learning is social and "it requires developing the disposition, demeanour, and outlook of the practitioners." While this very well captures the process of apprenticeship, professional, and most workplace learning, it also applies to general education.

❐

43

Health Education in School

Generally to all the living things, health is very important to peaceful life. With out health anyone cannot live comfortable. The overall population has very little consideration towards health. A learning about health is essential to improve and keep up the strength of an individual and gatherings and to have a solid existence. It's our duty to instruct students on health. This is possible by giving changes to pick up information, abilities and attitude on health. Health education is essential if people are to learn how to live health lives and avoids diseases. Health education can show everyone that good health and health services are a basic human right. All the category people should know about health. Especially students must be known about it, because the students only can change our society to healthy and wealthy. So as a teacher, we should make awareness to students in school for better life and better society. So I would like to write about Health Education in School.

HEALTH EDUCATION

Health education is a profession of educating people about health. Areas within this profession encompass environmental health, physical health, social health, emotional health, intellectual health, and spiritual health, as well as sexual and reproductive health education.

Health education can be defined as the principle by which individuals and groups of people learn to beave in a manner conducive to the promotion, maintenance, or restoration of health.

The joint committee on Health Education and Promotion Terminology of 2001 defined Health Education as "any combination of planned learning experiences based on sound theories that provide individuals, groups, and communities the opportunity to acquire information and the skills needed to make quality health decisions."

The World Health Organization defined Health Education as "comprising of consciously constructed opportunities for learning involving some form of communication designed to improve health literacy, including improving knowledge, and developing life skills which are conductive to individual and community health."

WHY NEED HEALTH EDUCATION?

Health education assembles students' knowledge, abilities, and positive attitudes about health. Health education educates about physical, mental, passionate and social health. It persuades students to improve and keep up their health, avoid illness, and decrease dangerous practices.

Nowadays students can easily affect sickness by more environmental and food factors. More students take unhealthy food like fast food, and take smoking, and they are not take food in correct time and also correct level. Some students will eat low level food and some students will take extra food. Students take the activities as a fashion. There is no awareness in themselves. These are more important factors for illness.

Health educational program and guidance help students learn abilities they will use to settle on solid decisions all through their lifetime. Effective educational module result in positive changes in conduct that lower student risks around: liquor, tobacco, and different medications, damage counteractive action, mental and passionate health, nutrition, physical action, avoidance of sicknesses and sexuality and family life.

Health education advances learning in different subjects. One study demonstrated that perusing and math scores of third and fourth grade students who got far reaching health education were fundamentally higher than the individuals who did not. All in all, solid students adapt better. Various investigations have appeared more beneficial students will in general improve in school. They have higher participation, have better evaluations, and perform better on tests.

PRINCIPLES OF HEALTH EDUCATION

Credibility

Health education makes the students to credibility. Students should be believe themselves and will be credibility.

Interest

Interest is the main principle in health education because without interest we cannot do anything.

Participation

We cannot ignore the participation concept. In society each and every person will be participate in each and every happen.

Motivation

Health education having the principle of motivation. Motivation is the best key for do any work better.

Learning by Doing

It is the main problem among students. mostly students are leaning by read and memory the printed lines in text books. So they cannot understand and realise the concept easily. So through health education we can improve the educational concept and knowledge will get by practical method.

HEALTH EDUCATION IN SCHOOL FOCUS ON

- Caring for oneself and others
- Making healthy decisions and taking control over life's circumstances
- Preventing leading causes of death, disease and disability like tobacco use, drugs and alcohol, violence and injuries, unhealthy nutrition, HIV/ AIDS.
- Influencing health-related behaviours.

IMPACT OF HEALTH EDUCATION AMONG STUDENTS

Health education teachers about physical, mental, emotional and social health. It motivates students to improve and maintain their health, prevent disease, and reduce risky behaviours. In general, healthy students learn better. Numerous studies have shown that healthier students tend to do better.

CONCLUSION

Health education is significant addition to the curricula of schools because health is a source of major concern. The existence of health problems can disrupt the opportunities for learning in the sense that it can disrupt classroom attendance and overall state of mind. Increasing awareness among the student body can reduce the risk of educational disruptions. The development of attitudes at a young age can increase the probability that behaviours will be altered and a more balanced lifestyle is developed. So Health Education should be important to students in school atmosphere.

❐

44

Contribution of Education to build a Value based Society

Abstract

Education is the social institution through which society provides its members with important knowledge, including basic facts, job skills and cultural norms values. Education and Society are interrelated. The mode of education and the type of education everything depends upon the society we live in. Therefore, education carries greater importance than ever in today's society. This paper attempts to highlight the function, values and importance of education and society.

Introduction

Education is an important aspect that plays a huge role in the modern, industrialized world. People need a good education to be able to survive. Fortunately, more and more people realize how important education is for future generations. At the same time, governments all around the world are spending money on a good education system, and people are actively encouraged to win scholarships and continue their studies.

Each of us spends a big part of our childhood in education. People need a high level of education to have a better life in the future. Parents are also eager to send their kids to school and hope that they succeed in life. Everyone knows that people who have higher studies are very likely to get professional work in the future. It does not only allow people to read or write it also offers them the opportunity to have a good life, communicate better, develop new technologies and support the economy.

Function of Education in the Society

Education is the most crucial aspect of society which should be given great attention for it to become the powerful tool to make every individual become the catalyst of change. Changes are rampant on the society, but all of those are needed to make the society progressive and functional. Society and every individual should work hand in hand so that no one would be set aside and become outdated knowing that we are now living in a highly modernized society. In order to achieve that, everyone should be aware on the functions of education in the society.

Social Control and Change

Society is said to be dynamic and progressive and not a station. Education helps every individual to develop their skills that are needed to control and change the society positively. Social environment is where the child's personality can be fully developed that is why it should be conducive enough for them to grow into a better person.

Reconstruction of Individual's Experiences

Education is life that is full of different experiences which would make every person become an agent of change that is essential for the society. This helps them to reconstruct all their experiences in life as well adjust with environmental changes.

Development of Moral and Social Value

Moral and social values affect every individual in dealing with the society. Through proper education, they would be given the chance to acquire moral and social values which would help them become the reason for the society to achieve positive changes towards success.

Providing Equality and Opportunity

Discrimination should be lesson if every person would be given proper education which is needed for providing equality and opportunity. We cannot deny that educated people are more successful in life and have greater opportunities in life that is why every educational institution is providing good quality of education for people to become successful in their career.

Training Ground for leadership

The quality of an individual in being a leader can be developed through education that they can be used in participating in the spheres of political, educational, social, and religious activities.

Inculcation of Social and Civic Responsibility

Education is the best tool for the rising education to become aware and understand their duties and rights of having a democratic country where everyone is given the chance to express and be treated equally.

National Integration

People living in different countries are diverse that is why respect of language, color, physical environment habits, dress, and caste should be adhere.

Career Advancement

There is a direct correlation between the level of education that a person has and the likelihood of finding a decent job. Nowadays employers are looking to hire people who have a high-level of education. Although that's not compulsory for all positions, most employers prefer candidates that have qualifications in a certain field. The level of education of a person can show a particular interest in a field, and this is a logical thing. Even though experience is vital in most cases, nothing compares to having a degree in a certain field. Education does not mean just time spent in school. It essentially means a set of skills, motivation, and self-discipline.

Character Building

Education is one of the main factors that allow people to grow and develop as individuals. It teaches people important life values, and it opens their mind to a lot of interesting aspects of life and not only. Classrooms are ideal places for healthy discussions on all kinds of subjects. At the same time, education encourages people to develop their social skills, problem-solving skills, and creative skills. In order to become a genuine individual one has to pick the right education system. Parents need to pick the best school for their children.

Backbone of Society

All developing countries must have a good education system. Poor standards will usually cripple the society. However, educated people will always find a solution to their problems. Therefore, education plays one of the most important roles in the development of nations. Modern society is based on people who have high standards and knowledge which allows them to implement the best solutions for different problems. After all, education means innovation. Innovation and creativity can only occur when people are skilled enough to know how to operate with different technologies and machines.

Those are the functions of education in the society and the lives of people who are needed by the society to empower changes. Life is full of challenges and problems which make every individual neglect what their social responsibilities are. This is the main reason why the society is having a hard time to progress but this can be solved through the help of good quality of education to make people acquire the needed knowledge and develop their innate skills that can be used to be good citizens in their own ways.

The Value of Education in Society

Education is very important and highly valued in today's society; it is also necessary for success in life. Education is supposed to provide students with the necessary skills that prepare them for the world of work later in life. The education system also serves to teach individuals the values and morals of society. Government should pay serious attention to education and support it economically although this is sometimes not the case. Students must be equipped with knowledge and skills which are needed to participate effectively as member of society and contribute towards the development of shared values and common identity; the education system serves this purpose

Although these sociologists have debated the purpose and function of the educational systems, most agree that access to educational opportunities has a profound effect on individual life chances and attainment. Specific education policies and practices such as school choice, curriculum differentiation, school finance, and school assignment shape the range of educational opportunities available to students. Differences by social class, race/ethnicity, and gender exist. The central question is whether or not schools function to promote social mobility, achievement, and economic well-being or whether or not schools function to reproduce social inequalities. Although educational attainment is related to an individual's family background (socioeconomic status), the public education system is supposed to function as an equalizer for those who cannot afford private education.

The importance of Education in our Society

In our culture today, there is a huge emphasis on education, especially higher education. Society basically says the more educated you are, the better off you are. That is pretty much true if you live by the means of society. The basic idea that education, especially a college education, is something that people should pursue even into their adult years is not by any means a new idea. Every society has specialized individuals who fulfill certain positions that require extended education. In some cases, these people are known as shamans, priests, or professors or they may be doctors, mechanics, blacksmiths, or artists. In all these professions, some form of higher education is necessary. It could come from an apprentice or rigorous private study, or it could take the form of a formal higher education. Whatever the form, the meanings is the same, i.e. gain knowledge and use it.

CONCLUSION

Many sociologists have observed that there is a strong relationship between education and society. Any society requires a good education system. The leaders of tomorrow are formed and inspired today. However, their leadership can only start by acquiring life lessons and having potential. According to me any day education is something that equips man with the necessary thing that is required for him to life his life without depending on anyone.

❐

45

Distance Education' and 'E-Learning': Not the samething

Higher education systems all over the world are challenged nowadays by the new information and communication technologies. Already in 1989 SorenNiper in his classic analysis identified three generations of distance education: the first was correspondence teaching; the second was multi-media teaching - integrating the use of print with broadcast media, cassettes and to some degree computers; and the third generation was identified with the new interactive communication technologies.

Many policy makers, scholars and practitioners in higher education use the terms 'distance education' and 'E-learning' interchangeably as synonyms. It is important to mention that the various forms of learning through ICT are defined in the relevant literature by at least a dozen different terms, such as web-based learning, computer-mediated communication, telematics environments, E-learning, virtual classrooms, online instruction, I-Campus, electronic communication, cyberspace learning environments, computer-driven interactive communication, distributed learning, borderless education. In this article, all forms of learning/teaching through ICT are referred to as 'E-learning'. However, distance education in most higher education systems is not delivered through the new electronic media, and vice versa: E-learning in most universities and colleges all over the world is not used for distance education purposes.

This article discusses the distinct differences between 'distance education' and 'e-learning' in higher education settings by comparing some of their major characteristics. It examines the reasons why most distance education on the university level all over the world is still provided through the more 'traditional' media of print and broadcasting, in spite of the many advantages E-learning provides for distance teaching purposes. The article analyzes the erroneous assumptions on which many exaggerated predictions as to the future impact of the ICT were based upon, and it concludes by highlighting future trends of 'distance education' and 'e-learning' in academia.

Distance Education and E-learning at University level - Three Distinctive Differences

Distance education at university level has existed since the early half of the nineteenth century (Bell and Tight 1993). The idea of a distance teaching university adopts the opposite course of a campus-based university. Instead of assembling students from dispersed locations in one place, it reaches out to students wherever they live or wish to study. E-learning, on the other hand, is a relatively new phenomenon and relates to the use of electronic media for a variety of learning purposes that range from add-on functions in conventional classrooms to full substitution for the face-to-face meetings by online encounters. Below three distinctive differences between 'distance education' and'e-learning' are examined in relation to: remoteness and proximity between the learner and teacher in the study process; relevant target populations; and cost considerations.

1. **On Remoteness and Proximity**

   'Distance education', by its very definition, denotes the physical separation of learners from instructor at least at certain stages of learning process.

   Holmberg, one of the leading researchers in the field of distance education, defined 'distance education' as characterized by non-contiguous communication, meaning that the learner and teacher are separated not only in space but also in time. Education and pure distance education are extremes that rarely exist. Many distance education providers use face-to-face tutorials, summer schools and laboratory sessions, whereas many conventional universities utilize independent study and guided learning by tutors and a variety of media.Daniel's interpretation of the term 'distance education' embraces all forms of instruction in which classroom sessions are not the primary means of education. Distance education is mostly homework, with occasional work in class; whereas conventional education is mostly classwork with occasional work at hog process, as two of the major characteristics of distance education. In other words, in 'distance education' students are usually taught as individuals, not in groups, and are separated physically from both the teacher and other fellow students. In some cases, groups of students are taught by a distant teacher, mainly in the framework of teleconferencing and other broadcasting media.

2. **Target Clienteles**

   A second distinctive characteristic of distance education is its attention to the needs of special clienteles that for a variety of reasons cannot attend a face-to-face gathering, a school or a conventional campus.

3. **Cost Considerations**

   A third major characteristic of distance education at university level in recent decades has been its ability to broaden access to higher education by providing economies of scale.

Why is it Difficult to Implement E-learning in Large Distance Teaching Institutions?

The new technologies are most attractive for distance teaching. They have the potential to overcome three major problems of traditional education.To rescue the isolated students from their loneliness by providing interaction with teachers, professors and tutors, as well as with other peer students throughout the study process; to provide easy access to libraries and other information resources, which was nearly impossible in the past; and to update the self-study materials on an on-going basis.

Some Erroneous Assumptions as to E-learning Applications

1. **Space and Time as Barriers to Overcome**

   One of the erroneous assumptions as to the fast spread of e-learning was based on the notion that the need to attend a physical campus at given times is perceived as a barrier to overcome by most students.

2. **The urge of Universities to Extend their Student Population**

   A second erroneous assumption regarding the impact of the new electronic media on the academic world was based on the notion that most universities have an urge to expand their boundaries and to extend their student clienteles, if only possible.

3. **Lack of Clear Problems as a Problem**

   The third erroneous perception is that the merits of the new technologies are so great, that they will be adopted easily and eagerly by policy makers and practitioners in the academic world without any need to define a clear vision of problems they might solve or what parameters in higher education they could improve.

On the future of 'distance education and e-learning' in higher education - concluding remarks

This article examined the distinct differences between 'distance education' and 'e-learning' in higher education, and clarified the erroneousassumptions on which many exaggerated predictions as to the sweeping effects of the new electronic media were based. Though it is likely that in the upcoming decade more and more providers of distance education will incorporate various forms of e-learning in their learning/teaching apparatus, still the differences between 'distance education' and 'e-learning' will remain noticeable. The boundaries between 'distance education' and 'e-learning' will blur in some areas, but they will never totally merge. Both phenomena will grow in the future, but mostly for different reasons and in different directions.

❒

46

Enhancing Life Skills through Distance Mode

Education is a continuous process of development from 'womb to the tomb'. Several thinkers hold the view that education starts even before birth. Every year, every month, every day and every minute, step by step a person learns. In the modern world no one knows what tomorrow will bring and so every individual must equip himself in every moment of his life to meet the new challenges in life. Education must at all stages become self-education, so that with the provisions of education acquired at school, the adult will continue his education throughout life with all the means at his disposal- the library, the reading room, camps, tours, mass media, clubs, institutions etc. Lifelong education is acquired through formal, non-formal and informal means. Education provides a way of life. It develops certain values. A person may possess high literacy and even high degrees but he may be regarded as uneducated if he lacks human qualities. Education is concerned with the development of character and personality.

Education aims at developing the knowledge, moral values and understanding required in the walk of life. The purpose of education is to develop well-informed, intensive and well-equipped citizens of the society and also to develop the human being, not an individual alone. There are qualities required by everyone to live good, well-adjusted and harmonious life. These qualities are developed only through education which demands,

- Creative Thinking
- Coping with Emotions
- Coping with Stress.

Objectives of Education

1. To emphasize the unity of knowledge could provide success in life.
2. To create a new system of education for social progress and to promote values of emotional and social integration.
3. To develop environmental awareness and to adjust with the changing situations.
4. To bring about a synthesis between cultural values and scientific values and to incorporate these values, ideals and principles in various life situations.
5. To provide the right kind of leadership in all walks of life, to identify gifted youth and help them develop their potential to the maximum.
6. To respect the dignity and worth of man by giving him equality of rights and opportunities.
7. To realize that truth always triumphs and leads to human progress and prosperity.

Education in Real-life Setting

One feels that distance education does not have the kind of recognisable and apparent structure that formal education possesses. It seems to be amorphous, supine and bloodless, lacking the obvious dynamism that an oral communicator necessarily imparts. While it is true that it suffers from an absence of a certain kind of vitality which only the presence of a teacher can generate, it nevertheless compensates for this by making use of as many inputs to 'learning as are possible and by structuring itself around the actual learning experience of the students. The recent developments in the telecommunication and computer technologies have increased the possibilities of teacher-student dialogue and peer group interaction. Through e-mail and internet facilities, collaborative learning has become a reality. Given the access to these facilities, distance learners would feel less lonely Defining Distance Education and alienated. If some sort of face-to-face teaching-learning component in the forms of summer schools and contact programmers can be arranged, the loneliness of distance learners can be reduced still further.

Definitions of Distance Education

Wedemeyer (1977) has used the terms 'open learning', 'distance education' and 'independent study' in his works, but favors the last term consistently. He defines 'independent study' as follows: Independent study consists of various forms of teaching-learning arrangements in which teachers and learners canny out their essential tasks and responsibilities apart from one another, communicating in a variety of ways. Its purposes are to free on campus or external learners with the opportunity to continue learning in their own environments, and developing in all learners the capacity to canny on self-directed learning, the ultimate maturity required of the educated person.

Peters (1973) defined distance education as a method of imparting knowledge, skills and attitudes which is rationalized by the application of division of labor and organizational principles as well as by the extensive use of technical media, specially for the purpose of reproducing high quality teaching materials which makes it possible to instruct great numbers of stud.

Imparting life Skills through Distance Mode

In distance education provides various subjects. These subjects are included that attitude and skills and knowledge. In addition to this the students of distance education should learn various life skills for their successful life. Because in regular mode teachers regularly taught the life skills in different ways in higher education also. But this aspect has been neglected in the distance mode. Some people are good at learning, some people are better at being practical oriented. So, distance education provides different kinds of knowledge of needs, aspirations and limitations of the people by improving their social and cultural welfare. In distance education could play important and viable roles in improving life skills of learners.

CONCLUSION

In distance education, self instructional materials, contact classes, assessment and value education are the most important activities definitely play a vital role in enhancing life skills. Today, ''Sarva siksha abiyan" provides elementary education to all. Distance education is a boon to higher education to feat their goal.

❐

47

ICT Based Classrooms for Teaching and Learning Process

However, with the rapid progress in technology and the advancement in learning systems, it is now embraced by the masses. The introduction of computers was the basis of this revolution and with the passage of time, as we get hooked to smartphones, tablets, etc, these devices now have an importance place in the classrooms for learning. Books are gradually getting replaced by electronic educational materials like optical discs or pen drives. Knowledge can also be shared via the Internet, which is accessible or, anywhere, anytime.

In teaching and learning process, we have a lot to choose from the world of technology: Television, Radio, Computers, the Internet, Email, Blogs and Audio Cassettes, Power Point, Videos. The last two eras have witnessed a revolution due to commencement of technology, and has changed the dynamics of educational institutes, and has also influenced the educational system and the way people interact and work in the society. This rapid rising and development of information technology has offered a better pattern to explore the new teaching model.

The educational system may need to utilize and compete with the new Information and communication technologies and benefit from them. There are lots of possibilities of such utilization such as: using simulation and animation to present some of the complex boring problems in a more appealing format.

Such techniques are particularly useful for teaching kids within primary schools in early ages.

The educational technology is expected to become an important part of the curriculum, students must become proficient in accessing and using electronic resources. This paper labels how to ICT based learning techniques such as e-learning, blended and web-based learning that could help the students to develop their thinking skills and problem solving ability skill of learners.

E-LEARNING

A learning system based on formalised teaching but with the help of electronic resources is known as E-learning. While teaching can be based in or out of the classrooms, the use of computers and the Internet forms the major component of E-learning. E-learning can also be termed as a network enabled transfer of skills and knowledge, and the delivery of education is made to a large number of recipients at the same or different times. Earlier, it was not accepted wholeheartedly as it was assumed that this system lacked the human element required in learning.

CHARACTERISTICS OF E- LEARNING

1. E-learning is Learner-Centric Learning: The learner centric e-learning model makes an array of resources available to the learner, who is free to choose when, where and how to learn.
2. E-learning for lifelong learning: With increasing access to technologies and its ever increasing sophistication this approach to learning facilitates lifelong learning among various stake holders.
3. E-learning is Flexible Learning: E-learning has historically been linked with distance education and flexible learning.
4. E-learning is Social: E-learning seeks to foster collaboration and peers interaction. Various e-learning technologies facilitate various types of collaboration among learners and teachers.
5. E-learning Involves Effective Communication: The effectiveness of e-learning also depends on establishing two-way communication between teachers and learners, and among learners themselves.

Synchronous E-learning

In Synchronous E-learning, communication occurs at the same time between individuals and information is accessed instantly. This is commonly supported by media such as Video Conferencing, Virtual Classrooms and Chat sessions. The most familiar form of synchronous electronic communication is real time two way text-based online chat, which is widely used in e-learning.

Asynchronous E-learning

As you are familiar with the use of E-mail which is also a two way communication, here the flexibility is that the sender and receiver of the message need not be online at the same time.

Advantages of E-learning

1. **On-Demand Availability** enables students to complete training conveniently at off-hours or from home.
2. **Self-Pacing** for slow or quick learners reduces stress and increases satisfaction.
3. **Interactivity Engages** users, pushing them rather than pulling them through training.
4. **Confidence** that refresher or quick reference materials are available reduces burden of responsibility of mastery.

Disadvantages of E-learning

- **Technology Dependent:** Learners will need access to a machine of minimum and specification as dictated by the e-learning supplier or access to a service with a high bandwidth to transfer the course materials in a timely way.
- **Material Incompatibility:** Some materials designed for one particular system will not function properly on another (for example, the Apple Macintosh and the Windows PC). Standards will help in the area.
- **Unsuitable for Certain Types of Training:** Any skill that relies heavily on inter-personal contact although these courses could be supplemented by e-learning.
- **Expensive:** Start-up cost of an e-learning service is expensive and the cost of production of online training materials is very high.

BLENDED LEARNING

Blended learning e-learning is being combined with traditional classroom methods and independent study to create a new, hybrid teaching methodology. Many use terms like hybrid, mixed, or integrative to describe the same trend.

In a blended-learning course, for example, students might attend a class taught by a teacher in a traditional classroom setting, while also independently completing online components of the course outside of the classroom.

Advantages

- Blended learning can provide the convenience, speed and cost effectiveness of e-learning with the personal touch of traditional learning.

- Students can prepare for, consolidate and recall classroom experiences online, while gaining the benefits of interaction with teachers and students via an actual or virtual classroom.
- Student learning and retention rates improve without sacrificing the convenience, cost-effectiveness and customization of self-paced Web-based coursework.

MULTIMEDIA BASED LEARNING

The use of multimedia described here makes use of print texts, film and Internet to develop and enhance skills and knowledge. Through their interactions with multimedia texts on topic of interest, students become increasingly familiar with concepts. The students become actively engaged in the process of meaning construction within and across different media. Thus they greatly increase their overall knowledge base, as well as their ability and skills, facilitating their performance in future Study.

CONCLUSION

The information and communication technology can only be as good as its teachers and students.One of the approaches for improving the personalization in the e-learning process is ensuring access to appropriate e-learning materials, according the individual learning style of the student. The learning style is the way of adoptions and procession of the information. Every person develops preferred and successive behaviour and concrete approaches for studying. The ICT based leaning such as e-learning and blended learning is very effective for teaching and learning process. This is connected with three processes, These all the techniques use in the classrooms giving the students the tools for self-learning, which will give them the opportunity to study according to their own capabilities, learning style, knowledge and skills, to choose the type of the e-learning material and the way of presentation of the new material, according to their own interests, needs and learning style.

❐

48

ICT Based Education

The education has vital role in building the society. Education determines standard of society. The quality education helps to empowering the nation in all aspects by providing new thoughts, the ways of implementation of various technologies and so many such things. The quality education is basic need of the society. There are number of effective teaching & learning methodologies in practice. Technology is the most effective way to increase the student's knowledge. Here comes the role of ICT in the education sector! Being an academician I cannot imagine education without ICT. Nowadays ICT (specially an internet) plays imminent role in the process of integrating technology into the educational activities.

What is ICT?

ICT is an acronym that stands for "Information Communication Technologies". Information and communication technologies are an umbrella term that includes all technologies for the manipulation and communication of information. ICT considers all the uses of digital technology that already exists to help individuals, business and organization. It is difficult to define ICT because it is difficult to keep up the changes they happen so fast. ICT is concern with the storage, retrieval, manipulation, transmission or receipt of digital data. The definition taken from the guidance in the QCA schemes of work for ICT is "ICTs are the computing and communication facilities and features that variously support teaching, learning and a range of activities in education."

Objectives of ICT Implementation in Education

1. Improvement in learning achievement
2. Reduction of adult illiteracy rate, with sufficient emphasis on female literacy.
3. Expansion of provisions of basic education and training in other essential skills required by youth and adults
4. Increased acquisition by individuals and families of the knowledge, skills and values required for better living and sound and sustainable development.

Role of ICT in Higher Education

1. To increase variety of educational services & medium
2. To promote equal opportunities to obtain education & information.
3. To develop a system of collecting & disseminating educational information.
4. To promote technology literacy.

ICT as a Change Agent in Learning Process

1. **Conventional Learning Process**

   In the process of conventional learning emphasis was given on contents. It follows the particular course structure/syllabus for many years. Accordingly the subject wise textbooks & reference books have been written. By using relevant material to the subject teachers supposed to teach through lectures and presentation. Teachers used their lesson plans, tutorials, different way of assessment to evaluate student performance etc

2. **Competent Course Structure / Syllabus**

   It is the need of the day to improve quality & structure of the syllabi by enforcing competency & performance based approach towards it. To include advance technology and practical approach is also on of the imp. One such curricula requires,

   1. Access to information types & different forms.
   2. Student-centered learning though information access.
   3. Learning environment concentrated on information access & inquiry.
   4. Real life examples.
   5. Teachers as mentors rather that content experts.

The role of ICT in the education at higher level recurring and unavoidable. It is challenge to integrate ICTs with universities, into their strategies and educational process. It should be implemented at national & international level. It will be helpful to improve qualify and flexibility, the widening access to the field of tuition. Many universities are providing distance education by creating N/w through mutual partnership.

Change In The Way of Learning

We discussed ICTs are cause to make a move from a teacher centered learning to competency based learning. Universities are also responsible to make supporting changes in the way students are learning. Traditional way of learning is based on Tran missive modes. Use of ICT in education also affects the way students learning. The following points are particular forms of learning.

1. **Students Centered Learning:** With the help of technologies it is possible to promote transformation of education from teacher centered inst. To students centered inst. e.g.
    - Increased use of web as a source.
    - Internet users can select the experts from whom they will learn.
    - Process will become problem – based learning.
    - The proliferation of capability, competency and outcomes oriented curricula.

    ICTs in education acts as a change agent. It supports independent learning. Students become immersed in the learning process by using ICT.
2. **Supporting Knowledge Construction**

    The emergence of ICTs as a learning technology unknowingly insists to think on alternative theories for learning. The conventional teaching process has focused on teachers planning and leading students through a series of in structural sequences to achieve desired outcome. This way of teaching follows the planned transmission of knowledge though some interaction with the content as a means to consolidate the knowledge acquision. It depends on the process of personal understanding. In this domain learning is viewed as the construction of meaning rather than memorization of facts. Use of ICTs provide many opportunities through their provision and support for resource based, student centered learning. It acts to support various aspects of knowledge construction and as more and more stud. Employ ICTs in their learning process, the more pronounced impact of this will become.

The Impact of ICT on place 'When' & 'Where' to learn

In the past, there was no or little choice for students in terms of method & manner in which programs have been delivered. Students typically being forced to accept what has been delivered. ICT applications provide many options & choices in the same case.

1. **Any Place learning**

   The use of ICT has extended the scope of offering programs at a distance. The off-campus delivery was an option for students who were unable to attend the campuses. Today, many students are able to make this choice through technology – facilitated learning settings. e.g.

   - In many instances traditional classroom learning has given way to learning in work-based settings with students able to access courses and programs from their workplace. The advantages of education and training at the point of need relate not only to convenience but include cost savings associated with travel and time away from work, and also situation and application of the learning activities within relevant and meaningful contexts
   - The communications capabilities of modern technologies provide opportunities for many learners to enroll in courses offered by external institutions rather than those situated locally. These opportunities provide such advantages as extended course offerings and eclectic class cohorts comprised of students of differing backgrounds, cultures and perspectives.
   - The freedoms of choice provided by programs that can be accessed at any place are also supporting the delivery of programs with units and courses from a variety of institutions, There are now countless ways for students completing undergraduate degrees for example, to study units for a single degree, through a number of different institutions, an activity that provides considerable diversity and choice for students in the programs they complete.

2. **Any Time learning**

   In case of geographical flexibility, technology, facilitated educational programs also remove the temporal constraints. It is the good opportunity for stud. To undertake education anywhere, anytime & any place.

   - Through online technologies learning has become an activity that is no longer set within programmed schedules and slots. Learners are free to participate in learning activities when time permits and these freedoms have greatly increased the opportunities for many students to participate in formal programs.

- The wide variety of technologies that support learning are able to provide asynchronous supports for learning so that the need for real-time participation can be avoided while the advantages of communication and collaboration with other learners is retained.
- As well as learning at anytime, teachers are also finding the capabilities of teaching at any time to be opportunistic and able to be used to advantage. Mobile technologies and seamless communications technologies support 24x7 teaching and learning. Choosing how much time will be used within the 24x7 envelope and what periods of time are challenges that will face the educators of the future

The Role of ICT in Enhancing the Development of Basic Education and Literacy

We take the same broad definition of ICT to include radio, television, satellite, fixed and mobile telephone, fax, computers and CD-ROMs and the internet. The ICTs can be divided into two groups: traditional or old ICTs (namely, radio and TV) and the new ICTs (namely, the Internet and telecommunications). Learning through new ICTs is also called E-learning. Recent studies show the enormous potential of E-learning, especially in industrialized countries. In April 2001, MIT announced that learning materials and syllabi for all courses were being put on the Internet for anyone to use – recognizing the power of the Internet and that knowledge is for sharing. E-learning has the following advantages:

1. Access to the learning programme any time convenient to the learner.
2. Learners can be at any place to log on.
3. Asynchronous interaction providing participants and tutors with time to prepare their responses leading to succinct and to-the-point interaction and on-track, thoughtful and creative conversations.
4. Enhanced group collaboration creating shared electronic conversations which can be more thoughtful and permanent than voice conversation. Aided by group coordinators, these sessions can be powerful for learning and problem solving.
5. New educational approaches can be used. For example, faculty from anywhere in the world, faculty teams with different specialties can be put together and innovations of teachers can be shared along themselves for improvement and adaptation

The Use of ICTs to Support basic Education

We shall examine below how and where ICTs, both new and old, can enhance education for all in developing countries. As in the case of higher education mentioned in the previous section, there are four ways ICTs can support basic education – (i) supporting education in schools, (ii) providing non formal education for out-of-school children and adults, (iii) supporting pre-service distance education of teachers and their in-service professional development, and (iv) enhancing the management of schools. These are detailed below.

Supporting Education in Schools

ICT can provide access to information sources, enable communications, create interacting learning environment and promote change in methods of teaching. Quality and access to up-to date and relevant materials can be improved while offsetting some costs of textbooks. However, the improvement in quality resulting from the new ICTs is yet to be justified with the cost in developing countries. Radio is still the most cost effective ICT for enhancing quality in school education. However, with the falling cost of hardware , maintenance and Internet access and increasing e extension of telecommunications and power infrastructure, it is expected that the benefits of using new technology in the schools of developing countries will exceed the costs. Supporting non-formal education for out of school children and adults

Empirical evidence demonstrates that radio and television, the traditional ICTs are cost. Supporting pre- and in- service teacher education. The high demand for teachers calls for the rapid supply of trained teachers. Distance education of teachers is an essential medium to achieve education for all. Radio and television (radio more than television) still remain popular means because of low costs. However, teacher education using new ICTs are increasingly becoming popular because of the possibilities of the 'multiplier effect', greater interactivity between students and tutor, opportunities for learners to proceed at their own pace , at any place and at any time, the possibilities of combining video, audio and texts to improve delivery and quality of instruction and finally the possibilities of establishing teacher resource centers with access to power and telecommunications equipped with computers and Internet facilities. Regional initiatives. Effective means to reach out-of-school children and adults where the costs are spread over a large number of learners, in the regions of conflict and for refugees. If the purpose of ICT is to reach children and adults who cannot go to school for remoteness and/or for opportunity costs, radio and television are more likely to widen access than the new ICTs which may not be available to them. However, basic education is more successful when delivered in the mother tongue and traditional ICTs may be less economic because of the small number of learners. The possibility of two-way communications with new ICTs makes them more attractive where the target group has easy access to them, for example, in peri-urban areas.

Supporting pre- and in- service teacher education. The high demand for teachers calls for the rapid supply of trained teachers. Distance education of teachers is an essential medium to achieve education for all. Radio and television (radio more than television) still remain popular means because of low costs. However, teacher education using new ICTs are increasingly becoming popular because of the possibilities of the 'multiplier effect', greater interactivity between students and tutor, opportunities for learners to proceed at their own pace , at any place and at any time, the possibilities of combining video, audio and texts to improve delivery and quality of instruction and finally the possibilities of establishing teacher resource centers with access to power and telecommunications equipped with computers and Internet facilities. Regional initiatives.

CONCLUSION

The role of ICTs in the education is recurring and unavoidable. Rapid changes in the technologies are indicating that the role of ICT in future will grow tremendously in the education. 1. By observing current activities and practices in the education, we can say the development of ICTs within education has strongly affected on a. What is learned? b. How it is learned? c. When & where learning takes place d. Who is learning and who is teaching. 2. ICT also focuses modification of the role of teachers. In addition to classroom teaching, they will have other skills and responsibilities. Teachers will act as virtual guides for students who use electronic media. 3. Ultimately, the use of ICT will enhance the learning experiences of students. Also it helps them to think independently and communicate creatively. It also helps students for building successful careers and lives, in an increasingly technological world.

❐

49

Relationship between Social Skill and School Climate

While school can be a positive social experience for many children, for others it can be a nightmare.School is not only a place where children learn reading, writing and math. It is also a place where they learn to get along with other people and develop social skills. Social skills are the skills we need to interact adaptively in our cultural environment. Although students don't get grades on social tests from their teachers, their peers are constantly giving them "grades" on "social tests" every day. If a child does well on these "tests", he is apt to be well liked and happy. He will enjoy school and look forward to coming to school. If a child fails these tests, she is apt to feel disconnected and left out.

Failing a social test can be more painful to a child than failing a reading or science test. For some children, social skills can be the hardest subject to pass in school. Social skills play a very important role in a child's emotional health and well-being. Without friendships, school can be a very unhappy, lonely place that a child might want to avoid.

Children are born with innate social competencies just as they are born with other innate strengths and weaknesses in abilities such as attention, memory, language and motor skills. Weakness in these other skills can negatively affect a child's social competency. For example, children who have attentional problems may have trouble listening and attending in conversations, be unable to inhibit the impulse to talk or say things at inappropriate times. Children with memory problems may have difficulty following a conversation because they cannot remember what was just said. Children with language and communication difficulties are especially vulnerable to social problems. They may have difficulty keeping up with the pace of a conversation, especially when there is a group of children talking. Children with autism and Asperger's syndrome are especially ill equipped to deal with social situations.

Social Status at School

Just as with other abilities, children vary widely in how well they are able to form friendships and gain peer acceptance. Because students grade each other, children gain different levels of social status at school. Social status represents the child's standing or position relative to other members of the class.

Some children are well endowed with social skills. They are popular and very well liked by all or most of their peers. Some seem to have a knack for making friends and getting along with others. They are very friendly and outgoing and always seem to be at ease around people. Other children are popular because they are on the school football team, play in a band, can draw very well or are really good-looking. Popular students are typically the leaders at school. They are self-confident and influential.

Many students are not really considered popular but are pretty well liked by their peers and have a number of friends. This group of children usually comprises the majority of the students in a class. These likeable children feel good about how they relate to others but may, at times, worry about what their classmates think of them.

Some children are shy, quiet and timid. They may have one or two close friends but not a large group of friends. While other students like them, they do not get involved in many activities in or out of school. They tend to feel awkward or uncomfortable around people they don't know very well. Shy children usually aren't unhappy about how they get along with others but wish that they could feel more comfortable and be more involved. Some shy children become anxious in social situations.

Other students are ignored or unnoticed by their peers. No one really dislikes or likes them. These children are not the ones picked first for activities, but they are not the ones that are teased or bullied either. They are usually social adept. Some of these children don't like being ignored but others don't mind because they are more interested in solitary activities or prefer interactions with adults more than with peers.

The children who have the most social difficulty at school are those that are rejected by their peers. Other children really don't like them and may not treat them well. Rejected children are those that are picked on, laughed at, talked about, teased and bullied. They are widely disliked, excluded from activities and may be ostracized by their peers.

Another group of children are viewed in varying ways by different students. Some students like them a lot, others ignore them and others reject them. They are considered controversial.

Children are rejected by their peers for many reasons. It may be hard to like them because of their misbehavior. They seem mean and may bully other students, get into fights, act out in class or frequently get into trouble. Aggressive children have little idea of how their disruptive behavior affects their relationships with others. Other children are rejected because they are withdrawn, passive and anxious in the presence of their peers. They spend much of their time in isolation. Other children are rejected because they are different. They may look different, dress differently or learn differently. Their clothes, haircut or mannerisms may not match the current vogue. They may be "klutzes", short, overweight or have a physical handicap. They may have trouble learning in the same ways as most children and be thought of as dumb or stupid. Unfortunately, these children are often the targets of teasing and bullying by more popular and socially accepted students.

Sometimes popular students may find that they can enhance their social status by leading the offense against children with social skill problems. Other students who want to gain the favor of popular students willingly collaborate against their rejected classmates, only increasing the humiliation and despair that rejected students feel. Adults in their roles as parents, teachers and school administrators should intervene swiftly when they see vulnerable children become the targets for more socially adept children.

While it can be a problem to have no friends in school, it can also be a problem to need friends too much. Many children who are rejected by their peers are unhappy. They feel alone and believe that no one cares about them. Some view acting out as their only way to get the attention they desire from others. In their minds, getting negative attention is better than getting no attention at all. Some children who are rejected by their peers are so desperate to be liked that they will do anything to be accepted. They may join gangs, use drugs and even commit crimes to gain peer acceptance and a sense of belonging in a group. Being accepted by a group is the only way that these children can feel good about themselves. They cannot tolerate social isolation and are terrified of being left out.

Other children don't mind being left out sometimes and don't need to be liked by everyone. They believe that not everyone needs or wants to be popular. Some children want to be different and should be admired for their individuality and willingness to be who they are. These children are not socially inept and are usually not the targets of teasing or bullying.

Communication Skills

Good social skills require good communication skills. Because we communicate verbally and nonverbally, both of these types of skills contribute to how well students relate to their peers. Children with language problems often have trouble socially because they have difficulty understanding the words that other children use and/or putting their ideas into words to express these ideas to others. They can't find the right words to use or easily put them together in a way that makes sense. They may have trouble understanding or telling jokes. They may not know the current jargon or idioms that their peers use. They may also have trouble keeping up the pace of conversations, particularly in a group. It is hard for them to jump into a conversation.

Other children, who may have good language skills, have trouble with nonverbal communication. They can't "read" body language, facial expressions or tone of voice. These children interpret words literally and may miss the majority of the intended communication. Much of accurate communication depends on nonverbal cues and gestures. To communicate competently, a child must be able to process the whole message sent by another and integrate the verbal and nonverbal components of the message.

Children with verbal and nonverbal communication difficulties often resort to temper tantrums or "meltdowns" to communicate emotions such as anger and frustration. They may appear uncooperative, fresh or rude and may be called oppositional and/or defiant. Helping these children improve their communication skills can greatly improve their social skills and level of peer acceptance.

Social Skills

Social inability can be a lifelong problem. Therefore it is imperative that social skill deficits be identified early and addressed in much the same way as we identify and address children's learning problems because social incompetence can be more debilitating and detrimental to success in life than learning problems.

There are several types of social skills that must be mastered for a child to be socially adept. These range from the ability to initiate, maintain and end a conversation to reading social signals to more complex skills such as solving problems and resolving conflict. The following examples represent some of the fundamental principles of relating well to others. Children with social skill deficits can be taught these skills directly by parents, teachers and/ or professionals using the strategies of modeling, role-playing, rehearsal and practice.

Greetings

Children develop relationships with peers by interacting with them. The first step in a social interaction is greeting someone. We not only greet others with words like "Hi!" or "How are you?" but with facial expressions, tone of voice and gestures such as a nod or a wave. Children with social inability may not say hello to people they know. They may walk right past them and not even look at them. If they do speak, they may not make eye contact and may simply look down at the floor. If they do say hello, it might not be in a very friendly tone of voice or with a smile. The nonverbal parts of greeting someone are just as important as the words. It's not so much what you say but how you say it that lets people know you are glad to see them.

Initiating Conversation

After you have greeted someone, you usually have a conversation with them. In order to carry on a conversation, a child must be able to initiate the conversation, maintain it and close it appropriately. This requires good listening and attentional skills, as well as the ability to take turns and probe for missing information. Sometimes children cannot think of anything to talk about. When you can't think of anything to say, it can be good to ask the other person a question. The question can be about them or what they think about a movie or event that everyone is talking about. Sometimes when children don't know what to say, they begin by talking about themselves or about something that the other person is not interested in. If they keep talking without giving the other person an opportunity to enter the conversation, or if they keep talking about themselves or something uninteresting to the other person, the person is likely to get tired of listening. He may walk away and even avoid future conversations with the child. Being a good conversationalist requires turn-taking and reciprocity. You have to listen as well as talk. If you don't show an interest in what the other person has to say, he probably won't be interested in talking to you. Impulsive children often have trouble knowing when to talk and when to listen.

Understanding the Listener, Part I

Once a conversation is initiated, in order to maintain it, it is important to understand the audience you are talking to. Children with social inability often have difficulty adapting what they say to their listener. A socially adept child quickly and unconsciously identifies and categorizes his listener, measures what she planned to say against the anticipated response of the listener, and then proceeds, alters or avoids what she had planned to say. She knows that you don't talk to authority figures in the same way that you talk to peers. Socially inept children can't change their words or tone of voice to match their audience. For example, saying goodbye to a teacher with "Catch you later, dude!" would be inappropriate and could result in a detention. Adults often call children who have problems reading their audience disrespectful. Other students may view them as strange if they use stiff and formal language that is more suitable to conversations with adults than peers. A misread of the listener often leads to a misunderstood message and potential social rejection.

Understanding the Listener, Part II

To converse in a socially appropriate manner, children must be able to take the perspective or point of view of the other person, i.e., think the way they think. To do this a child must pretend that he is the listener and think about what he needs to hear to understand what is being said. For example, a child might say, "I finally got finished." and not provide the details of what he started. Many children assume that other people think and feel the way that they do. These children may appear insensitive and selfish, although this is not their intent. They may also appear "dingy" because they seem to be coming from another planet when they speak. When your audience has to guess what you are talking about, they are apt to feel uncomfortable and may be reluctant to converse with you.

Empathizing

Empathy is similar to perspective taking but means that you are able to feel what the other person feels. Empathy allows you to really connect with other people. For example, if a student got an A on a math test and her friend got a D, she wouldn't brag about her A to her friend because she knows it will make her feel bad because she didn't do well. She could empathize with her by saying something like "That's a bummer." Other children often think of children who lack empathy as mean, unkind or self-centered.

Reading Social Cues

It is very important to read social cues in a conversation. Cues are the hints and signals that guide us to the next thing to say or do. Social cues can be verbal or nonverbal. Verbal cues are the words that the other person is saying. Tone of voice is an important part of verbal cues. For example, "Oh, great!" can mean that something is really terrific, or if said sarcastically, can mean that something is awful. Nonverbal cues are things that we see rather than hear in a conversation, such as body language and facial expressions. For example, if a friend's facial expression changes from a smile to a frown and his body gets stiff when you are talking about a new CD that you bought, you might want to change the topic or ask him if what you said upset him. Good detectives pay very close attention to nonverbal cues.

Previewing

Conversations also require that you preview or think about what effect your words or actions may have on your listener before you say or do them. If you think that the impact will be negative, you can adjust what you might say or do. Impulsive children often have trouble with previewing and are unable to stop and think before they say or do something. For example, if a group of children was talking about the football game last week, it would be inappropriate to interject a sentence about the math exam next week. When you walk in on the middle of a conversation, it is always a good idea to listen for a few minutes before entering the conversation. If your friends were complaining about not being able to drive their parents' cars to the dance on Friday, it wouldn't win any points with them to say, "Get real! Did you really think that your parents would let you take their car to the dance?" Doing this would be tactless and insensitive.

Problem-Solving

Problems and conflict are often a part of social interactions. Someone may not agree with you, get angry at something you say, insult you or become aggressive toward you. How you react to these conflicts depends on how good your problem solving skills are. Children who are not good social problem solvers have trouble settling conflicts and disagreements. They get mad easily and may not speak to someone because they are mad at them. It has to be "their way or the highway". They always want to win no matter what the cost, even if that means losing a friend. It often also means making an enemy, which creates additional social problems. Conflicts cannot be avoided and are often necessary to "clear the air". Turning a conflict from a "win-lose" situation to a "win-win" situation is the best way to resolve conflict. This requires negotiation and compromise, give and take, but results in a situation that all parties can live with and helps maintain friendships.

Apologizing

Everyone makes social mistakes at one time or another. A person with good social skills is confident enough to make a sincere apology for his error. This is a courageous act and is the quickest and easiest way to correct a social blunder. Children with weak social skills may have trouble saying they are sorry because they can't lose face. They are afraid that others may see them as weak.

They might also be too proud, or feel stupid or foolish if they apologize. In reality, other people usually have a higher opinion of someone who apologizes for making a mistake.

Teaching Social Skills

Children with verbal and nonverbal learning disabilities often have social problems at school. These children struggle academically and socially. While schools address children's learning problems, they often neglect children's social needs and rely on parents and/or professionals to handle these problems. A lack of social skills and the inability to connect with others, form friendships and resolve conflicts can lead to more failure and distress for students than academic problems can.

How Parents Can Help

Parents typically play the major role in teaching children social skills. Many children acquire social skills on their own. They don't really need help. For children who do need help, there are many good self-help books on the market to assist parents in improving their child's social abilities. Parents can directly teach social skills by modeling, role-playing and providing opportunities for their child to rehearse and practice new skills. Parents should encourage and praise the child for successfully using a new skill. Professionals typically intervene only when children are having substantial social difficulty with peers. These individuals can implement structured, guided and effective programs that often involve group work with peers. Children must then generalize the skills they learn in the group to school and other personal social situations.

How Teachers Can Help

School is the place that children spend the majority of their time with peers. It is, therefore, a natural and perfect setting for children to learn and practice social skills. While teachers don't have to teach a class in social skills, they can take advantage of every opportunity to help children improve their social skills. They should be alert to teasing and bullying and aware of children that are rejected or ignored by their peers. They should work cooperatively with the children's parents to prevent the humiliation, embarrassment and distress that befall these children. Teachers can be valuable facilitators in helping children gain social competency. Pairing a socially inept child with a socially adept child, involving children in cooperative instead of competitive learning exercises, identifying and acknowledging the strengths of all children, understanding social weaknesses and creating an environment in which diversity is accepted and celebrated can greatly enhance all children's social abilities, sense of belongingness and self-esteem not just in the classroom but in life. ❐

50

ICT in Education

The education has vital role in building the society. Education determines standard of society. The quality education helps to empowering the nation in all aspects by providing new thoughts, the ways of implementation of various technologies and so many such things. The quality education is basic need of the society. There are number of effective teaching & learning methodologies in practice. Technology is the most effective way to increase the student's knowledge. Nowadays ICT (specially an internet) plays imminent role in the process of integrating technology into the educational activities. ICTs have an important role to play in changing and modernizing educational systems and ways of learning(Saravanakumar, AR, 2016). ICTs can enhance the quality of education in several ways, by increasing learner motivation and engagement, by facilitating the acquisition of basic skills, and by enhancing teacher training.

THE EFFECTIVENESS OF ICTS IN EDUCATION

ICTs are a potentially powerful tool for extending educational opportunities, both formal and non-formal, to previously underserved constituencies—scattered and rural populations, groups traditionally excluded from education due to cultural or social reasons such as ethnic minorities, girls and women, persons with disabilities, and the elderly, as well as all others who for reasons of cost or because of time constraints are unable to enroll on campus.

Anytime, Anywhere

One defining feature of ICTs is their ability to transcend time and space (Padmini Devi,K.R & Saravanakumar,AR., 2018). ICTs make possible asynchronous learning, or learning characterized by a time lag between the delivery of instruction and its reception by learners. Online course materials, for example, may be accessed 24 hours a day, 7 days a week. ICT-based educational delivery (e.g., educational programming broadcast over radio or television) also dispenses with the need for all learners and the instructor to be in one physical location. Additionally, certain types of ICTs, such as teleconferencing technologies, enable instruction to be received simultaneously by multiple, geographically dispersed learners (i.e., synchronous learning).

Access to Remote learning Resources

Teachers and learners no longer have to rely solely on printed books and other materials in physical media housed in libraries (and available in limited quantities) for their educational needs. With the Internet and the World Wide Web, a wealth of learning materials in almost every subject and in a variety of media can now be accessed from anywhere at anytime of the day and by an unlimited number of people. This is particularly significant for many schools in developing countries, and even some in developed countries, that have limited and outdated library resources. ICTs also facilitate access to resource persons, mentors, experts, researchers, professionals, business leaders, and peers—all over the world.

ICTs help Prepare Individuals for the Workplace

One of the most commonly cited reasons for using ICTs in the classroom has been to better prepare the current generation of students for a workplace where ICTs, particularly computers, the Internet and related technologies, are becoming more and more ubiquitous. Technological literacy, or the ability to use ICTs effectively and efficiently, is thus seen as representing a competitive edge in an increasingly globalizing job market.

BENEFITS FOR TEACHERS

1. ICT facilitates sharing of resources, expertise and advice
2. Greater flexibility in when and where tasks are carried out
3. Gains in ICT literacy skills, confidence and enthusiasm.
4. Easier planning and preparation of lessons and designing materials
5. Access to up-to-date pupil and school data, any time and anywhere.
6. Enhancement of professional image projected to colleagues.
7. Students are generally more 'on task' and express more positive feelings when they use computers than when they are given other tasks to do.

8. Computer use during lessons motivated students to continue using learning outside school hours.

BENEFITS FOR STUDENTS

1. Higher quality lessons through greater collaboration between teachers in planning and preparing resources.
2. More focused teaching, tailored to students' strengths and weaknesses, through better analysis of attainment data.
3. Improved pastoral care and behaviour management through better tracking of students.
4. Gains in understanding and analytical skills, including improvements in reading.

Comprehension

1. Development of writing skills (including spelling, grammar, punctuation, editing and re-drafting), also fluency, originality and elaboration.
2. Encouragement of independent and active learning, and self-responsibility for learning.
3. Flexibility of 'anytime, anywhere' access (Jacobsen and Kremer, 2000)
4. Development of higher level learning styles.
5. Students who used educational technology in school felt more successful in school, were more motivated to learn and have increased self-confidence and self-esteem
6. Students found learning in a technology-enhanced setting more stimulating and student-centred than in a traditional classroom
7. Broadband technology supports the reliable and uninterrupted downloading of web-hosted educational multimedia resources
8. Opportunities to address their work to an external audience
9. Opportunities to collaborate on assignments with people outside or inside school

BENEFITS FOR PARENTS

Easier Communication with Teachers

- Higher quality student reports – more legible, more detailed, better presented
- Greater access to more accurate attendance and attainment information
- Increased involvement in education for parents and, in some cases, improved self-esteem
- Increased knowledge of children's learning and capabilities, owing to increase in learning activity being situated in the home

Parents are more likely to be Engaged in the School Community

- You will see that ICT can have a positive impact across a very wide range of aspects of school life.

THE USE OF ICTS HELP IMPROVE THE QUALITY OF EDUCATION

- **ICTs can Enhance the Quality of Education in Several Ways:** by increasing learner motivation and engagement by facilitating the acquisition of basic skills, and by enhancing teacher training. ICTs are also transformational tools which, when used appropriately, can promote the shift to a learner-centered environment.
- **Motivating to learn:** ICTs such as videos, television and multimedia computer software that combine text, sound, and colorful, moving images can be used to provide challenging and authentic content that will engage the student in the learning process. Interactive radio likewise makes use of sound effects, songs, dramatizations, comic skits, and other performance conventions to compel the students to listen and become involved in the lessons being delivered. More so than any other type of ICT, networked computers with Internet connectivity can increase learner motivation as it combines the media richness and interactivity of other ICTs with the opportunity to connect with real people and to participate in real world events.
- **Facilitating the Acquisition of Basic Skills:** The transmission of basic skills and concepts that are the foundation of higher order thinking skills and creativity can be facilitated by ICTs through drill and practice. Educational television programs such as Sesame Street use repetition and reinforcement to teach the alphabet, numbers, colors, shapes and other basic concepts (Padmini Devi,K.R & Saravanakumar,AR., 2018). Most of the early uses of computers were for computer-based learning (also called computer-assisted instruction) that focused on mastery of skills and content through repetition and reinforcement.
- **Enhancing Teacher Training:** ICTs have also been used to improve access to and the quality of teacher training. For example, At Indira Gandhi National Open University, satellite-based one-way video- and two-way audio-conferencing was held in 1996, supplemented by print-materials and recorded video, to train 910 primary school teachers and facilitators from 20 district training institutes in Karnataka State. The teachers interacted with remote lecturers by telephone and fax

CONCLUSION

ICT is an extended term for Information technology which is a technological source to make information available at the right time, right place in the right form to the right user. Earlier, one had to wait for the newspapers to get the information across the world. Now with the smarter technology, information can be accessed from anywhere using smart-phones and gadgets. All this is made possible with the help of Information and Communication Technology.

❐

51

Virtual Laboratory Revels the Reality

The flipped classroom is known by various names including the inverted classroom, and more simply, the flip. Origination stories differ, but most credit Jonathan Bergmann and Aaron Sams, high school chemistry teachers from Colorado, who began using recorded lectures in 2006. The flip evolved out of a history of experimentation with the concept of hybrid, or blended learning and problem based learning, using active learning techniques and new technologies to engage students. The flipped classroom has two defining components: moving the lecture outside of class, usually delivered through some electronic means, and moving the practical application assignments, formerly homework, into the classroom (Educause, 2012). There are many other optional components that arguably optimize this structure and provide enhanced learning opportunities to students, creating a wide variation in practice ("Flipped classroom offers," 2011). The lecture format has varied and evolved from slides, audio, podcasts, or narrated presentations, to video casts that may also incorporate animations, screen captures, and other multimedia content. The classroom component is varied as well, with different learning expectations, engagement techniques, levels of student autonomy, and other variability (Sams, 2011). In fact, instructors have taken countless paths to teaching with the flip because the learning context and objectives determine which features are most useful (Bull, Fester, &Kjellerstrom, 2012).

Khan Academy, Coursera, TED talks, and even YouTube are online resources associated with the flipped classroom, providing access to recorded lectures, instructional videos, and sometimes other interactive elements for teaching and learning. In many cases instructors implementing the flip depend on these resources to provide the lecture content (Bull, Ferster, & Kjellstrom, 2012). Sourcing of content from outside may be helpful for those who lack presentation skills, extensive subject knowledge, or need an outside perspective to enrich their course. Scott McLeod, a leader in educational technology and the Director of Innovation for Prairie Lakes Area Education Agency 8 in Iowa, notes that these large educational video sites are innovations that were not created by established education groups but instead came from outside "to fill the vacuum" that educators had left (as cited in Tucker, 2012, p.83), leaving the possibility that as this learning model grows, educators may take back the reigns.

Virtual Laboratory

It also intends to develop a complete Learning Management System where the students can avail the various tools for learning, including additional web-resources, video-lectures, animated demonstrations and self-evaluation. There is also a component wherein costly equipment and resources are shared, which is otherwise available to only a limited number of users due to constraints on time and geographical distances.

Seven IIT's (Delhi, Bombay, Kanpur, Kharagpur, Madras, Roorkee and Guwahati), IIIT Hyderabad, Amrita University, Dayalbagh University, NIT Karnataka, and College of Engineering, Pune, are the institutions participating in the project.

The Project intends to cover physical sciences, chemical science and various branches of engineering like electronics and communications, computer science and engineering, electrical engineering, mechanical engineering, chemical engineering, biotechnology engineering and civil engineering.Relax time constraints, adapting to pace of each student, if there was insufficient time in lab.

WHY USE THE FLIP?

Instructors of all kinds cite strengths of the flipped model, including efficient use of class time (Cole, 2009), more active learning opportunities for students (Gannod, Berg &Helmick, 2008), increased one-on-one interaction between student and teacher (Lage, Platt, &Treglia, 2000), student responsibility for learning (Overmyer, 2012), and addressing multiple learning styles ("Flipped classroom offers," 2011; Gallagher, 2009; Gannod, et al., 2008). Each of these features has implications for student learning and may be more strongly or weakly demonstrated depending on the specific implementation.

As curriculum requirements grow, instructors are pressured to make more efficient use of class time. In the flipped classroom, students can get the most out of class time by spending it on practical application, not on inactive lecture (Cole, 2009). Lecture content can be provided just as well through electronic means. Perhaps it can even be improved because professors may be obliged to make video lectures a manageable length.

WHO IS USING THE FLIP?

Flipped classroom experimentation is happening in many disciplines, and the examples referenced in this review span from engineering to life sciences to business to statistics. These disciplines often depend largely on students understanding underlying principles and theoretical concepts before being able to engage in practical application or problem solving (Gannod, et al., 2008), which is why using the flip is attractive for them. Overmyer observes that the model is useful "where content is usually more technical and linear" (2012, p.46).

Martin notes (as cited in Berrett, 2012) that the humanities have long taught by focusing class time on discussion, since the subject matter lends itself to this model. Although not identical to the flipped classroom, students do complete readings before class, in order to be prepared for engaging in guided discussion with their instructor and peers.

THE FLIP IN HIGHER EDUCATION

The flipped classroom appears to have originated in a middle school environment, and the majority of literature exploring its use is focused on K-12. There are plenty of examples of and interest in its use in higher education, however. In this environment, we hope to prepare students for jobs or make them capable of applying concepts learned in the classroom to real life situations. Flipped classroom pedagogy also prioritizes student ability to apply learned concepts in problem solving. Lage, et al., in one of the earlier and most widely cited articles on flipping the classroom in higher education, transformed their economics teaching with the "inverted classroom" approach, accommodating the classroom diversity instructors are increasingly facing (2000). In many cases, higher education instructors don't seek to build a flipped classroom; they stumble upon it after working to build a more engaging learning experience that takes advantage of the technology currently available, like Dotson and Diaz, who compare their assignment redesign to the "classroom flip" based on a desire to use active learning and technology to extend students' education outside of the classroom (2008, p. 4). Others identify the model as one that meets their pedagogical needs, like Findlay-Thompson and Mombourquette, who articulate that "application, analysis, and evaluation" skills are the needs satisfied by a flipped course redesign (2014, p.65).

CONCLUSION

The virtual laboratory is now a days focus the real situation and scenes in science education. The teaching learning process the role of virtual – laboratory the most predominant role . Most of the cases the students unable to imagine the real motions. This virtual laboratory can occurs and improve the understanding level of students. it can be motivated to the both teacher and students.

❐

52

Educational Innovation in Distance Education

The word innovation is derived from the Latin word 'innovare', which means 'renew' or 'alter'. Innovation is the first attempt to carry out a new idea or invention into practice. In simple language we may say that innovation is the successful implementation of creative ideas within an organization or system. In this view, the creativity of an individual is the starting point for innovation. Broadly, an action can be identified as an innovation if it is new and useful to the system; increases the efficiency of the system; is cost effective; and is compatible/adaptable with other similar systems.

Two Innovative Models for Program

An innovation is defined as "an idea, practice, or object that is perceived as new by an individual or other unit of adoption" (Rogers, 1995, p. 11). Whether you are making decisions about use of database management tools, merging technological tools, communication tools to develop teaching¬learning communities, or learning outcome/assessment tools, we hope that our "toolkit" can provide innovative approaches in distance learning program development and delivery.

In today's competitive world, the success of theDLESdepends upon innovations, which would increase the efficiency and quality of the system? For this, a concerted study of the diverse areas of the DLESis required, which should be followed by introducing innovations in it. This can be done through the identification, adaptation and introduction of the existing innovations in the system or through the introduction of new innovations.

1. **Merging Technologies to Deliver Instruction**

   Web¬supported instruction is becoming more commonplace in today's colleges and universities Distance education continues to expand because of growth of the Internet, increased capability and flexibility of web¬based tools, increased proficiency in basic Internet skills, and shrinking barriers with respect to accessing and using the Internet. Distance education methods include those that permit any education received by a student to occur when the teacher and the student are separated by location and/or time.

   Distance education relies on the students' abilities to be self¬directed and internally motivated. This type of education is particularly appealing to students whose lifestyle (time and distance constraints) does not allow them to take advantage of traditional classroom methods. To optimize methods of delivering instructional programs, a need exists to examine continually technologically mediated delivery strategies; Which is to say, how can teaching be improved through the use of technology? Web course tools (e.g., static and dynamic Web pages, threaded discussion groups, email, chat, instant messaging, streaming media/video, animations, application sharing, IP audio/video conferencing) are being adopted and used increasingly by teachers to optimize delivery of instructional material. Web¬based instruction can be classified into one of three categories: Developed, dependent, or supported.

   The overall instructional design process can be viewed as a continuum where the teaching and learning process is constantly evaluated and improved using experiences gained in developing and delivering instruction. The application of learning tools and technologies is not a linear process, but in fact, a circular one. As can be seen from the above diagram, traditional learning has been delivered in a classroom setting assisted by certain technology: first with chalk and blackboards, whiteboards with markers, overhead projectors and similar assistive tools. A second stage of "distance learning" took place in a television studio of sorts with several learners, usually in grouped settings, or "remote sites." The learning technology, however, remained essentially the same with the exception of delivery by closed circuit television. An extension of the ITV model came from broadcast television (or distribution by video tape) and support to an asynchronous learning environment by using some form of computer¬supported telecommunications. As webbased and other computer¬supported learning tools became available, they have been adapted to the distance learning processes, and have resulted in the development of learning delivered fully online, without the intervention of traditional classroom or television technology.

2. **Managing Electronic Course Materials**

In distance education courses managing electronic course materials, student participation, student achievement, and course evaluations can be problematic. Fortunately, Web course tools, such as WebCT™ and Blackboard™ have built in features that facilitate management of course materials, student access, and student achievement. With Web course tools, students are able to access grades and determine their progress in the course; access and print course materials; and create an interactive online learning environment between and among students and instructor through email, threaded discussion, online testing, and study guides.

The Universities database¬model deconstructs individual programs and courses to identify components necessary for the creation of effective teaching and learning communities. Each learning object or module is identified and the necessary content, technology, communication and assessment tools required to effectively deliver and measure instruction are entered into a database. Each module represents a self¬contained unit that should become a seamless part of a learning package. Modules may focus on a particular narrow area within the province of a faculty member subject matter expert, or could interface with and call upon modules from other areas or disciplines in a nonlinear manner.

Evaluating the effectiveness of instruction and the course can also be accomplished using Web course tools. The need to ensure anonymous evaluations has led institutions to use online instruments that write to a password protected database that is only accessible to those responsible for collecting and reporting such data. This method of evaluation can easily and efficiently collate, aggregate and manage large datasets.

Effective Strategies to Develop Teaching¬Learning Communities

Developing and delivering courses, curricula, and programs at a distance requires faculties and administrators to consider many factors including how to overcome barriers to effective and efficient implementation of distance education courses, curricula, and programs. Moore (2001) noted that to be successful in delivering online courses, faculty must: allow student to student interaction with minimal faculty intervention; engage students in regular assignments in order to monitor progress and intervene when needed; provide specialized attention to students with low levels of selfdirectedness; and help students become more self-directed.

Students in distance education courses and programs often feel isolated and apprehensive. This may be due to lack of student to student and student to faculty contact. Recent studies on retention have indicated that creating satisfying and rewarding social experiences may be as important to retention as academic and intellectual factors. Specifically, the program attempts to: provide timely and appropriate interaction between students and faculty, and among students; provide appropriate training in methods and technologies for interaction for faculty who teach and for students who learn at a distance; encourage interactive teaching and learning that fosters critical dialogue, integrative learning, mentoring, cooperative peer learning, and group out¬of class activities; use e¬mail or Web¬based sites to inform students about opportunities for interaction in person¬to¬person or in distance settings; and monitor synchronous and asynchronous interactions between faculty and students to assess the total duration and system of engagement.

The database¬model at University of Houston integrates communication tools in the course/program developmental process. Instructional designers are assigned to work with faculty to develop an instructional plan that addresses the need for faculty¬student and peer¬to-peer interaction. Decisions regarding the nature and type of communication required and the technology that will be used to facilitate interaction are made jointly by faculty and the instructional designer based on the complexity of the course, the maturity and experience of the target student population, and the likely value¬added of each communication opportunity. In addition, a customized, animated online tutorial is available for all students using WebCT to train them in the use of chat rooms, discussion boards, and the exchange of course materials/assignments using the drop box. An online tutorial is provided to faculty with an emphasis on pedagogical issues associated with the development and delivery of distance learning courses/ programs.

Alternate forms of Assessment

Determining, measuring and verifying competencies needed by students to complete the stated objectives of a course are difficult but necessary tasks. Teachers are continuously seeking appropriate techniques to document student growth and learning during a course. Assessment of outcomes is essential, though it is also important to understand the point from which the learner is coming. This can call for the development of tools for pre¬assessing learner levels of understanding as a general baseline of knowledge, or as a baseline for approaching various learning modules or topics.To establish a baseline, and to ensure that each group had a similar starting point, a pre¬assessment test was administered to each learner.

CONCLUSIONS

Several innovative programs have been offered by different ODL universities. These include gardening, child labor eradication, personality development, museum studies, life coping skills, horticulture, natural resource management, vocational skills, mushroom cultivation, water treatment, and sustainable communitydevelopment. These programs encourage capacity building and impart knowledge to a layperson. Various other innovative programs on special education, such as parent education, parenting skills, child psychology, school phobia, school psychology, staff development, aromatherapy, Reiki etc. are offered all over the world. These can be offered in India through the DLES system.

❐

53

Classroom less Techniques in Distance Education

Students interested in pursuing options among global distance learning programs should start by doing some research into the credibility of programs. Each country has its own standards and criteria for distance education programs and the 'world council for distance learning schools' (WCDLS) provides further accountability. As long as the school and its program fulfil those requirements , they receive the credentials necessary to indicate they meet high quality standards and students will benefit from investing their money ,time effort there while earning degrees that are equivalent to those earned in traditional schools.

Traditionally, distance learning took place through correspondence. Students received their study materials via the post and worked through these materials at their own pace. However, recent developments in technology have led to an increase in the variety of distance learning resources that are available. This turn has made it possible for different types of distance learning to emerge. It is now possible, for example, for students to attend web-based lectures and to download their study materials from the internet.

WAY OF DISTANCE LEARNING

As its name suggests, distance learning is an activity that takes place outside of the traditional classroom. In an informal setting, typically in the learner's own home, and in a less structured format, distance learners do all their reading, studying, completing assignments, taking tests, and submitting work at a distance from the related school. Technology has raised the quality of individualized distance instruction. The use of various forms of electronic media increases time effectiveness and improves the delivery of information. Video, audio, and computer-based applications may enhance the product received by the independent learner. Electronic delivery can occur using synchronous communication, in which class members participate at the same time, or asynchronous communication where participants are separated by time (Romiszowski, 1993).

CLASSROOM LESS TECHNIQUES IN DISTANCE EDUCATION

Video/audio models of distance education include broadcast television, cable television, satellite, microwave, fibre optics, and audio graphics. The most widely used format is broadcast and cable television (Parrott, 1995). However, developments in satellite and fibre optic systems have produced other successful programs. The interactive capability of many of these networks has produced a distance classroom that is nearly identical to a regular classroom. Teachers and students can interact through both two-way video and one-way video with two-way audio systems. The recent development of Desktop Video Conferencing (DVC) which brings interactive video capability to the desktop computer, further enhances learning opportunities.

The linking of computer technology through the use of the Internet or CD-ROM with television transmission provides a potentially new dimension to distance education. This technique can link university professors to high school teachers, or to physically disabled students, in a distance setting (McLean, 1996).

Another form of interaction is the use of computer conferencing. This method utilizes asynchronous communication in such forms as an e-mail list group, an Internet discussion group, or other types of conferencing software. Asynchronous methods of communication are especially appealing to the learner who has difficulty scheduling specific time- and place-bound course work.

Key Elements To Successive Classroom Less Techniques In Distance Education

Garrels (1997) describes five critical elements for successful teaching at a distance:

1. **Instructor Enthusiasm**- This requires animation and comfort in front of the camera, or with the technology utilized. Faculty support and interest are critical to the success of distance learning endeavours.
2. **Organization**- Teaching materials must be prepared in advance; timing, variation, and smooth transitions must be planned. Instructors should allocate from 3 to 5 hours of preparation for each hour of distance instruction. Great attention to detail is required long before the actual classroom activity occurs.
3. **Strong Commitment to Student Interaction**- Whatever the modality used to teach at a distance, the instructor must encourage and facilitate on-going communication between the students and the instructor.
4. **Familiarity with the Technology used in the Class Format**- Faculty development is important before beginning any distance activities, and instructors should be trained in video use, computer use, or other forms of instructional technology used.
5. **Critical Support Personnel** - Production staff, graphic designers, and technical staff members will help the instructional setting produce successful teaching at a distance.

Suggestions To Improve Classroom Less Techniques In Distance Education

- Begin the course planning process by reviewing the literature on distance education research.
- Before developing something new, check and review existing materials for content and presentation ideas.
- Make sure you understand the strengths and weaknesses of various delivery systems (audio, video, data, print, etc.) not only in terms of how they are delivered (satellite, microwave, fiber optic cable, etc.) but in terms of learning styles and course requirements.
- Hands-on training is critical for both teacher and students. Consider a pre-class session in which the class meets informally using the delivery technology and learns about the roles and responsibilities of technical support staff.
- At the start of class, hold a straightforward discussion to set rules, guidelines, and standards. Once procedures have been established, consistently uphold them.

CONCLUSION

The primary role of the student is to learn. Under the best of circumstances, this challenging task requires motivation, planning, and the ability to analyse and apply the information being taught. When using the classroom less techniques in a distance education setting, the process of student learning is more effective.

❒

54

Academic Stress and Adjustment Level among the Higher Secondary School Students

Stress is a situation which is so difficult to avoid. The topic is being discussed not only in our daily conversations but has become enough of a public issue to attract wide spread media attention whether it is the, radio, television, newspapers or magazines, casual conversation. The stress figures everywhere. Different people have different views about it, as stress can be experienced from a variety of situation. It varies from person to person or situation to situation. Even the amount or impact of stress differs from person to person. Sometimes, even the same situation is perceived differently by different people. Some respond to the stress very easily and some others react seriously. But in most of the cases, it will be moderate. The early researchers on stress address themselves mostly to the understanding of the meaning of stress and delineating effects of stress. Stress has been found to act as a tonic when it is in mild form. When intensity of stress increases it lead to deleterious effects both on the body and mind. Today the examinations are taken seriously more by the parents than by the students. As the day of examination approaches, the parents worry more about the child's achievement and their undue anxiety often results in pressurizing the children to study hard even by cutting down their time for play and recreation or even relaxation.

NEED FOR THE STUDY

Academic Stress plays a vital role in the student's life and it accounts for variation in performance and achievements for success. Some amount of academic stress is essential in mobilizing the potentialities of the individual to work more efficiently. The problem of Academic Stress requires a study of all the dimensions and implications in detail and plan strategies for either prevention, or reducing the intensity of the problem initially at the school level and future to manage either at the individual level or in the group setting. Several studies reported that school students are experiencing more stress. A major stress for higher secondary school students is amount and complexity of material to be learned. It can lead to students being unable to perform to the best of their abilities in education. Stress within the students may not only affect the physical and emotional well-being of a student and their families, but also affects the educational institution where they are studying because it may impair the academic relationship between students and the institutions. So there is a need to have psychologists to handle common psychological and academic problems.

OBJECTIVES OF THE STUDY

The Objectives of the study are as follow.

- To find out the level of Academic Stress and Adjustment level among the higher secondary school students.
- To find out the level of significant difference between the Academic Stress and Adjustment level among the higher secondary school students with respect to their background variables such as Gender, Locality and Medium of institution.
- To find out the level of significant relationship between the Academic Stress and Adjustment level among the higher secondary school students.

HYPOTHESES OF THE STUDY

The Null Hypotheses have been framed and they are as follow.

- The Academic Stress and Adjustment level in the among higher secondary school students is low.
- There is no significant difference between the Academic Stress and Adjustment level in the among higher secondary school students with respect to their background variables such as Gender, Locality and Medium of institution
- There is no significant relationship between the Academic Stress and Adjustment level in among the higher secondary school students.

METHODOLOGY OF THE STUDY

The present study belongs to Social Survey Method and Stratified Random Sampling Technique was followed to select the sample for the study.

i. **Tools Used**

Two types of tools were used in the present study. According to Lazarus (1961), the two tools were developed and standardized by SIVA RATHNAM REDDY (2017) in namely,

- Academic Stress Scale (ASC)
- Adjustment Level Scale (ALS)

The tools were revalidated by investigators. Then the questions were taken for data collection. The students were asked to make a tick mark for the correct answer in a separate answer sheet. It was decided to give two marks for positive answer, one mark for undecided answer and no mark for negative answer. The reliability of the tool was established by following split half method. The value of 'r' was found to be 0.67, which revealed that the developed tool of Academic Stress and Adjustment Level was highly reliable.

ii. **Selection and Size of the Sample**

The investigators have selected a sample of 480higher secondary school students from 10 various higher secondary school students at Vellore District in Tamil Nadu.

iii. **Data Analysis**

Data was analyzed by using Mean, SD,'t'-test, and Pearson's product moment correlation for the present study. The descriptive and inferential analysis results are framed in the following tables.

TABLE. 54.1: Mean and Standard Deviation for Academic Stress and Adjustment Level Scores among the Higher Secondary School Students

S.No	Category	Variables	Size of the sample	Mean	SD
1	Academic Stress	Gender	480	83.4	17.8
		Locality	480	80.6	15.32
		Medium of School	480	83.4	18.5
2	Adjustment level	Gender	480	56.4	11.41
		Locality	480	54.1	7.62
		Medium of School	480	56.4	11.52

From the Table 54.1 the obtained Maximum and Minimum Mean and SD values of the Academic Stress and Adjustment Level Scores are 83.4and 18.5 and 54.1 and 7.62.

TABLE. 54.2: Significance Difference between Male and Female Higher Secondary School Students in theirAcademic Stress

Gender	N	Mean	SD	't'- value
Male	240	89.48	19.382	7.459**
Female	240	77.32	16.201	
** Not Significant at 0.01 Level				

The table 54.1 shows that the't' value, 7.459** is not significant at 0.01 level. The result reveals that there is significant difference between the level of Academic Stress among the Male and Female Higher Secondary School Students. The Male students are having high level of Academic Stress than the Female students. Hence, the framed null hypothesis is found to be rejected.

TABLE. 54.3: Significance Difference between Urban and Rural Higher Secondary School Students in their Academic Stress

Locality	N	Mean	SD	't' value
Urban	300	91.97	15.178	15.765**
Rural	180	69.13	15.477	
** Not Significant at 0.01 Level				

Table 54.2 shows that the't' value, 15.765** is Not Significant at 0.05 level. The Urban Students are having significantly higher level of Academic Stress than the Rural Students. Hence, the framed null hypothesis is found to be rejected.

TABLE. 54.4: Significance difference between Tamil and English Medium Higher Secondary Students in their Academic Stress

Medium	N	Mean	SD	't' value
Tamil	240	79.55	19.240	4.569**
English	240	87.25	17.671	
** Significant at 0.01 Level				

From Table 54.3, it is clear that the't' value is 4.569** and is significant at 0.01 level. The English medium Students are having significantly higher level of Academic Stress than the Tamil medium Students. Hence, the framed null hypothesis is found to be rejected.

TABLE. 54.5: Significance Difference between Male and Female Higher Secondary Students in their Adjustment level

Category	N	Mean	SD	't' value
Male	240	58.83	11.831	4.745**
Female	240	53.89	10.991	
**Significant at 0.01 Level				

Table 54.4 shows that the't' value, 4.745** is Significant at 0.01 level. The result reveals that there is a significant difference between Adjustment level of Male and Female Higher School Students. The Male students are having high Adjustment level than the Female students. Hence, the framed null hypothesis is found to be rejected

TABLE. 54.6: Significance of the Difference between Urban and Rural Higher Secondary School Students in their Adjustment level

Category	N	Mean	SD	't' value
Urban	300	63.16	7.958	25.462**
Rural	180	45.03	7.294	
* Significant at 0.01 Level				

The above table 54.5 shows that the't' value, 25.462 is Significant at 0.01 level. The Urban Students are having significantly higher Adjustment level than the Rural Students. Hence, the framed null hypothesis is found to be rejected.

TABLE. 54.7: Significance of the Difference between Tamil and English Medium Higher Secondary School Students in their Adjustment level

Category	N	Mean	SD	't' value
Tamil	240	54.49	11.968	3.558**
English	240	58.23	11.080	
** Significant at 0.01 Level				

The above table 54.6 shows that the't' value, 3.558 is Significant at 0.01 level. The English medium Students are having significantly higher Adjustment level than the Tamil medium school students. Hence, the framed null hypothesis is found to be rejected.

TABLE. 54.8: Significant Relationship between Academic Stress and Adjustment level of the students among the Higher Secondary School Students

Classification	N	'r'
Academic Stress and Adjustment level	480	0.79
**Significant at the level of 0.01 levels		

The above table 54.7 show sthat the 'r' value, 0.79 is significant at 0.01 level. Pearson's product moment correlation was worked out. The coefficient of correlation calculated is 0.76, which is positive and high. Hence the formulated hypothesis "There is no significant relationship between Academic Stress and Adjustment level" is rejected. This shows there is close relationship between Academic Stress and Adjustment Level of the students.

EDUCATIONAL IMPLICATIONS OF THE STUDY

When the student is having high academic stress, he or she cannot adjust well to the situation, so their development will be hampered and affects their success. It is necessary to estimate the academic stress and adjustment level of students for proper guidance. The teachers and administrators should have proper knowledgeonstudent's stress and adjustment level in academic matters for proper planning and execution of various schemes and their implementation. Even to respond to the new schemes for students, the students should be free from stress and adjust to the new environment. Guidance and counseling services in schools may be started to reduce stress.

CONCLUSION

Academic Stress plays a vital role in the student's life and it accounts for variation in performance and achievements for success. It is necessary to estimate the academic stress and adjustment level of students for proper guidance. Guidance and counseling services in schools should be started and also various programmes to reduce stress should be hosted.

❐

55

Integration of Digital Technology in Classroom Instruction

Digital Technologies have touched every sphere of our life in the present world. The society is highly sensitive to create knowledge-intensive environment to efficiently create, share, use and protect knowledge. Educational Institutions are gearing up to provide information networks to students with access to digital resources. Digital Technology is a powerful tool for problem-solving, conceptual development, critical thinking and evaluation which help to make the learning process much easier for the students. To be effective in the Classroom Instruction, Teachers should acquire the knowledge and skills to adapt to the new electronic technological tools like Computer Assisted Instruction (CAI), On-line Learning, Virtual Learning, e-Learning, m-Learning, Blogs, Videoconferencing etc. which are student-cantered, collaborative, which aims to achieve high academic standards.

VARITIES OF DIGITAL TECHNOLOGICAL TOOLS

The following are some of the digital Technological tools that can be used effectively in the Classroom Instruction like e-Learning, m-Learning, Computer Assisted Instruction (CAI), Virtual Learning, On-line Learning, Blogs, Podcasting, Videoconferencing etc.

1. **E-Learning**

   E-learning which refers to the electronic learning promotes innovative strategy in teaching methods with information of diversified learning environment. It has more variety of information resources in learning experience with the use of Multimedia and non-verbal presentation by teaching material which encourages more and more self-learners to continue life-long learning without limitation of space, time and profession. It is a single point of access that serves as a gateway to variety of e-resources.

2. **M-Learning**

   Mobile Learning is termed as m-learning which is enabled by the use of portable computing devices such as PDA's, Palmtops, Smart Phones, and tablet PC's communicating over wireless networks. The use of computing in teaching and learning is being extended to spaces beyond the traditional classroom and within the classroom, the teachers and learners are gaining more flexibility and new opportunities for interaction with each other through Short Messaging Service (SMS), downloading the course-content where lessons are provided in bit sized format, a fact which is appealing to busy students through Blue-tooth connectivity easily without Internet connectivity.

3. **Computer Assisted Instruction (CAI)**

   It is a development of systematic programmed learning and teaching machine. It is a self-instructional device with the principle of automization. CAI is "Computer applications applied to traditional teaching methods such as drill, tutorial, demonstration, simulation and instructional games". It is an effective medium and an indispensable aid in the teaching-learning process.

4. **Virtual Learning Environment (VLE)**

   VLE is a set of teaching and learning tools designed to enhance a students' learning experience by including computers and Internet in the learning process. The principal components of VLE package include curriculum mapping, student tracking, On-line support for both teachers and students.

5. **On-Line Learning**

   It is synonymous with Web-based learning where learning is fostered via World Wide Web (WWW) only with Internet connectivity. It is pedagogy of On-line teaching and learning. The various strategies of Instruction was followed through On-line learning such as Conversing, Discussing, Mentoring, Questioning, Debating, Sharing data which is the necessary components for the teaching-learning process in the

Classroom Instruction. The other important features of On-line learning are Analysing, Seeking, Collecting, Organising and Synthesing, On-line information of knowledge resources towards the evolutionary growth of open, flexible, anytime and anywhere in learning.

6. **Blogs**

The term 'Blog' is a blend of the term, 'web' and 'log' leading to 'web log', which finally becomes "Blog". Blog as an educational tool can be integrated in multifaceted manner to accommodate all learners. As they are easy to create and update efficiently they can be used to inform students of classroom requirements, post handouts, notices, home work and assignments or act as a question and answer board. It provides conversation between the batch-mates in larger classes. A teacher can create and manage a blog to his/her professional interest and disseminate academic information and give instruction to their students on-line. The information or instruction through Blogs can be accessed by the students through the Internet connectivity everywhere even after the classroom hours

FEATURES OF DIGITAL DEVICES

The digital devices now play a major role in our lives in the following ways.

1. Digital Media Players have become the preferred way of listening to music, much of it downloaded from online music stores.
2. Mobile Phones, particularly Smartphone have become a major mode of communication. They can be used for voice calls, texting and even video calls.
3. Video Games Consoles can obviously be used to pay video games, but many of them also provide Internet access and can play optical media, such as CDs and DVDs.
4. Tablet Computers provide many of the facilities of laptop systems and can also be used for Internet access and for playing audio or video files.
5. Digital Cameras are used to take pictures which can later be transferred to a computer for editing. They range from simple snapshot cameras to professional models.
6. Digital Videos Cameras can be used to record and store video older modes often recorded to magnetic tape or optical media – more modern models record to hard disk.

CHALLENGES OF DIGITAL TECHNOLOGIES

There are certain challenges which are to be followed while using in the field of education they are as follow.

1. The applications of digital technology that have yet to be proven to be effective when compared to more traditional classroom learning contexts. Teachers and schools need to think carefully about when, why and how to use technologies as well as evaluating their efficiency and effectiveness.
2. There is a 'digital divide' – the divide between those who have access to digital technology and the internet, and those who do not use in.
3. Implementing and then maintaining technology is costly particularly as systems can quickly become out of date.
4. There may be problems with the existing infrastructure.
5. The hacking of personal information, access to illegal or banned materials and distractions from learning all being high on institutional agendas.
6. Some uses of technologies can be harmful. The poor posture and eyestrain are common problems when working at desktop computers for prolonged periods.

TEACHERS SUPPORT

It is viewed that the teachers attitude towards digital technology has been changed which may be due to the cause of frequently attending in-service training on application of digital technologies in the field of education being conducted by higher authorities. They are getting strength by way of enriching themselves and cooperating themselves to the system of education in all the way.

Teachers can make the best use of technology in the classroom by developing their awareness of a range of digital technologies and considering carefully both how and why they can be used to support students' learning. Effective selection of software and devices is only part of the story. The consideration of what learning will be achieved and how the technology may help is fundamental to its effective deployment.

BENEFITS OF DIGITAL TECHNOLOGY

The digital technologies are helping the system of education in so many ways to the teachers, students and administrators. Some of them are as follow.

1. Digital technology has changed the way we work, communicate with friends and colleagues, and entertain ourselves. Option of recording music and movies to optical media, such as CD-ROMs or DVD-ROMs and playing them back using a CD or DVD player.

2. Photography has become an important application area for digital technology. Instead of taking pictures on film, which then needs to be submitted for processing and subsequently printed, one can use digital cameras that can store images in a digital format.
3. These digital images can then be transferred to a computer, where editing operations like clipping, resizing and adjustment of colour or brightness can take place. Some editing operations can even be carried out on the digital camera itself. Rather than printing pictures we can now share those by uploading them to picture-sharing sites.
4. Digital technology can be used to record and share videos, using a range of devices such as camcorders, mobile phones and webcams. Clips can be uploaded to video-sharing web site, such as YouTube or Vimeo, and displayed on social networking sites. Video editing software can be used to edit digital video by adding or deleting scenes and applying special effects.
5. Digital technology has also transformed communication, particularly in the business world. Video conferencing is now commonplace, eliminating the need to travel long distances to attend meetings. It can also be useful in a social context, allowing easy communication with friends or family in faraway locations.

CONCLUSION

Transition, Transformation and Revolution are the scenario of today's educational system. All process of learning is soon crossing boundaries and barriers. So, it require a change in knowledge competencies and skills to deal with technological advancement in networking which is necessary to establish a network between students, educators, parents, institution and libraries and the world over. The four approaches which adopted in the technology such as emerging, applying, infusing and transforming will represent a continuum. The main purposes of implications of the study is to make knowledge free and seamlessly available to all those which need it for educational matters at anytime, anywhere and accessible from any device.

❒

56

Blended Learning Opportunities in Higher Education

BLENDED LEARNING APPROACH: AN INTRODUCATION

Blended learning (BL) describes a learning environment that ether combines teaching methods, delivery modes, media formats or a mixture of all these. It also refers to the integrated learning activities such as a mixture of online and face-to-face learning. In other words, Blended learning is a mixture of e-learning and traditional types of learning. It is mentioned as the integrated combination of traditional learning with web-based online approaches, the combination of media and tools deployed in an e-learning environment and the combination of a number of pedagogical approaches. Among the benefits of blended learning reported by recent research were (i) provide students with more control over learning; (ii) To foster critical thinking; (iii) To excel online assessment system and computer tutorials.

OBJECTIVES OF BLENDED LEARNING APPROACH

Three are varieties of objectives for implementing a blended learning program, as follows.

- Improved learning over either pure traditional classroom learning or pure e-learning
- Increased convenience (time, place and so on)

- The cost savings may result from perhaps reducing the number of instructors
- The e-learning component of a blended learning program can help ease the classroom space needs by have in students learn more from outside the classrooms. The freed-up classroom space can potentially be used for other purposes.

ELEMENTS IN BLENDED LEARNING APPROACH

Blended learning includes a combination of computer-based and/or online and face-to-face elements, and a mix of formats, media and methods, so the most appropriate and effective approach can be used for each part of the learning experience.

Formats

- To work face-to-face with students work independently in a self-paced way
- The place could be something like a classroom, community centre room, conference hall, computer lab, etc.
- The students may work some of the time in a computer lab
- The students may join online learning communities and discussions
- Learners attempt web-based tutorials or activities

Media

Students of the Higher Education may utilize CDs, videotapes, audio tapes, books, newspapers, television, radio, online chat, computers, web sites, and games.Some of these media (for example, newspaper or games) are available or usable online or as a physical resource.

Methods

- One can work one-on-one with students
- Student may setup group projects
- he students of the Higher education may put different groups together to work on similar topics or project

CATEGORIES OF BLENDED LEARNING APPROACHES

The categories of blended learning approaches are as follows.

Enabling blends

Primarily focus on addressing issue of access and convenience – for example, blends that are intended to provide additional flexibility to the learners or blends that attempt to provide the same opportunities or learning experience but through a different modality.

Enhancing Blends

Allow incremental changes to the pedagogy but do not radically change the way teaching and learning occur. This can occur at both ends of the spectrum. For example, in a traditional face-to-face learning environment, additional resources and perhaps some supplementary materials may be included online.

Transforming Blends

Blends that allow a essential transformation of the pedagogy – for example, a change from a model where learners are just receivers of information to a model where learners actively construct knowledge through dynamic interactions. These types of blends enable intellectual activity that was not practically possible without the technology.

BENEFITS OF BLENDED LEARNING APPROACH IN CLASSROOM

The following are the benefits to blended learning approaches.

- Students can participate at any time
- Students can collaborate on their own time
- It can provide reduction in costs, ime, labour, stress, etc.
- Course documents are available to learner 24 hours a day
- Flexible classroom scheduling
- Class goals can easily be met
- Uniformed class for multi-section offerings
- Effective use of class time
- Enhanced computer literacy among students and instructors
- Using the World Wide Web resources to support class activities
- Supply students with additional learning materials if they need them
- Increase the quality of communications between the instructor and learner
- Using interactive programs that produce quick feedback and an advice for any remedial work

DIFFICULTIES TO BLENDED LEARNING APPROACH

Despite the advantages, there are some difficulties with blended learning. These can be reduce or overcome. To avoid these points might reduce the quality of teaching in this mode. These might include:

Bias

Some people have difficulty using or accepting teaching methods that are unfamiliar or unconventional. In the case of computer mediated learning, some people cannot use computers well or prefer to avoid using them. Blended learning can be adapted to suit not only the learners but also the teachers.

Faculty Difficulties

Faculty compensation and initial difficulties to cope up with the leaning requirement to teach in this mode. Not all instructors are as effective in teaching blended courses.

Lack of Means

One may not have enough time, money, equipment, etc. E-learning classes cannot function if instructors and students cannot operate the necessary hardware and software. Some schools may not have enough computer rooms for every teacher to use one, a school may not even have computers at all, or a teacher may not have the time or skills to create computer activities for lessons. Training is not done properly because of lack of time with use of technological tools.

Poor Mixes

Learning methods and tools need to be used well in conjunction with each other. Careful thought needs to go into making a good blend.

Computer difficulties: Students might have different computers with different bandwidth capabilities. Students using only speed computers than others.

CONCLUSION

A common feature in blended lessons is that students work in pairs or groups to complete a task. Education is not just information transfer but also skill development and social interaction. Students learn from each other as they help one another through the tasks and observe each other as work. Blended learning can provide reduction in costs, time, labour, stress, etc. Normally this is achieved by using computers. Materials kept on line are easier to access, distribute, and reproduce. Material can be accessed instantly from many locations at any time. This saves not only time, it also saves money that would be used for printing and distributing, and natural resources that would become paper waste. In addition it saves learners from losing, forgetting, or having to carry texts. Teachers can more easily share work with other teachers, and teachers can more easily modify and upgrade his material. A blended learning approach can make his teaching easier.

❐

57

ICT in Open and Distance Education

Distance education is the education provided into at a distance. That is unlike the formal system, the teaching learning process is not mostly conducted in a room or in a institution, a distance is maintained between the teacher and the taught. It is a kind of non formal education in which there are no restrictions of age, class, duration, even qualification etc for a degree. There are flexibility in all aspects of education from admission to examination distance education was started and even now it's known in various names such as instruction through correspondence, home study, postal tuition, external study, off campus study, open learning, open school, open university and so on. Distance education has an important role in the Universalization of educational opportunities. The flexibility and innovativeness of the distance learning system are particularly suited to the diverse requirements of the pluralist clientele.

Open learning, which covers a wide range of innovations and reforms in the educational sector that advocates flexibility to the learner with regard to entry and exit; pace and place of study; method of study and also the choice and combination of courses; assessment and course completion. The lesser the restrictions, the higher the degree of openness. The Open learning system aims to redress social or educational inequality and to offer opportunities not provided by conventional colleges or universities. Educational opportunities are planned deliberately so that access to education is available to larger sections of the society. Thus, ODL is a term which accepts the philosophy of "openness" and uses the "distance mode" of learning.

Pressure

Pressure on institutions of higher learning is tremendous, and all the central, state and "deemed to be" universities, and institution of national importance, have not been able to meet the need for increasing aspiration for education. Increasingly, private initiative for higher education is being called for, through the private universities, bill is still lying in the parliament awaiting clearance. A large number of private institutes have come up and increasing number of such institutions is being accorded the status of "deemed to be" universities by the University Grand Commission.

Funding

Funding has been a major issue. With decreasing resource allocation for higher education, universities are required to mobilize additional resources from increasing student's fees, and or tapping other sources like expansion of university industry linkages and offering distance learning programmes.

Quality and Accreditation

Quality and accreditation are other issues as well as infrastructure, pedagogic, financial and other resources to be utilized not only to the optimum level but also conform to agreed upon standards so that the inputs, process and outputs are under constant scrutiny for improvement in respective areas. NAAC and the NBA are responsible for institutional and programme evaluation, and for providing accredited status to institutions of higher learning. Universities are also required to conform to the standers set by various other councils.

Globalization and Global Pressure

Globalization and Global Pressure for "reform" have led universities to rethink about the curriculum, instructional strategy involving more ICT enabled education, expansion of training and continuous professional development or "lifelong learning" provisions, international student needs, and quality benchmarking. This involves competition and formation of strategic alliance. While many of the universities are getting into more of strategic planning only a few have adopted holistic planning initiative which involves system-wide implementation of especially ICT enabled teaching, research, extension, management, services and evaluation.

Curriculum Designing

Curriculum Designing is still central issues in universities. While most have no even updated and transformed in the pattern suggested by the university grants commission through their curriculum development cells, there is also an increasing need to diversity curriculum and course structures to meet emerging specialized need for education and training research. Though many of the central agencies like the UGC, ICSSR, SCIR, ICMR, ICAR and others have significant funding for discipline research, the quality of doctoral programmes has not increased significantly.

Continuing Professional Development

Continuing professional development in various professions and professional development of college and university teachers are areas of significant concern to educational planners and administrators. Many of the universities do not have programmes tailored made for continuing professional development and training needs of various economic and development sectors.

Employment

Employment higher and further education, while in gainful employments, is still a true phenomenon. Further, most of the campuses face the problem of students and employee unrest.

STEPS INTO INTEGRATION OF ICT

Integrating information and communication technology in open and distance teaching- learning process involve in the following steps:

- Awareness
- Fundamental Knowledge
- Proper training
- Implementation/Put into Practice
- Follow-up activities

Fundamental knowledge

To create and insert the basic knowledge of the modern technology those are involved in teaching and learning towards teachers. The basic knowledge is

- Nature of media
- Use of media in teaching learning process and
- Implementing the media in teaching

Proper Training

It is needed to give proper tainting to teacher about the equipment and instrument, which are utilized and involved teaching.

Implementation/Put into Practice

After receiving the training, the teachers should implement his training in his teaching and evaluation.

Follow-up Activities

While implementing new technology, there may so many difficulties and experiments arise. These may be eradicated through sharing and consulting the expert.

ADVANTAGES OF ICT

The numbers of advantages of ICT in respect of academic and administration aspects in the distance education are discussed below. In the terms Academic Aspects.

- Enhance faculty & student engagement
- Information-gathering
- Provides immediate feedback
- Reinforces motivation for teaching improvement
- The document tracking system can be applied this helps the learners to get efficient and more cost effective service.
- In the terms of Administration Aspects
- The admission of students and registration of students can be done through on-line.
- Digitization of students' records makes storage and retrieval of information easy and simple.
- Payment of fees can also be done through on-line, it reduce the dubious activities of some account clerk.

DRAWBACK IN OPEN AND DISTANCE LEARNING

The only drawback ODL since its conception is the testing of material, whether quiz, test or examinations, online courses have had difficulty controlling cheating because of the lake of teacher control. In a classroom situation, a teacher can monitor students and visually uphold a level of integrity consistent with an institutions reputation. With distance learning, the students are removed from supervision completely. Integrity issues concerning testing can be addressed by requiring students to take examinations in a controlled setting or there may be an enforced time limit. Examinations can be held at a common location so that professors can supervise directly. Better still would be offering secure exam software and packages to help professors to manage their students more effectively.

CONCLUSIONS

Educationists and researchers believe that the problems would be solved on the gap between the existing labor force of the country and the expected labor force of the global market along the created opportunities using of Open and Distance learning technologies. The measures will assure that knowledge and skill based labor force of India will develop qualitatively and quantitatively.

❐

58

Education and Society

Society has its own structure with different interrelated parts. There are five pillars which are holding the society .There is a functional relationship with education with other sub system. Interrelationship and interactions must be stronger. Each and every society has its own norms, values, culture, tradition, which are moulded and shaped by education. Education is a strong foundation for the developing socicty. Many like Leo Tolstoy, Antonio Gramsci, Paulo Freire, Brasil Bernstein, Ivan Illich, Pierre Bourdein, Rabindranath Tagore, Sarvepalli Radhakrishnan, M.K Gandhi etc.

The Influence of Society to Education Progression

Education of any society has direct correlations with its socio-cultural factors. The process of education evolved in its social structure, social norms and values system. School is one such creation of human society to transfer the existing cultural content from one generation to next generation. In informal setting, socialization is a process through which community transact or educate their members about the norms and values of the society. Traditionally, education provided by religious institutions like Christian missionaries, Islamic Madharasa, Buddhist monasteries and other religious organizations. These institutions have the special feature and they inculcate their religious ideals. These are not limited established religions, each community transmit their norms and values. In this process of education and socialization, education and society have close association since inception of society itself. On the one hand, education prepares individual to perform different social roles in society.

The Influence of Education to Social Progression

Education is a social concern. Its objective is to develop and awaken in the child the physical, intellectual and moral states which are acquired of the individual by the society. Education is to eradicate inequality in the society. It is a double-edged tool which eliminates the effects of socio-economic inequalities. Education is important in the creation of any democratic existence of the society. It enhances Geo-Political stability. It imparts knowledge to elect a ruler. Promotes tolerance, minimises conflicts. Acts as a passport and increases hope for the future and is also a powerful tool.

Role of School

The school prepares young people for this transition. Schools operates on meritocratic principle, status is achieved on the basis of merit. Like Durkheim, Parsons also argue that the school represents society in miniature. By reflecting the operation of society as a whole, the school prepares young people for their adult roles. As part of this process, schools socialise young people into the basic values of society. These values have important functions in society as a whole.

Parsons sees the educational system as an important mechanism for the selection of individuals for their future role in society. Thus schools by testing and evaluating students, match their talents, skills and capacities to the jobs for which they are best suited. The school is therefore seen as the major mechanism for role allotment.

Women Education

Rapid expansion of education among women is established in spite of many obstacles. To some extent education is a source of social mobility for the despondent groups. Distance education is a fast growing and wide-spread trend. This offers flexible learning ways, can contribute considerably making higher education more accessible to adults. Many are unable to participate in on-campus education. This trend facilitates the adult women learners in higher education.

Various Forms of Education

There are various forms and varieties of education which have been brought about by the needs of modern society. Universal education, adult education, vocational and scientific education are the various forms and varieties of education. This is due to social needs and aspirations.

CONCLUSION

Education and society have close association since inception of society itself. On the one hand, education prepares individual to perform different social roles in society, whereas on other hand, society and culture determines system of socialization and the nature of education to be imparted to the members. Each society, from simple to the complex one, has its own system of educating their young generation and accordingly the institutions are developed. Above mentioned, last two sections are devoted to this understanding. First, education carries many social functions in society to transmit culture and knowledge. This alone makes mankind different than other animals of earth. Secondly, society has plays detrimental role in the process of education.

❒

59

E-Governance in Higher Education Institutions: Need of the Hour

A good higher education system is required for overall success of a nation. Electronic Governance (e-Governance) is one much mechanism that can help societies, governments and institutions to become more efficient in the delivery of services.e-Governance is the use of Information and Communication Technologies (ICT) for the planning, implementation, and monitoring of government programs, schemes, and activities. UNESCO (2011) has defined "E-governance may be understood as the performance of this governance via the electronic medium in order to facilitate an efficient, speedy and transparent process of disseminating information to the public, and other agencies, and for performing government administration activities.". In the Indian context, former President of India, A P J Abdul Kalam defined e-Governance as "A transparent smart e-Governance with seamless access, secure and authentic flow of information crossing the interdepartmental barrier and providing a fair and unbiased service to the citizen". Ramganesh et al., 2016 in their study state that e-Governance solution in the field of educational sector has changed the total policy of administration, which is designed to make the system easy accessible, time saving and economic.

E-Governance: Major Challenges

Mittal & Kaur(2013) view, as the usage of Information Technology is growing very fast, Higher education institution is making many efforts to provide services to its stakeholders through e-Governance. However poor IT infrastructure is not up to the work in education. Also there are several problems can be enumerated as follows,

- **Poverty** - Accessing Internet is a costly affair for the poor who struggle for their livelihood in developing countries like India. Required infrastructure in the form of installing the necessary telephone lines needed for internet or email access is equally unaffordable in most poor countries.
- **Technical Illiteracy** - There is general lack of technical literacy as well as literacy in countries like India.
- **Language Dominance** - The dominance of English on the internet constrains the access of non-English-speaking population. In the case of India, 95 percent of the population does not speak English. Due to such overwhelming dominance of English over these communication channels, computers and the internet are quite useless in Indian villages.
- **Unawareness** - There is general lack of awareness regarding benefits of e-Governance as well as the process involved in implementing successful G-C, G-G and G-B projects.
- **Inequality** - Inequality in gaining access to public sector services between various sections of citizens, especially between urban and rural communities, between the educated and illiterate, and between the rich and poor.
- **Infrastructure** - Lack of necessary infrastructure like electricity, internet, technology and ways of communications will affect the speed which delays the implementation.
- **Impediments for the Re-Engineering Process** - Implementation of E-Governance projects requires lots of restructuring in administrative processes, redefining of administrative procedures and formats which finds the resistance in almost all the departments at all the levels.

On the whole, there are several challenges and barriers that can delay progress of e-Governance implementation. This section, briefly discussed the most important and common challenges and barriers based on the implementation.

E-governance: Major issues

Alshehri & Drew (2010) stated that the developing countries like India people are poor and infrastructure is not up to the work. There are several reasons under such condition it becomes very different to provide government services to the people, here are some reasons as below:

A. **Technical Issues**

- **Interoperability**: The interoperation of various state governments, the various ministries with in a state government is a critical issue. Integration of data is main problem, how to capture the data in web based form and how to transfer it in common format for processing and sharing the information.
- **Privacy:** privacy of any transaction or information provided by the citizen to the government agency must be ensured. Otherwise the information can be misuse by the private sector or competitors and the users may be reluctant to access the services provided.
- **Security:** Transaction security is another major problem in E-governance. The tax, fine and bill payment must be secured and the system design should be full proof.
- **Authentication:** The authentication of citizens requesting services, needs to be verified before they access or use the services. The digital signature plays an important role in providing the authenticity but this is expensive and requires frequent maintenance.

B. **Economic Issues**

- **Cost:** Implementation, operations and maintenance cost of service provided should be low enough for high cost benefit ratio.
- **Maintainability:** IT has been continuously evolving and software are frequently upgraded. Thus the system must be compatible and maintainable for easily fulfillment of emerging needs.
- **Reusability:** E-governance should be considered as nationwide plan and the implemented modules must be reusable by other administrations.
- **Portability:** The primary requisite for portable applications is independence of components from hardware or software platforms, to help in possible reuse by other administrations.

C. **Social Issues**

- **Accessibility:** E-governance service should be accessible for anybody from anywhere at any time. Even if internet population is growing exponentially, there is a very big portion of the population who may not able to access e-governance for various reasons.

- **Usability:** All the users may not be expert of ICT transactions or the technology used for e-governance. Therefore the service provided must be usable or user friendly. To make the system usable, the guidance of operation may be provided to the users.
- **Acceptance:** E-governance requires reconfiguration of internal and external structure of public sectors. The main aim is to improve the system efficiently and to provide high quality services to the citizens. E-governance is for citizen convenience, instead of convenience of government.
- **Use of local languages:** The access of information must be permitted in the local languages for user comfort. There should be language software or some other technologies to translate the information from English to local languages.
- **Awareness in Rural Areas:** in India, there are very high percentage of villages where awareness of E-governance is required since large portion of rural populations are not aware of new technologies and computer educations.

E-Governance: Advantages

Higher educational institutions may have various requirements that include computerization and management of processes such as registration, admission, student information, classes, time table, transport, attendance, library, salary, examinations, performance, grades, hostels, security and reports Suklabaidya & Sen (2013). Following are the advantages of e-Governance,

- **E Services–** The main aim is to improve the delivery of serviccs to students by providing interactive services. Some examples of interactive services are: requests for documents, requests for certificates, issuing admit cards and id cards. After the implementation e-governance, we improve the delivery of services to students, faculty &stakeholders.
- **E-Participation–** Active alumni students, experienced teachers, stakeholders can involve in decision making process for quality education in rural area.
- **Improved Education System** - E-governance in education sectors allows use of information and communication technologies with the aim of improving education, improve information, service delivery, encourage student participation in the decision making process, making administration transparent and effective and give universities a new channel of educational deployment. Also, the system can obtain feedback from industry and students to modify course curriculum if deemed appropriate by the authorities.

- **Increasing Transparency** - The aim of e governance to share information with the college, teachers, students and stakeholder. Governing body can involve in decision making for education development.
- **Innovative Teaching Tools–** The new technologies offer vast opportunities for progress in all walks of life. With the introduction of new technological initiatives the structure of higher educational institutions has changed. The changing role of lecturers, the changeable learning environment and the design of eLearning facilities all contribute to a potentially more flexible organizational structure of higher education. This has been possible by technological implementation based environments such as bulletin boards, virtual lectures and e Libraries and video conferencing.
- **Private Public Participation–** Public-Private-Partnership (PPP) arrangement tasks include design and development of application software, population of data and content in the regional language, procurement and installation of networking and computer systems, deployment of software and delivery of services.
- **Centralized Information-** E-Governance has provided electronic information infrastructure to simplify service delivery, reduce duplication, and improve the level and speed of service at a lower cost. The centralized information approach of e- Governance keeps all information at one place in electronic form. This approach of making information secure prevents it against any theft or leakage.
- In summary, the online methods enable more effective education and offer significant advantages over traditional services. It will be help in the betterment of the higher education in the country and increase the number of employable students.

E-Governance: Indian Government Initiatives

- E-Governance initiates several programsand policies which promote the usage of ICT in
- Education. It predicts that there are many benefits for the students, learner and the teachers.
- National Academic Depository (NAD) is an initiative of MHRD to maintain a national-level database of all academic qualifications from secondary school certificate to university and professional certificates.
- National E-Governance Plan (NeGP)

The Mission of the National E-Governance Plan (NeGP) is to focus on Education sector that Provide greater opportunities of access to higher education with equity to all eligible persons and in particular to the vulnerable sections.

Developing Library Network (DELNET)

The Developing Library Network (DELNET), promoted by the National Informatics Centre, Department of Information Technology, Ministry of Communications and Information Technology of the Indian government, is an example of e-governance in the field of library and information science.

National Electronic Library (NEL)

The Government of India has also taken a decision to provide access to a National Electronic Library (NEL) to its citizens including students and teachers in schools, colleges and universities. Most resources in NEL would be available in open access to every citizen of India without any restrictions.

Digital India Program

The vision of Digital India aims to transform the country into a digitally empowered society and knowledge economy. A programme on digital literacy would be taken up at the national level and Massive Online Open Courses (MOOCs) shall be developed and leveraged for e-Education.

CONCLUSION

E-Governance is one of the major factors for making the rapid changes in our society. The use of ICT can develop education quality, expand learning opportunities and make education accessible. The introduction of innovative technological applications in higher education institutions is associated with changes, not only at the level of teaching and learning, but also in carrying out administrative tasks in colleges. E-governance initiates several programs and policies which promote the usage of ICT in education (Kumar, 2012). As the usage of Information Technology is growing very fast, Indian government is making many efforts to provide services to its citizens through e-Governance. Although Indian government is spending a lot of money on e-Governance projects but still these projects are not successful in all parts of India because unawareness in people.

❐

Bibliography

1. Brine, Alan an Feather, John. (2002). Supporting skills development – LTSN-ICS. In 68th IFLA Council and General Conference Bangkok, Thailand, 18 – 24 .
2. Casey, D. (1998). Learning "From" or "Through" the Web: Models of Web Based Education. (http://www.acm.org/pubs/citations/proceedings/cse/282991/p51-casey/).
3. Dibbon, David. (2000). Innovative Teaching Working Group: A Proposal. Education 4361. December 10. Gilbert, L. & Moore, D.R. (1998). Building Interactivity into Web Courses: Tools for Social and Instructional Interaction. Educational Technology, May-June, 29- 35.
4. Adams, J. C. & Aaron A. A (1998). Web-based testing: A study in insecurity, World Wide Web 1, p193-208
5. Javed Wasim, et al.(2014). Web Based Learning. International Journal of Computer Science and Information Technologies, Vol. 5 (1), 446-449.
6. Wang, M. (2000). Evaluating the Usability of Web-based Learning Tools. Masters thesis, Department of Computer Science, University of Victoria.
7. Baytak, A., Tarman, B., & Ayas, C. (2011). Experiencing technology integration in education: children's perceptions. International Electronic Journal of Elementary Education, 3(2), 139-151.
8. Bulman, G. and Fairlie, R. W. (2016). Technology and Education: Computers, Software and the Internet. National Bureau of Economic Research, NBER Working Paper No. 22237.

9. Keser, H., Uzunboylu, H., & Ozdamli, F. (2012). The trends in technology supported collaborative learning studies in 21st century. World Journal On Educational Technology, 3(2), 103-119.
10. Downes, S. (2004). Educational Blogging, Educause Review 39 (5) pp. 14-26. Retrieved from http://www.educause.edu/pub/er/erm04/erm0450.asp
11. Duffy, P. & Bruns, A. (2006). The use of blogs, wikis and RSS in education: A conversation of possibilities. Proceedings of the Online Learning and Teaching Conference 2006, Brisbane: September 26.
12. Hooker M (2009) Concept Note: The Use of ICT in Teacher Professional Development, Accessed on 16th January 2016 from http://www.gesci.org/old/files/docman/TPD Workshop-Concept Note.doc
13. ICT in Education - An online course available at ICT in Education accessed on 4th Jan, 2016.
14. Bharadwaj, R.L (1998). "Percieved parenting of Rejection Acceptance and Adolescents value conflicts". *Indian Psychological Review,* Vol.1, pp.256 - 266.
15. Ciarrochi, Joseph, said Terri, Deame, Frank. P (2005), when simplifying life is not is bad. The link between rigidity, stressful life events and mental health in an undergraduate population *British Journal of Guidance and counseling,* V33/2, pp.185 - 197.
16. Journal of American College of Health (2005). "The mental health needs of today's college students, challenges and recommendation". Helder publications, *Helen Dwight raid education foundation,* V53/4 p.157, Jan-Feb. 2005.
17. Kathuria M (1974)."Personality determination of vocational maturity and cancer induciveness". *Dissertation abstracts.*
18. David Archer, Speech delivered at 'Financing Education 2030' in Beirut Lebanon on May 2018.
19. Malala, Speech delivered by Malala Yousafzai at United Nation Conference in12th July, 2013.
20. Mandela, "Lightning your way to a better future: Speech delivered by N R Mandela at launch of mindset Network", 2003.
21. Berta Esteve Volast, (2007), "Gender discrimination and Growth: Theory and Evidence from India," London, London School of Economics and Political Sciences.
22. Seguino, Stephanie. (2006). "Gender Equality and Economic Growth: A Cross-Country Analysis", World\Development, Vol. 28, No. 7, pp. 67-71.

23. https://ihds.umd.edu/sites/default/files/WhiteRutherKahn.pdf
24. https://www.undp.org/content/dam/undp/library/Poverty%20Reduction/Inclusive%20development/Humanity%20Divided/HumanityDivided_Ch5_low.pdf
25. Ablodun, Fadeyi Olalekan, (2008). 'Distance Learning and Women Marginalisation: The Gender Orientation perspective' The fifth Plan – Commonwealth Forum on Open and Distance Learning University of London UK 13-17 July.
26. Chaudhary, Pratima (1995). Women's Education in India-Myth and reality, Haranand publications, New Delhi.
27. Empowering Women through Distance Learning in India. Paper presented at Fourth Pan Commonwealth Forum for Open Learning Conference, Sunset Jamaica Grande Resort, Ocho Rios, Jamaica, 30thOctober-3rdNovember.http://pcf4.dec.uwi.edu/viewpaper.php?id=329 (Accessed on 27 December, 2016)
28. Moore, M. G. (1989). Distance Education: A learner's System, Lifelong Learning.
29. Bates, A. W. (1991). Interactivity as a criterion for media selection in distance education
30. Moore, M. G. (1989). Distance Education: A learner's System, Lifelong Learning.
31. Mind weaves: communications, Computer, and distance Education.
32. Pradeepkumarmisra,(2013),"*pedagogical quality enrichment in OER – based courseware: Guiding principles*", Open praxis,vol.5,issue.2,pp123-134.
33. Robert A. Desharnais, Melvin Limson,(2007), "*Designing and Implementing Virtual Courseware to Promote InquirybasedLearning*", MERLOT Journal of Online Learning and Teaching, Vol. 3, No. 1,
34. Saraswathi.G and Leo Stanly.s(2019), "*Usage Of Digital Learning In Enhancing Conceptual Clarity And Retention", Page No, (99)*Cognitive and techno Pedagogical skills for 21stCentury learners,Nationalconference, Alagappa university.
35. Amutha, S., and John Kennedy, S. (2015). Awareness onTechnology-Based Education by the Student Teachers. *International Journal of Scientific and Research Publications,* Volume 5, Issue 9.
36. Beena et al, (2012). A Study on the ICT Awareness of M.Ed. Trainees .*Mgt.Eco.Res.,* Vol. 3(4), pp. 573-578.
37. Deivam, M., (2016). ICT Literacy among B.Ed Teacher Trainees. *InternationalJournalofMultidisciplinaryEducationandResearch,* Volume 1, Issue 3, Page No. 05-08.

38. Moore, M.G.(1989). Distance Education: A learner's System, Lifelong Learning,Vol.12, No.8 pp8-11.
39. RiyaTiwari and Swati Tikam(2016). Awareness and Use of ICT by B. Ed. Ravishankar University, *Journal of Ravishankar University,* Part-A, 22,pp.44-48,
40. Yang andHao (2012). ICT in English Schools: Transforming Education? *Technology, Pedagogy and Education,*Vol.21,No.1 ,pp.101-118.
41. Anderson, L. W., & Krathwohl, D. R. (2000). Taxonomy for learning, teaching, and assessing. New York: Allyn and Bacon.
42. Anderson, R. E., & Plomp, T. (2002). Proposal for IEA SITES module 3. Amsterdam: International Association for the Evaluation of Educational Achievement.
43. David, P. A., & Foray, D. (2003). Economic fundamentals of the knowledge society. Policy Futures in Education.
44. Hargreaves, A. (2003). Teaching in the knowledge society. New York: Teachers College(2007).
45. Jonassen, D. H. (1999). Computers as mindtools for schools: Engaging critical thinking .
46. Merrill. Kohyama, K. (1968). Introduction to information society theory.
47. Burton, J.K., Moore,D.M., & Magliaro, S.G. (2003). Behaviorism and instructional technology. In D. Jonassen (Ed.), *Handbook of research on educational communications and technology* (2nd ed., pp. 3-36). New York, NY: Routledge/Taylor & Francis Group.
48. Duffy, T.M.& Cunningham,D.J.(1996). Constructivism: Implications for the design and delivery of instruction. In D.Jonassen(Ed.), *Handbook of research on educational communications and technology* (1st ed.,pp.1-31). New York, NY: Routledge/Taylor & Francis Group.
49. Huitt,W.(2009). Humanism and open education. *Educational Psychology Interactive.* Valdosta, GA:Valdosta State University.Retrieved [date],from http://www.edpsycinteractive.org/topics/affect/humed.html
50. Kirschner, P. A., Sweller, J., & Clark, R. E. (2006). Why minimal guidance during instruction does not work: An analysis of the failure of constructivist, discovery, problem-based, experiential, and inquiry-based teaching. *Educational Psychologist,* 41(2), 75–86.
51. Arbaugh, J.B., (2008), "Introduction: Blended learning: Research and practice", Academy of Management Learning & Education 7, no. 1: 130–1.
52. Charles, D., and P. Anthony., (2007), "Blended learning: Research perspectives", Needham, MA: Sloan Center for Online Education.

53. Haddad, W., & Drexler, A. A. (2002), "Technologies for Education: Potentials, Parameters, and Prospect", AED, Paris UNESCO, Washington D.C
54. Brundtland, G.H. (1989) 'Developing distance education', in Developing distance education. Report from the fourteenth world conference. Oslo; ICDE.
55. St. meld. nr. 40 (1990-91) Fra visjon til virke. Om huger tanning. Oslo: Ministry of Church, Education and Research.
56. IRDAC (1990) Skills shortages in Europe, IRDAC opinion.
57. EADTU (1988) Report on long-term developments, Heerlen, Netherlands.
60. Atkins, D, E.; Brown, J, S. and Hammond, A, L. (2007), A Review of the Open Educational Resources (OER) Movement: Achievements, Challenges and New Opportunities,
61. Bell, Steven.(2017). "Research Guides: Discovering Open Educational Resources (OER): Home".guides.temple.edu. Retrieved on 2019-03-08.
62. UNESCO.(2005).Open Content for Higher Education. Retrieved from http://www.unesco.org.
63. UNESCO. (2012). Paris OER declaration. Retrieved from unesco.org/ on 2019-03-08.
64. Gaba, ashok; Li , wei (2015), Growth and development of distance education in India and china: a study on policy perspectives, Open Praxis, Vol. 7 issue 4, pp-311-323.
65. Ritimoni Bordoloi (2018), transforming and Empowering higher education through open and distance learning in India, Asian Association of Open Universities Journal, Vol. 13. No1 PP. 24-36
66. Santi kundu (2014), Open and distance learning Education its Scope and Constraints in India Scenario, IOSR Journal of Humanities and social Science . Vol. 19,issue 4 pp 1-05
67. Bonk, C.J. (2002). *Online Teaching in an Online World.* Education at a Glance: United States Distance Learning Association (USDLA) Journal, Vol. 16(1).
68. Carnevale, D. (2004). *Professors Seek Compensation for Online Courses.* Chronicle of Higher Education: Information Technology. Volume 50(49), pp- A27.
69. Irani, T. (2001). *Targeting distance education students: influences on traditional-ages students intent to enroll in a distance, education course.* United States Distance Learning Association. Vol. 15(11), pp- Reference
70. Abanikannda, M.O. (2016). Enhancing Effective Chemistry Learning Through Hypermedia Instructional Mode of Delivery. *European* Journal *of Educational Research,* 5(1), 27-34.

71. Ameritech, (1996, February). Ameritech Distance Learning [WWW document].
72. Escoffery, C., Miner, K. R., Adame, D. D., Butler, S., McCormick, L., & Mendell, E. (2005). Internet use for health information among college students. *Journal of American College Health,* 53(4), 183-188.
73. Hammond, N., & Bennett, C. (2001). Discipline Differences in Role and Use of ICT to Support Group-Based Learning. *Web Journal of Computer Assisted Learning,* 18(1), 55-63.
74. Katz, D., & Kahn, R.L. (1966). *The social psychology of organizations.* New York: John Wiley.
75. Kovalan, A. (2006). Effect of difference strategies of Web-Based instruction in the context of practicing Yoga online. *Doctorial Thesis,* Bharathiar University.
76. Improving Quality of Distance Education in India – Prof. S.C. Sahoo
77. https://www.distancelearningportal.com/articles/241/moocs-online-distance-learning-for-everyone-including-you.html
78. http://www.cilt.uct.ac.za/sites/default/files/image_tool/images/83/CILTPAPERS/FA_MOOCs_final%20Sept2015.pdf
79. https://www.researchgate.net/publication/320038196_An_Overview_of_MOOC_in_India
80. http://www.indiaeducation.net/online-education/all-about-moocs-massive-open-online-courses-india-abroad.html
81. https://www.higher-education-marketing.com/blog/distance-education-moocs
82. https://www.linkedin.com/pulse/how-employers-view-mooc-certificates-2018-carolyn-mcintyre
83. Improving Quality of Distance Education in India – Prof. S.C. Sahoo
84. https://www.distancelearningportal.com/articles/241/moocs-online-distance-learning-for-everyone-including-you.html
85. http://www.cilt.uct.ac.za/sites/default/files/image_tool/images/83/CILTPAPERS/FA_MOOCs_final%20Sept2015.pdf
86. https://www.researchgate.net/publication/320038196_An_Overview_of_MOOC_in_India
87. http://www.indiaeducation.net/online-education/all-about-moocs-massive-open-online-courses-india-abroad.html
88. https://www.higher-education-marketing.com/blog/distance-education-moocs
89. https://www.linkedin.com/pulse/how-employers-view-mooc-certificates-2018-carolyn-mcintyre

90. Fiona Copland, Sue Garton and Anne Burns, Challenges in Teaching English to Young Learners: Global Perspectives and Local Realities, TESOL Quarterly, Vol. 48, 2014.
91. Basu, A. Sinha,A. Saha,A & Pal, A (2012). Novel Approach in Distance Education using Satellite Broadcast. Proceedings of 3rd International Conference on E-Education, E-Business, E-Management and E-Learning. IPEDR vol.27 © (2012) IACSIT Press, Singapore
92. Gakhar, K. & Kour, H.(2012). Scenario of Present Education System: A Comparative Study Of Haryana And Its Neighbouring States. International Journal of Social Science & Interdisciplinary Research Vol.1 Issue 8, www.indianresearchjournals.com
93. Won Kim & Timothy K. Shih (2003): "Distance Education: The Status and Challenges", in Journal of Object Technology, vol. 2, no. 6, November-December 2003.
94. Warsi, J. (2004), "conditions under which English is taught in Pakistan: An Applied Linguistic Perspective." SARID Journal, 1 (1), 1-9, retrieved from http://
95. Centers for Disease Control & Prevention, (2007). National Health Education Standards.
96. Nagarajan. k., Natarajan. S., (2013). Health Education, Education in the Emerging Indian Society.
97. Bechtel, W. & Abrahamsen, A. (2010). Dynamic mechanistic explanation: computational modeling of circadian rhythms as an exemplar for cognitive science. Studies in History and Philosophy of Science, 41, 321-333.
98. Coltheart, M. (2012). Dual-route theories of reading aloud. In J. S. Adelman (Ed.), Visual word recognition, volume 1: Models and methods, orthography and phonology (pp. 3–27). Hove, UK: Psychology Press.
99. Snowling, M. J. &Melby-Lervåg, M. (2016, January 4). Oral language deficits in familial dyslexia: A meta-analysis and review. Psychological Bulletin. Advance online publication. http://dx.doi.org/10.1037/bul0000037.
100. Dignmarti Bhaskara Rao. (2001). Information Technology. New Delhi: Discovery Publishing House.
101. Karpaga Kumaravel.R. (2002). Integrating Technology into Teaching and Learning, Tiruchirappalli: Society for Educational Technology, Research and Development (SETRAD).
102. Palaniappan. V.P. (1988). Computer and Educational Technology. New Delhi: Sona Printer.

103. Sampath. et al. (1984). Introduction to Educational Technology. New Delhi : Sterling Publishers Pvt. Ltd.
104. Caine, R. N., & Caine, G. (2006). *Meaningful learning and the executive functions of the brain. The Neuroscience of Adult Learning, 5(3).*
105. Wolfe, P. (2001). Brain Matters: *Translating Research into Classroom Practice, Alexandria, VA: ASCD.*
106. *How the Brain Learns a Second Language,* Retrieved from brainconnection.brainhq.com on 21.03.2019.
107. Emrah Ekmekçi(2015), *"Distance education in foreign language teaching: evaluations*
108. *from the perspectives of freshman students",* Retrieved from www.sciencedirect.com on 15.03.2019.
109. Bates, A. W. (1995). Technology, Open Learning and Distance Education, London:Routledge, 29-31.
110. Dupagne, M., and Krendl, K. A., (1992). Teachers' attitudes toward computers: A review of the literature. *Journal of Research on Computing in Education,* 24(3), 420-429.
111. Falchikov, N and Boud, D., (1989).Student Self-Assessment in Higher Education: A MetaAnalysis, *Review of Educational Research,* 59(4), 395-430
112. Beyer, B. K. (2008). What research tells us about teaching thinking skills. The Social Studies, 99(5), 223-232. Retrieved from ERIC database. (EJ812510)
113. Irfaner, S. (2006). Enhancing thinking skills in the classroom. Humanity & Social Sciences Journal, 1(1), 28-36.
114. Marshall , S and Mitchell, G. (2003) Potential Indicators of Science Education Process.
115. 'Investigating Science Education in the Society' International review of Science Education and Society,Vol.1, No.2, 2017.
116. Anderson R. (2002). Guest editorial: International studies on innovative uses of ICT in schools *Journal of Learning* (18) 16-21.
117. Drent M. Meelissen M(2008). Which factors obstruct or stimulate teacher educators to use ICT innovatively? Computers & Education 51 (5) 187-199.
118. Chia J. Duthie B.(1993).Primary children and computer-based art work. Their learning strategies and context Art Education 46 (6) 23- 35.
119. shby,J.Sadera,W.A.,McNary, S.W. (2011). 'Comparing student success between developmental math courses, offered online, blended, and face-to-face' Journal of Interactive Online Learning10 (3).

120. [3]Bersin, J. (2004). The Blended Learning Book: Best Practices, Proven Methodologies, and Lessons Learned. USA: John Wiley & Sons, Inc
121. Ashby,J.Sadera,W.A.,McNary, S.W. (2011). 'Comparing student success between developmental math courses, offered online, blended, and face-to-face' Journal of Interactive Online Learning10 (3).
122. Basu, Kaushik (2002), "Ideology, Economics and Labour Market Policy"
123. Dhankar. N. (2010). Education In Emerging Indian Society. New Delhi: APH Publishing Corporation.
124. Pathak, K. R. (2007). Education in the Emerging India. New Delhi: Atlantic Publishers.
125. Siddiqui, M. H. (2009). Philosophical and Sociological foundation of Education. New Delhi: APH Publishing Corporation, APM Publication Corporation.
126. Thakur, A. S., and Berwal, S. (2007). Education in Emerging Indian Society. New Delhi: National Publishing House.
127. David, P. A., & Foray, D. (2003). Economic fundamentals of the knowledge society. Policy Futures in Education.
128. Hargreaves, A. (2003). Teaching in the knowledge society. New York: Teachers College(2007).
130. Garg BS, Zodpey SP. Status paper on public health courses in India. India, New Delhi: WHO Country Office; 2006. pp. 6-17.
131. World Health Organisation. (1998). List of Basic Terms. Health Promotion Glossary. (pp.4). Retrieved My 1, 2009, froogym.
132. Iammarino NK, et al. Int Health Educ. 1980. The School Health Curriculum project: A study of frequency of participation to impact.
133 Report of the Health Survey and Development Committee. Vol.1. Delhi: Manager of Publications; 1946. Government of India; pp. 158-75. (Chairman: Sir Joseph Bhore), New Delhi.
134. Abarmowitz, A.I. (1983). Social determinism, rationality and partisanship among college students. Political Bahavior, 5,353-362.
135. Bartlett, F.C. 1932 Remembering: *A Study in Experimental and Social Psychology.* Cambridge, England: Cambridge University Press.
136. Blakemore, K.and Cooksey, b. (1981). A Sociology of Education for Africa. London: George Allen & Unwin.
137. CM. (2001). Disturbing the Educational Universe: Universities in the Digital Age Dinosaurs or Prometheans? Report of the President for the Academic Year AFT (2000).
138. Distance Education: Guidelines for Good Practice. Washington D.C.: American Federation of Teachers. 2000-1, MIT.

139. AFT (2001). A Virtual Revolution: Trends in the Expansion of Distance Education. Washington D.C.: American Federation of Teachers.
140. Lal Madan (2005). Essential of Educational Technology, Anmol publications PVT.LTD., New Delhi
141. Leon A and Leon M. (1995) Fundamental of Information Technology, Vikas Publishing House PVT.LTD., New Delhi.
142. Ashvini Joshi. Multimedia: A Technique in Teaching Process in the Classrooms, Sri Satya Sai College of Engineering, Bhospal (India).
143. Cohen, C. (2000). Raise Your Child's Social IQ: Stepping Stones to People Skills for Kids. Silver Springs, MD: Advantage Books.
144. Coie, J. D., Dodge, K. A., and Coppotelli, H. (1982). Dimensions and types of social status: A cross-age perspective. Developmental Psychology, 18, 557-570.
145. Levine, M. D. (1998). Developmental Variation and Learning Disorders: Second Edition. Cambridge, MA: Educator's Publishing Service, Inc.
146. Bikas C. Sanyal, "New functions of higher education and ICT to achieve education for all", International Institute for Educational Planning, UNESCO, 12 September 2001
147. Joanne Capper, "E-learning growth and promise for the developing world", In: "TechKnowLogia", May/June, 2001
148. Padmini Devi, K.R & Saravanakumar, AR.(2018).Impact of ICT (Information and Communication Technology) in Enhancing Quality of Education, Review of Research,Vol.7, Issue.7 ISSN No: 2249-894X
149. Campbell, B., Collins, P., Hadaway, H., Hedley, N. and Stoermer, M. (2002). Web3D in Ocean Science Learning Environments: Virtual Big Beef Creek. In Proceedings of the 2002 Web3D Symposium HTML Abstract/ PDF Full paper
150. Froitzheim, Konrad (), Communication Technologies for Virtual Laboratories HTML (does not really address the core problem, but looks at communication tools for participants).
151. R. Giegerich, D. W. Lorenz, ViSeL: An interactive Virtual Laboratory for DNA Sequencing, Tagungsbandzum Workshop "Multimedia-Systeme" imRahmen der GI-Jahrestagung 1998, S.53-S.65, Magdeburg, Hrsg.: H.J. Appelrath, D. Boles, K. Meyer-Wegener, 09/1998. Word
152. Jensen, Nils, Gabriele von Voigt, Wolfgang Nejdl, Stephan Olbrich (2004), Development of a Virtual Laboratory System for Science Education, Interactive Multimedia Electronic Journal of Computer-Enhanced Learning, 6 (2). HTML.
153. Agarwala, A. N. & Singn, S. P. (1992). The Economic of Underdevelopment. Ibadan: University Press.

154. Haralambus, M. Holborn, M. &Heald, R. (2007). Sociology, Themes and Perspectives (7th Edition). London: Heaper Collins Publishers Ltd. Kosemani,
155. J. Orubite, O. K.A. (1995). History of Nigerian Education: A Contemporary Analysis. Port Harcourt: Abe Publishers.
156. Lockheed, M. (1994). Improving Primary Education in Developing Countries. A World Bank Publication. New York: University Press.
157. Mead, M. (1968). In Ahluwalia SP and Bais, H. S. (2010). Education and Challenges. APH Publishing Corporation. New Delhi.
158. Garrels, M. (1997). Dynamic relationships: Five critical elements for teaching at a distance. Faculty Development Papers. Available online at: Indiana Higher Education Telecommunication System (http://www.ihets.org/distance_ed/fdpapers/1997/garrels.htm l).
159. Mr. R. Selvaganapathy & Dr. A .Edward William Benjamin. Multimedia in Learning Chemistry at Higher Secondary level. RESEARCH REVIEW- International Journal of Multidisciplinary. Volume-04, Issue-02, February -2019. ISSN: 2455-3085 (Online).
160. McLean, D. D. (1996). Use of computer-based technology in health, physical education, recreation, and dance. ERIC Digest 94-7. Washington, DC: ERIC Clearinghouse on Teaching and Teacher Education. ED 390 874
161. Lyn Corno, Eric M.Anderman (2012), Handbook of Educational Psychology.
162. Bajwa and Nameet Virk (2006), "Academic achievement in relation to personality stress and well-being".
163. Bengalee, M.D (1974). "Facing modern educational challenges" published by Deepak publications, Bombay, First edition.
164. Claes, M.E. (1992). Friendship and personal adjustment during adolescence Journal of adolescence, 15, 1, 39.
165. Gohil (2008). Teaching Blogs on-line. Retrieved from www.Teachingblogsonline.com
166. Kumar, K.L. (2008) Educational Technology – A Practical Textbook for Students, Teachers, Professionals and Trainers.
167. Manas, R.P. (2010). ICT- Enabled Teacher Education: A Challenge, University News, 48 (20) May 17-23, pp 19-24.
168. Natchimuthu, K. and Vijayakumari, G. (2007). Modern ICT Trends in Teaching Technology, EduTracks, Vol.6, No.6, Feb 2007, pp 18-20.
170. Anadakrishnan (2018).Higher Education of India. A Critical Viewpoint. University News,56(41), 3- 5.

171. Cottrell, D., & Robison, R. (2003). Blended learning in an accounting course. Quarterly Review of distance Education, 4(3), 261-269.
172. Driscoll, M. (2002, March 1). Blended: learning: Let's get beyond the hype. E-Leaning.
173. Graham, C.R., Allen, S., &Ure, D. (2003). Blended learning environments; A review of the research literature. Unpublished manuscript, Provo, UT.
174. William Dharma Raja, B and Anandan, K. (2010) *Educational Technology, A P H Publishing Corporation,* New Delhi.
175. Anandan.K (2010) *Instructional Technology in Teacher Education, A P H Publishing Corporation,* New Delhi.
176. Anandan.K (2010) *ICT in Distance Education, A P H Publishing Corporation,* New Delhi.
177. Barnard, J. (1992). *Multimedia and the Future of Distance Learning Technology.* Educational Media International, 29 (3), 139-144.
178. Habibur Rahman (014) The Role of ICT in Open and Distance Education, Turkish Online Journal of Distance Education-TOJDE, ISSN 1302-6488 Volume: 15 , No-4.
179. Kumar, A. (2012). E-Governance in Education Sector. *Gian Jyoti E-Journal,* 1(2). Retrieved from www.gjimt.com/GianJyotiE-Journal.htm
180. Mittal,P., Kaur,A.(2013) E-Governance - A challenge for India. *International Journal of Advanced Research in Computer Engineering & Technology (IJARCET),* 2 (3), 1196-1199. Retrieved from file:///C:/Users/a/AppData/Local/Temp/IJARCET-VOL-2-ISSUE-3-1196-1199_1-1.pdf
Ramganesh, E., Kirubakaran, E., & Gobi, R. (2016).m-Governance in Higher Education institutions: Technology Infrastructure for Cutting-edge Connectivity to stakeholders.
181. *IOSR Journal of Computer Engineering (IOSR-JCE), 18(2),* 116-120. Retrieved from www.iosrjournals.org

❏❏❏